SECOND EDITION

Global Marketing
and Advertising

SECOND EDITION

Global Marketing and Advertising

Understanding Cultural Paradoxes

Marieke de Mooij

Cross Cultural Communications Company

Foreword by
Geert Hofstede

SAGE Publications
Thousand Oaks ■ London ■ New Delhi

For information:

Sage Publications, Inc.
2455 Teller Road
Thousand Oaks, California 91320
E-mail: order@sagepub.com

Sage Publications Ltd.
1 Oliver's Yard
55 City Road
London EC1Y 1SP
United Kingdom

Sage Publications India Pvt. Ltd.
B-42, Panchsheel Enclave
Post Box 4109
New Delhi 110 017 India

Printed in the United States of America

Library of Congress Cataloging-in-Publication Data

Mooij, Marieke K. de, 1943–
Global marketing and advertising: Understanding cultural paradoxes /
Marieke de Mooij.— 2nd ed.
    p. cm.
Includes bibliographical references and index.
ISBN 1-4129-1475-2 (cloth) — ISBN 1-4129-1476-0 (pbk.)
    1. Target marketing—Cross-cultural studies. 2. Advertising—Cross-cultural
studies. 3. Consumer behavior—Cross-cultural studies. I. Title.
HF5415.127.M66 2005
658.8′02—dc22   2004026086

This book is printed on acid-free paper.

06   07   08   09   10   9   8   7   6   5   4   3   2

Acquisitions Editor:	Al Bruckner
Editorial Assistant:	MaryAnn Vail
Production Editor:	Diane S. Foster
Copy Editor:	Robert Holm
Typesetter:	C&M Digitals (P) Ltd.
Proofreader:	Scott Oney
Indexer:	Teri Greenberg
Cover Designer:	Janet Foulger

Contents

Foreword to the Second Edition

A naive set of assumptions, quite common in both business and academia up till the present day, is that people are rational in trying to maximize their income, but irrational in spending it. Producers are supposed to be rational; consumers irrational. And inside the business organization, managers are supposed to be rational; subordinates irrational.

There is something fishy in this reasoning because producers are consumers to other producers, and managers are subordinates to other managers. The aforementioned assumptions do not reflect observable reality but a perception process in which those in control define rationality in their way. The rationality described in the policies and textbooks is usually the rationality of the producers and managers.

More fundamentally, there is not such a thing as a universal rationality—a discovery which, for example, economists applying a "rational choice" model still have to make. What is rational or irrational to a person depends on that person's value system, which in turn is part of the culture that person has acquired in her or his lifetime. What people around the world value varies enormously: They include poverty next to maximizing income, togetherness next to individuality, cooperation next to competition, modesty next to assertiveness, saving next to spending, chastity next to sexual fulfilment, self-effacement next to self-actualization. Downsizing personnel in order to maximize a company's profits may be rational in one society—say, the United States of America—but not in another—say, Japan—in which the commitment of permanent employees is the company's main capital.

Marketing and advertising are basically about consumers, not about producers. Marketing and advertising theories based on producers' logic but missing consumers' logic are useless. Market research agencies try to bridge the gap between the two kinds of logic, and their excellence depends on their ability to make the producer think in consumers' terms. Even within one country this is not easy; it becomes extremely difficult if consumers are children of other countries' cultures.

In the broader area of management, ethnocentric approaches over the past 30 years have gradually lost support, if only because they proved ineffective, even fatal. International or comparative management has become a recognized subdiscipline of management education; no current management text or handbook can do without it, even if the treatment of the subject often betrays hidden ethnocentrism.

It is a paradox that in the areas of marketing and advertising theories, ethnocentrism has survived longer than in (general) management—a paradox because if there is one aspect of the business that is culture-dependent, it is consumer behavior. As Marieke de Mooij writes, there may be global products, but there are no global people. The success of a business in the end depends on how well its products reach customers whose behavior is affected by values that may vary in all kinds of unexpected ways from those of the business's managers.

One reason for the relative backlog of culture-conscious theorizing in marketing has undoubtedly been the complexity of the field. There is so much variance among consumers worldwide that people were tempted to believe prophets who assure us that we are basically all the same. This message enabled too many marketing managers to sleep in peace, even if they had to wake up to disaster.

Marieke de Mooij has grown to become one of the world's pioneers in the field of culture and marketing. She brought along a thorough experience base in advertising, extensive teaching and consulting experience in different parts of the world, and the ability to empathize with people in other countries. In the first edition of this book, she applied her insights into marketing and into culture, using state-of-the-art literature for both and her direct hands-on research into advertising practices in different countries. In this second edition, she adds much recent information about differences in consumer behavior and their development over time.

In the past, it has sometimes been difficult to get attention for cultural differences from CEOs who saw this subject as soft and wanted to be guided by facts. The present book shows enough hard facts about the role of culture in global marketing and advertising to lift the barriers to top management attention.

—Geert Hofstede
Velp, the Netherlands

Preface to the Second Edition

When I wrote the first edition of *Global Marketing and Advertising*, interest in the influence of culture on marketing and advertising was low. Global marketers were more interested in the similarities than in the differences across countries. This has changed. Most global companies have become aware of the fact that people are not the same across countries and that they are not becoming the same either. I have seen pan-European advertising campaigns slowly turn into local campaigns, obviously because they didn't work. Even Coca-Cola, the quintessential global advertiser, has localized product development and marketing communications.

Several times I have met marketing people who told me that my work had contributed to their decision making. Also, universities increasingly have adopted the book, and I have received many spontaneous thanks from students who enjoyed reading it.

Marketing, however, is in continuous flux, and a book that doesn't include recent developments is not taken seriously. So here is the second edition, which is not only updated with respect to literature and research data but restructured. Following the advice of anonymous reviewers, redundant chapters (9 and 11) were deleted, new topics were inserted, and others were expanded. Examples of new topics are the media, the Internet, and brand positioning. Consumer behavior is more extensively covered than in the first edition. Appendix A includes a list of countries with their Hofstede scores, which can be of use to students who want to do statistical analysis themselves. For this purpose, the notes include several references to secondary data that can be retrieved from the Internet. Appendix B provides a list of such resources.

The book includes twice as many illustrations as the first edition. These are both recent examples and classic advertising examples. In particular, award-winning TV commercials appear to be a strong reflection of culture.

I have tried to include all suggestions from users and reviewers. Some I could cover only superficially or not at all. I have, for example, not covered the legal aspects of communications. First, focus on legal aspects is a request that only comes from the United States, probably because of the density of lawyers in that country. Second, by covering the legal aspects of the world, I would end up with a book that would be too thick and too boring. Two other aspects that I could only cover superficially are global public relations and global integrated marketing communications (IMC). There is hardly any international literature on the two topics, so I have only touched on them by mentioning a few cultural aspects.

I have tried to cover many different countries and regions in the world, but a similar amount of data is not available for all areas, so relatively more examples are from Europe. The Hofstede model used throughout the book, however, permits generalizing phenomena, so understanding cultural relationships in one region can be extended to other regions.

For this second edition, I acknowledge the contribution by Dr. Arne Maas, the anonymous reviewers, all at Sage who contributed, and of course, all who helped with the first edition.

—Marieke de Mooij
www.mariekedemooij.com

Summary of the Book

This book describes the various problems and opportunities of culture in global marketing and advertising. It argues that the main dispute in global marketing and advertising should not be about the efficiency of standardization but about the effectiveness of cultural segmentation. Knowledge of cultural specifics or the value paradoxes is the basis of effective international marketing communication strategies.

Chapter 1 deals with the value paradoxes of different cultures. Value paradoxes reflect the core values of culture and can be effectively used in appeals in marketing communications.

Chapter 2 describes the various aspects of global branding: what makes a successful global brand and how global brands are perceived by consumers. It discusses the global-local dilemma and a few of the myths of global marketing: the assumed existence of global communities and convergence of consumer behavior.

Chapter 3 defines culture and describes various aspects of culture such as language, signs and symbols, imagery and music, and global culture.

Chapter 4 describes various classifications of culture such as concepts of time and high and low context. Hofstede's dimensions of national culture that are used throughout the book are described in depth.

Chapter 5 deals with the value concept as applied to marketing. Cross-cultural value research and value and lifestyle studies used in marketing are described. Examples of country-specific values are given.

Chapter 6 provides an overview of the influence of culture on various consumer behavior theories. Four aspects of consumer behavior are covered: consumer attributes (the self and personality), social processes (needs, motivation, emotion, and group processes), mental processes (perception, information processing, and decision making), and consumer behavior domains (product ownership and usage, brand loyalty, and diffusion of innovations).

Chapter 7 deals with advertising and the media. How we communicate is related to culture and so are advertising styles. The creation of advertising follows assumptions about how advertising works that are based on U.S. studies of how consumers process information. One section touches on culture and public relations. Both media use and use of the Internet are related to culture, and so is Web site design.

Chapter 8 describes the value paradoxes in advertising appeals and explains how appeals in advertising reflect culture. It also shows examples of advertising ideas and concepts that cannot travel.

Chapter 9 describes seven basic advertising forms, with many examples, and the degree to which they are related to culture related.

Chapter 10 deals with all aspects of strategy. At the corporate level, the mission statement and corporate identity are discussed, as well as product/market development across cultures. An important part is brand positioning across cultures, or the matching of identity and image, which across cultures is even more difficult than within cultures. Finally, several marketing communication strategies are reviewed, as well as the different strategies to be used at different stages of market development.

Appendix A provides a list
 of countries with scores for the Hofstede dimensions and income per capita. The data can be used by students for cultural analysis of consumption data or for making culture maps for products or brands.

Appendix B provides a list of secondary sources, most of them in the public domain and many retrievable from the Internet. Data from these sources can be used by teachers and students to provide their own empirical evidence of culture's consequences.

ONE

The Paradoxes in Global Marketing Communications

I n a meeting between the Duke of Wellington and Napoleon after the battle of Waterloo, Wellington is said to have reproached Napoleon with the words, "You fight for power, we fight for honor," and Napoleon is said to have answered: "Yes, one always fights for what one does not have."

One tends to fight for what one does not have; one needs to learn skills one does not have. What seems paradoxical is that skills that come automatically in one part of the world have to be learned in another part of the world. Although teamwork training is big business in the United States, there is hardly a market for it in Japan. Individualistic behavior comes spontaneously to Americans, but the Japanese have to learn it. The Japanese, for whom group values are so important, have to learn to be more self-reliant and to take greater responsibility for their own actions. Leadership is a concept that comes automatically to the French: You have it or you don't. There is no proper word for leadership in either the French or the Spanish languages. In the United States, leadership is an integral part of primary education; children in elementary schools take turns being class leader for the day and may be publicly honored for it. American leaders are the heroes of capitalism; they are admired, whether they succeed or fail. Japanese leaders are faceless.

Chaos is said to be a key ingredient of Silicon Valley's success. But chaos management has not been accepted as a management style in all of corporate America because it conflicts with the desire for control. It is paradoxical to suggest that the Germans would benefit by a bit more chaos instead of rules. The Germans cannot thrive on chaos. On the contrary, German life is highly structured.

Tradition and modernity are seen as contradictions in the West; in Japan, they go side by side. The Japanese can be conservative and at the same time attracted by new ways. Whereas in the West the old must be discarded and the new must be embraced, in much of Asia, the traditional is exploited, recycled into modern ways of life.

The Value Paradox

Paradoxical values are found within cultures and between cultures. Every culture has its opposing values. Equality is an American core value, yet in the United States in particular, the gap between rich and poor is widening. What is confusing in the global marketplace is that certain opposing values of one culture also exist in other cultures but in reverse. An example is the individual freedom-belonging paradox. Individualism is a strong element of American society, and so is the need to belong. It seems paradoxical that both freedom and belonging are strong values of a single culture. The explanation is that in an individualistic society where people want to "do things their own way," "go it alone," people tend to become lonely if they don't make an effort to belong. The reverse is found in Japan where belonging is an integral part of society, and it takes an effort to behave in an individualistic way. According to the American Society of Association Executives in Washington, D.C., in 1995 there were some 100,000 associations and clubs in America. Seven of every 10 Americans belong to at least one club.[1] There is no such phenomenon in Japan.

This is what I call a *value paradox*. Paradoxes are statements that seem contradictory but are actually true. Value paradoxes are found in the opposing values in value systems such as freedom-belonging, tradition-innovation, order-chaos. Value paradoxes are part of people's systems; they reflect the *desirable* versus the *desired* in life. On the one hand, one should not sin; on the other hand, most of us do sin now and again. We don't want to be fat, we should eat healthy food, yet we do eat chocolate or drink beer, and we get fat. Value paradoxes reflect the contradictory and meaningful things in life. A value paradox reflects a dilemma. It includes choice, preferring the thing one ought to do over what one wants to do or the other way round. Value paradoxes reflect people's motives and include the elements that trigger people's feelings and emotions, and thus they are used in marketing and advertising. Because the important value paradoxes vary by culture, value-adding advertising cannot be exported from one culture to another without losing effectiveness.

The value "belonging" is frequently found in American advertising, particularly in the sentimental, emotional form. But appeals to individualism, such as "go your own way," "made for the individual," and egoism are found next to the quintessential American homecoming feelings. Both go together. For the Japanese, belonging is such an implicit part of life that it is not a value to be used as an appeal in Japanese advertising. The opposite will be of greater importance: individuality or independence, which expresses the desire to be oneself, to be able to succeed. Advertising often appeals to what is lacking in society. Where family values are lacking, advertising will show happy families. The happy family is a popular item in North American advertising but less frequently used in Japanese advertising.

Those who do not understand the value paradoxes in global cultures may easily delude themselves and think that the world is becoming one global culture with similar values. There may be similar values, but one culture's values may be the reverse of those in another culture.

It is the complexity of multiple paradoxes that makes communication in the global marketplace so difficult. Not all paradoxes are as obvious as the individual freedom-belonging paradox. The West-East paradoxes are strongest and seemingly obvious, but there is also a variety of paradoxes within regions. Within Europe, value paradoxes vary from freedom-order in Germany to freedom-affiliation in the Netherlands and freedom-dependence in France. The Germans cherish individual freedom, but too much freedom leads to disorder. The Dutch and Scandinavians value individual freedom, but affiliation needs are sometimes stronger. For the French, individual freedom goes along with dependence on power holders. When asked about the need for information, in the south of Europe consumers say they want more information than they say they do in the north, but they don't use it. If you ask them which information sources they have consulted before making a purchase, more say "none" in the South than in the North. This can be explained by culture (see Chapter 7).

People's value paradoxes are part of the culture of the country in which they grow up. It takes some reflection to discover one's own value paradoxes, and it is much more difficult to find the value paradoxes in other cultures. The value paradox concept is an integral part of this book. Examples of paradoxes in appeals in advertising will be given in Chapter 8.

The Global-Local Paradox

"Think global, act local" is a paradox. Thinking and behavior are equally influenced by culture. Someone who thinks globally is still a product of his or her own culture. Global thinking by a person of one culture may easily result in what is perceived as cultural imperialism by people of another culture. The way people think and perceive is guided by the framework of their own culture. One is inclined to see similarities from the framework of one's own culture. These similarities are often pseudosimilarities. They are based on what one wants to see, not on what is actually there. Perception of the phenomenon of Japanese individuality as a sign of Westernization of the Japanese is an example of such misperception. Watching young people worldwide drinking Coca-Cola or wearing jeans may result in thinking they are becoming the same, but there is ample evidence that to consumers the local is more meaningful than the global. For example, people increasingly prefer local music. In 2002 in the United States, 93% of music sold was by local artists. In Japan, it was 74% and across Europe over 50%.[2]

The Technology Paradox

Technological development is increasingly global, but the argument that technological development makes us global and leads toward similar needs for similar products is not correct. There is great variety in the adoption of technological innovations and usage of technological products. Developed Japan could be expected to have as many personal computers per capita as the United States, but it does not. In 2001, Japan had 35 computers per 100 people as compared with 63 in the United States, 46 in Canada, 37 in Britain, 43 in the Netherlands, 34 in France, 19 in Italy, and 17 in Spain.[3] Whereas in 2003, 35% of the Danes accessed the Internet every day, 17% of the British and only 4% of the Greeks did.[4] Cultural values can best explain these differences, in particular Hofstede's model of national culture that is used throughout this book. Statistical analysis of ownership and usage of technological products confirms that convergence of technology is not the same as convergence of people's values and habits. As early as the 1960s, the Canadian media philosopher Marshall McLuhan,[5] who coined the concept of the "global village," said that new media technology acts as extensions of human beings and enhances existing human activities. He said that the new media could make what is similar more similar and what is different more different. Indeed, technology reinforces the differences and together with increased wealth leads to divergent behavior instead of convergence. People will embrace new technology to do the things they are used to, but in a nicer or more efficient way. This will be discussed in further detail in Chapter 2.

The Media Paradox

The growing number of satellites is supposed to create a global village in which anybody can receive any TV channel. This is theory. In reality, there is no viewer freedom. Increasingly, local cable companies are deciding what local viewers will see: usually local programs. A satellite dish is no solution, as a variety of techniques and coding systems across countries makes it virtually impossible to receive what is available. In some ways, in the less technologically advanced, noncommercialized Europe of the past when the airwaves were government controlled, there was more freedom to receive television programs from other countries than there is with the new technology.

Paradoxes in Marketing Theory

The concept of marketing and many of the theories of consumer behavior with respect to consumption, buying, and communication originated in the United States and have been copied and used by teachers in many other cultures. There is little evidence of meaningful adaptations of these theories to other cultures. As a result, numerous students of marketing and advertising have learned marketing practice and theory that reflects American values and thinking patterns that may not always fit well in their own environment. This has led to many paradoxical concepts.

Local Markets Are People, Global Markets Are Products

Markets are people, not products. There may be global products, but there are no global people. There may be global brands, but there are no global motivations for buying those brands. The Sony Walkman is often used as an example of a global product, developed for global consumers with global needs, who would use it with similar motives. That is not true: There are two distinctly different motives for using that product. In the Western world, the motive is that of enjoyment of music without being disturbed by others. This was not the motive for Masaru Ibuka—cofounder with Akio Morita of the Sony Corporation—for inventing the Walkman. He wanted to listen to music without disturbing others.[6]

Advertisers take great pains to try to understand certain subcultures, such as youth culture, knowing that they can appeal to the young only if they address them in the right way. When it comes to addressing adult women or men of different national cultures with very different value systems, many advertisers suddenly think one standard message is sufficient. This is paradoxical behavior.

The decision to standardize has more to do with corporate culture than with the culture of markets and nations. Many global advertisers are not market oriented; they are product oriented. They search for that one universal great idea to sell their one standard product to assumed universal, global consumers. This is demonstrated by the fact that economies of scale are most often mentioned as cost-saving arguments for standardization. In reality, the cost of developing one standard idea that truly crosses borders is very high.

In order to get consensus over a "great idea" or "global platform," product managers, marketing managers, country managers, advertising managers, account supervisors, account directors, and creative directors of advertising agencies and the like in various countries have to get together, have to organize meetings and travel. Then, in the end, it appears that many adaptations are needed. Voice-overs or subtitles have to be made, pack shots must be changed, and texts have to be translated, adapted, or rewritten. Slogans developed for global use have to be translated, and in the end some translations appear to include subtle changes of meaning influenced by culture. An example is how Philips's statement, "Let's make things better," was translated into Spanish as *Juntos hacemos tu vida mejor,* into Italian as *Miglioramo il tuo mondo,* and into French as *Faisons toujours mieux.*

Not only do people of different countries speak different languages; their languages also represent different worldviews. Translations do not uncover the different worldviews, different ways of thinking, and different intellectual styles. International advertising consultant Simon Anholt[7] says, "Translating advertising copy is like painting the tip of an iceberg and hoping the whole thing will turn red." Advertising is more than words; it is made of culture.

The Universal and the Particular

Marketing and advertising textbooks generally draw from the social sciences: psychology, sociology, and economics. Theories developed in one particular culture are generally presented as universal and do not differentiate for the particularities of other cultures. Many of these theories draw from studies conducted in the United States yet are presented as universal. Americans also have adopted theories developed by philosophers of other cultures. For example, Freud's philosophy is found in many textbooks, regardless of the fact that a philosophy of someone of Austrian-Hungarian origin might not work as well in the Anglo-Saxon world. Rarely is the culture of origin of such concepts and theories taken into account when presenting them in books on consumer behavior. Motivational segmentation methods based on Freud's theories are offered to global advertisers,[8] although these theories are valid only for a limited number of cultures.

Some products are perceived as universal and culture-free, but the way they are used is not culture-free. Motives for using them vary. Certain global brands have become so ubiquitous that marketers think they satisfy universal needs. In reality, there are few truly global brands. Most reflect the culture of the home country. Coca-Cola and McDonald's reflect American values, and Gucci carefully keeps reflecting Italian culture.

Focus on a Unique Individual

Theories of buying behavior, decision making, and communication behavior generally describe individuals of Western societies, who are defined as unique personalities. When the influence of groups on individual buying behavior is considered from the sociological perspective, the individual is implicitly unique, as in Western societies. The group dynamics of Eastern societies are ignored.

The concepts of self and personality that are the basis of Western consumer behavior theories are drawn from Anglo-Saxon psychological research and include the hypothesis that people will buy products that are compatible with their self-concept or that will enhance their ideal self-image. Culture plays an important role in the construal of self and in the perception of ideal images. An example is the ideal woman's figure. Advertising in the Western world has been accused of propagating the ideal woman's figure as slim: The figure of the Barbie doll has become a white adolescent ideal. But even within the United States, the degree to which this is perceived as ideal varies: Contrary to white teens, black teens connect a full figure, rather than a slim one, with health and fertility.[9]

Modern branding theory was developed in the United States and the United Kingdom and uses concepts from Western psychology. Metaphors such as brand identity and brand personality are used and exported to countries in which words like *identity* or *personality* do not even exist in the local language. Asking people about "brand personality" in Asia will result in irrelevant answers.

The Paradoxes in Consumer Trends

The marketing and advertising profession thrives on trends, to point out what is new and fashionable. Many of what are presented as consumer trends to be exploited in marketing are based on value paradoxes. In the 1990s, for example, the trend of "cocooning"—withdrawing from social life into the home—was a reaction to a too competitive and individualistic life. One ought to go out into the world all alone and succeed, but in reality one wants the protection of the home. Also, hedonism as a trend with respect to food can never be a global trend. It is related to what the individual *should* do versus actually *does* do with respect to food: eating light products, remaining slim and healthy—or splurging. What is desirable or desired with respect to food and health varies by culture. There are few countries in which more extremes are found with respect to food and health than the United States—very thin next to very fat people and lots of junk food next to a variety of low-calorie foods. In France and Spain, food is more an element of social and family life.

"Trends," or temporary movements in society, may reflect a reaction to a too strong focus on the desirable. Trends or fads in business and management tend to reflect actual culture and of that culture the gap between the desirable and the desired. Chaos management may be the desired, but it conflicts with the desirable: control.

The Global Advertising Paradox

The anthropologist McCracken[10] points out that advertising works as a method of meaning transfer by bringing the consumer good and a representation of the culturally constituted world together within the frame of a particular advertisement. A creative director decides how the culturally constituted world is portrayed in an advertisement and the decision makers at the company decide if that view reflects their cultural framework. This begs the question of what advertising represents—the culture of the consumer or the culture of the company. To give an example: In German advertising, fewer humorous devices are used than in British advertising. Does this reflect that German consumers have less sense of humor? No, it does not. It reflects the risk-avoiding attitude of German management.

Ideally, effective advertising means that the values in the message match the values of the receiver. It is the culture of the consumer that should be reflected in advertising. Analysis of advertisements in international media such as *Newsweek, BusinessWeek,* and CNN shows that, in reality, international advertisers target international audiences with their home country's value system. Thus, the full potential of cross-border media is not used.

For a long time, international advertising strategists in the United States have thought that emotional or "feeling" appeals would travel better than "thinking" appeals because of the assumed universality of human values. Thus, much standardized international advertising has included appeals like happiness and love. Analysis of international advertising shows that this practice of using values in global advertising is mainly a U.S. practice. European companies focus more on innovative product attributes that are communicated in a culturally relevant way. This is discussed further in Chapters 7 and 10.

It is paradoxical that global advertisers prefer to develop what is universal instead of what should appeal to specific people in particular. In an age of increasing communication overload, people's selective perception mechanism will work harder. Add to that an increased amount of advertising reflecting cultural values that are not theirs, and not much imagination is needed to understand why advertising effectiveness is decreasing. On the one hand, advertisers know that advertising must be understood quickly, that instant recognition is necessary because there generally is little time to convey a message. On the other hand, global advertisers think they can export messages made for their own home culture to other, very different cultures. If they travel to other countries themselves, they employ travel agencies and read detailed travel guides. Yet they think that their messages can travel without guidance.

Effective Advertising Needs a Shared Culture

Common assumptions are that an advertisement will be effective if the viewer or reader decodes the advertisement successfully, if there is a meaningful transfer of "properties." The creator of the advertisement selects the elements of the advertisement according to his or her expectations about how the audience will respond, assuming shared cultural conventions. Receivers of the message must use the same conventions to evaluate the stimulus in order to be able to formulate the response. Thus, when developing one single idea for the whole world, or one global stimulus for different cultures, the assumption is that responses will be similar, too. This will only happen if sender and receiver share one culture. If there is no shared culture, the response is likely to be different from what is intended and expected. This does not result in effective advertising.

For cost efficiency reasons, companies prefer to standardize products and advertising. However, products may be similar, but usage and buying motives vary for most products. Levi's jeans may be the same all over the world, but for some they are the worker's outfit, for others they reflect an American lifestyle, whereas again for others they provide prestige. If buying motives for standardized products vary by country or area, how can a standardized advertising campaign be equally effective in all countries? Arguments for standardized advertising are all about standardizing the stimulus without taking into consideration the response to standardized stimuli. In this age of accountability, much is written about cost efficiency in the production of advertising, but little is written about the effectiveness of standardized advertising. The cost savings of a standardized campaign are easily offset by wasted media expenditures caused by less effective advertising messages. One of the reasons may well be that there is so little fundamental research on how advertising works. The relationship between advertising and culture will be discussed in Chapter 7.

How Advertising Works

There are continuous heated discussions among researchers across countries about how advertising works. Time and again, new models are developed. The assumption that the way advertising works may be related to culture is rarely included. Because the United States has a longer research history than other countries, its methods and styles are often used in cross-cultural advertising research. As a result, a characteristic of most studies is their "American-ness." Hypotheses are based on American assumptions, and research methodology is based on American conventions and philosophies of how advertising works. This is the ethnocentric approach. American concepts do not necessarily explain how advertising works in other cultures.

Diverse thinking patterns make advertising people think differently about how advertising works. Defining advertising primarily as "persuasive communication," for example, is typical of the Anglo-Saxon intellectual style, but it is not a universal way of thinking. I have been involved in advertising education in the Netherlands from 1971 onward, at a time when advertising theory was developed from American textbooks. The concept of persuasive communication, ubiquitous in American textbooks, has not become a core concept in Dutch advertising theory, although it is used in advertising effectiveness research by multinationals. The persuasion and "hard sell" models are specifically American. They are too often used as the basis for explaining how advertising works in other cultures.

An example of such cultural blindness is asking "how the persuasive process is supposed to work at the individual level in Japan."[11] Persuasiveness is not an ingredient of Japanese advertising, and the collectivistic nature of Japanese culture hardly includes an "effect at the individual level." Categorizing advertising according to hard sell versus soft sell is part of the American framework but is not practiced solely by American researchers. In fact, the practice is also adopted by researchers in other cultures where it does not apply.

The Research Paradox

By definition, value and lifestyle research is culture-bound, yet studies based on the value patterns of one culture are indiscriminately exported to other cultures. Value and lifestyle studies developed in the United States are used in Europe; and within Europe, studies developed in one country are sold to other countries as if equally valid. For example, Belgian value studies have been sold to the Netherlands, although the value systems of these markets are very different.

Although a large part of the world uses more visuals and symbols in advertising than words, the American term used for advertising research is *copy research.* This reflects a strong bias toward valuing the verbal and factual elements of advertising over the visual elements. The frameworks of researchers of one culture are systematically used to measure effectiveness in other cultures.

Much of the literature on the cross-cultural aspects of international advertising describes studies of advertising of different countries by comparative analysis of the content of advertising. The methods used are based on the conventions of the culture of the researcher, not on the culture of the material to be analyzed.

General findings of cross-cultural studies are that advertising styles vary widely across nations, but very few studies explain why. What these studies usually analyze is the stimulus, the symbols that a creative director has selected from her or his cultural frame of mind. Comparisons of audiences' assumed differences are usually crude. An example is comparing the United States, Europe, and Asia, or "developed" markets with "developing" markets, assuming that these categories include cultures with similar motivations or response patterns. There are few studies that attempt to match stimulus and response across cultures. In order to do this, the cultures of both the sender and the receiver must be studied.

When testing advertising, companies try to economize by selecting one or two countries in an area like Europe that should be representative of Europe. As the reader will discover when reading this book, this is very dangerous. One country is never culturally representative for the whole of Europe. An advertisement that is effective in France will not necessarily be effective in Germany or the United Kingdom.

The Culture Paradigm

Instead of converging with increased wealth, globalization, and technology, consumer behavior diverges across countries. As the British sociologist Anthony Giddens[12] says, "Globalization is the reason for the revival of local cultural identities in different parts of the world." With greater wealth, in what I call postscarcity societies,[13] consumers are increasingly able to express their values, and these values vary across cultures. In Europe, where countries are converging with respect to national wealth and where differences in consumer behavior are persistent, the only variable that can explain differences in consumer behavior across countries is culture. International marketers are only slowly becoming aware of the importance of culture. In the past, culture was viewed as something intangible that could not be quantified, but now several cultural models are available that help structure cultural differences. Such models will be discussed in Chapter 4. One of these models, by Geert Hofstede, allows quantifying cultural differences and will be used throughout this book to explain the various aspects of consumer behavior that are influenced by culture. This is important for CEOs and marketers of international companies who tend to ask for hard data when they want to develop international marketing strategies.

Conclusion

Those who believe that the future holds one global culture are deluded by value paradoxes that make the values of one culture seemingly similar to those of another, different culture. The most obvious example is the assumption that the Japanese are Westernizing because of increased focus on individuality. The global-local paradigm is another paradox: One cannot think globally; every human being thinks according to his or her own culturally defined thinking pattern. One can act globally, and that is what global companies do. When they globalize, they produce and distribute globally. For global communications, however, thinking must be local; to be effective it must focus on the particular, not on the universal.

In global marketing communications, we use the systems of one culture to develop advertising for other cultures. We use categorizations of one culture to describe others. We do not have one adequate global language by which we can reach global consumers. We find pseudo-similarities and think they are real and universal. We use one culture's motives to try to move people of other cultures. What we need is a new language to understand what moves people of different cultures, to develop systems to understand the differences and find the real similarities, which are few and far between. As a start, we have to learn to see the value paradoxes in the global marketplace and to understand them. This chapter has presented only a few examples. The rest of this book will focus on the value paradoxes used in marketing, branding, and communications; and tools will be presented for understanding the paradoxes for developing effective global advertising.

Notes

1. America's strange clubs: Brotherhoods of oddballs. (1995, December 23). *Economist,* 63.

2. Pepper, T. (2004, August 2). Building a bigger star. *Newsweek,* 52.

3. World Bank. (2003). *World development indicators.* Washington, DC: Author.

4. Jowell, R., et al. (2003). *European social survey 2002/2003* [technical report]. London: Centre for Comparative Social Surveys, City University.

5. McLuhan, M. (1964). *Understanding media: The extensions of man.* New York: McGraw-Hill, pp. 225, 268, and 276.

6. Morita, A., & Reingold, E. M. (1987). *Made in Japan.* Glasgow, Scotland: William Collins.

7. Anholt, S. (2000). *Another one bites the grass: Making sense of international advertising.* New York: Wiley, p. 5.

8. Callebaut, J., et al. (1994). *The naked consumer.* Antwerp, Belgium: Censydiam Institute.

9. Springer, K., & Samuels, A. (1995, April 24). The body of the beholder. *Newsweek,* 50–51.

10. McCracken, G. (1988). *Culture and consumption: New approaches to the symbolic character of consumer goods and activities.* Bloomington: Indiana University Press, pp. 71–89.

11. Johansson, J. K. (1994, March). "The sense of nonsense": Japanese TV advertising. *Journal of Advertising, 23,* 17–26.

12. Giddens, A. (2000). *Runaway world.* New York: Routledge, p. 31.

13. De Mooij, M. (2003). *Consumer Behavior and Culture.* Thousand Oaks, CA: Sage.

TWO

The Global-Local Paradox in Global Branding

One of the most discussed topics in global marketing and advertising is the choice between global and local, reaping the economic benefits of standardized production or accommodating local consumer needs and habits for greater effectiveness. The paradoxical aspect of this is that all marketers have learned that markets are people, which should translate into a local approach, but when they go global, they are production driven. They talk about products, brands, and markets, not about people.

The ubiquitous example of a global brand is Coca-Cola. Their global advertising campaigns have contributed to the success of the brand. Yet Coca-Cola is also increasingly localizing. To understand the global-local paradox in branding and advertising, this chapter discusses the various aspects of the global brand and the role of advertising in global branding.

Global Branding

In most categories, companies do not compete with products but with brands, augmented products that are differentiated and well positioned versus other brands in the category. In order to dominate, a global brand must be a leadership brand in all important markets in the world. Coca-Cola, for example, is sold in over 200 countries. Several brand consultants and advertising agencies such as Interbrand and Young & Rubicam compile annual lists of the most powerful brands worldwide, and Coca-Cola has repeatedly been number one. In 2004, it topped the Interbrand list of global brands with the highest brand value.[1] Another ranking is the annual Readers' Choice Brand of the Year survey, which recognizes brands that have the greatest impact on our lives. On this list, Coca-Cola ranked number four in 2003.

Google ranked first, Apple second, and the car brand Mini third. In the various regions in the world, different brands led the lists. In the United States and Canada, the first three brands were Apple, Target (a U.S. retailer), and Google. In Europe and Africa, the top three were Ikea, Virgin, and Nokia. In Asia and the Pacific, the three top brands were Sony, Samsung, and Toyota. In Latin America, the three top brands were Cemex (a cement company), Corona, and Bacardi.[2] This demonstrates that each region has its own important brands. Also, an annual study by Reader's Digest of the most trusted brands in 18 countries in Europe demonstrates that in many product categories, consumers trust local brands more than global brands.[3]

In global branding, the facets of the brands referred to are usually the formal brand identity (logo, symbol, trademark, brand name, colors, shapes), its positioning, its marketing mix, distribution, strategic principles, and advertising. The classic examples of global brands are rarely fully globally standardized. If we were to define a global brand as one in which all elements are standardized (identical brand name, package, and advertising worldwide), there are hardly any global brands—even Coca-Cola. What constitutes a global brand can be described as follows:

> A global brand is one that is available in most countries in the world and shares the same strategic principles, positioning, and marketing in every market throughout the world, although the marketing mix can vary. It has a substantial market share in all countries and comparable brand loyalty (brand franchise). It carries the same brand name or logo.

Such brands are also called global "megabrands." Examples are Coca-Cola, Nivea, L'Oréal, Nestlé, Gillette, Danone, Colgate, Volkswagen, Toyota, IBM, and Intel. According to our definition, Coca-Cola is the quintessential global brand, but the Coca-Cola company owns many successful local brands as well. On their Web site, they say, "We are meeting the demands of local tastes and cultures with nearly 400 brands in over 200 countries." Let's look at three of the characteristics of a global brand, as in the definition.

Illustration 2.1 McDonald's Tokyo, Japan

A global brand is available in most countries in the world. McDonald's, in 2004, offered its services via more than 30,000 distribution points in 119 countries, serving 47 million customers each day. The company has standard specifications for its technology, client service, hygiene, and operational systems. The arches are universal, but much else is localized, such as its products and most of its communications. Through the logo and color combination, it is recognized worldwide (see Illustration 2.1). Perhaps one of the causes of success of McDonald's in foreign markets is the fact that, next to maintaining a strong brand image and consistent service standards around the world, its advertising is local and its product offer has a local touch. Examples are the Kiwi Burger in New Zealand, the Maharaja Mac in India, the Prosperity Burger in Malaysia, the Teriyaki Burger in Japan, the McKroket in the Netherlands, McLaks (a grilled salmon burger) in Norway, and the Croque McDo in France, which refers to the popular French "croque monsieur," a hot ham and cheese sandwich. Advertising by McDonald's ties into local habits and symbols. In 2001, for example, advertising for McDonald's in France tied into "Astérix and Obélisk," the most famous historical cartoon of the nation. A standard formula doesn't mean that consumers use McDonald's in the same way. In some countries, McDonald's is the place to go for children's birthday parties, whereas in others it is the typical family restaurant (as it is announced in India, Illustration 2.2). In China, McDonald's is the place to go for a date because the typical Chinese restaurant with large-group tables doesn't provide the privacy needed. McDonald's with their tables for two does.

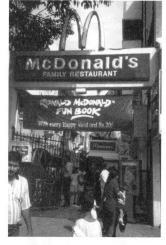

Illustration 2.2 McDonald's Mumbai, India

Global brands have a similar positioning in all markets. If the brand is a premium priced brand, it is premium priced around the world. If it is positioned vis-à-vis an age segment of the market, the positioning must be similar in every market. This is an ideal that cannot always come true, as the competitive environment of markets may vary, causing the need for adaptations in positioning. Yet real leadership brands must aspire to being leadership brands in all markets.

For most global brands, the product mix will vary to meet local consumer needs and competitive requirements. For example, both Coca-Cola and Pepsi-Cola increased the sweetness of their drinks in the Middle East where consumers prefer a sweeter drink. Other elements of the marketing mix such as price, promotion, appeal, media, distribution channels, and tactics may also vary. There are marked differences in the added values imputed to Coca-Cola by U.S. and non-U.S. consumers. In the United States, Coke is part of the social fabric of Americana, much like McDonald's. Non-American consumers drinking Coca-Cola outside the United States are quenching their thirst too, but they are drinking in a little bit of Americana as well. In non-Western societies especially, the brand helps make aspirational American lifestyles a little more approachable.[4] This "American-ness" can, however, be a handicap in countries that do not accept American values. As a reaction against American imperialism, Islamic groups in Europe have introduced their own cola brand called Mecca-Cola.

Procter & Gamble's Pampers brand was introduced in the United States in the late 1960s. Pampers created a disposable diaper market by providing a product that was more convenient than a cloth diaper. Pampers is now one of P&G's largest brands and is sold through a similar marketing strategy worldwide.

Global brands carry one brand name and/or logo. A global brand can carry one name or logo and thus be recognized worldwide, but the product may not be standard at all. An example is Knorr soups and sauces: The package with brand name and logo as found in supermarkets around the world provides the global brand image, yet the contents follow local tastes. Examples are goulash soup in Hungary and chicken noodle soup in Singapore. The logo and packages are similar worldwide, however, and can be recognized easily among competitive brands everywhere.

There are many brands that have all the characteristics of a global brand, yet they do not carry the same brand name everywhere. Sometimes the brand identity is global, but the names or symbols vary from one country to another, often for historical reasons. Examples are the different brand names of Unilever ice cream, many of which represent the names of the original companies Unilever acquired, yet the combination with the same logo makes them recognizable worldwide. Examples of names are Ola in the Netherlands; Olá in Portugal; Frigo in Spain; Langnese in Germany and Russia; Eskimo in Hungary; Algida in Poland, Greece, and Bulgaria; Eldorado in Italy; Good Humor in the United States; Wall's in the United Kingdom, Singapore, and Malaysia; and Streets in Australia. Illustration 2.3 shows examples from Poland, Germany, the Netherlands, Finland, Spain, and Denmark.

Illustration 2.3   Ice Cream Logos, Poland, Germany, Netherlands, Finland, Spain, Denmark

Names of Unilever's detergent brands are Surf and Wisk in the United States, Omo in the Netherlands and France, Skip in Spain, Persil in the United Kingdom, and Pollena in Poland. Reasons for using different names in different countries or regions may be legal, political, historical, or cultural, or due to language differences. The most important reason may well be to keep and leverage the brand names of an acquired company after having acquired it for its well-known local brand names. Companies buy other companies because of the brand name in which that company has invested for years, building an association network in the minds of consumers. Change would include loss of investment in the consumers' minds.

Perception of Global Brands by Consumers

The essence of a brand is that it is a name in the memory of consumers. It is a perceptual map of positive and negative associations, a symbolic language, a network of associations. Brands create meaning and identification. A brand's values must fit the mental mapping of people.[5] These values are conveyed by marketing communications. The brand owner has the opportunity to control the meaning the brand has for people. Marlboro used to be a brand for females and was turned into a male brand. Lucozade used to be an energy drink for feeble people and was repositioned as a sports drink.[6]

A universal function of a brand for customers is quality assurance. As a value, however, quality assurance is of varying importance in different cultures. Consumers in the south of Europe are more brand loyal than those in the north, and this difference can be explained by culture (see Chapter 6).

A brand may be sold worldwide and show all the characteristics of a global brand, but that does not necessarily make it a brand that is perceived as global by the consumer in all countries. A global brand usually has originated in a particular country. In some cases, in spite of being global, it is associated with that nation. This can be beneficial if the image of the country remains constant. In case of change, both upgrading (Japan from "shoddy" to "high quality") and downgrading ("American values" have become ambiguous; for some they are positive, for others negative) will influence the brand's image and acceptance.

There are few brands that are perceived as global by the consumer, and the importance of a global image varies by culture. Successful global brands can be perceived as local in certain countries: for example, Nivea, a brand of Beiersdorf in Germany, or Colgate, which originated in the United States. If a brand has been part of the family for generations, it has become ingrained in people's lives. It may well be that part of the success of a global brand is its integration into the local culture. It is the consumer who makes a brand successful by buying it and being loyal to it. Most strong global brands are old. The Colgate company began in 1806, Nivea originated in 1911, and Clorox in 1913.

Consumers have good memories, even for brands that have not been advertised for some time. Once a brand is known to consumers, it cannot easily be erased from consumers' minds.[7] An interesting example is the German cigarette brand Ernte 23, which had become very weak in West Germany from the 1980s onward. After the Berlin Wall came down, the brand became very strong in Saxony in former East Germany. People remembered the "good old days," which were expected to return after reunification.[8] The shampoo brand Pantene Pro V, for which P&G launched pan-European campaigns in the early 1990s, was still remembered by older people who knew it as the Swiss brand Pantene. Many strong brands, even if they are distributed worldwide, still have a strong national base and a very unequal market position in other countries, particularly in Europe. Danone, for example, is a prominent leader in France, but a challenger in Germany and the United Kingdom. In addition, many global brands do not have a global image in the home country. Heineken is a local brand in the Netherlands, but outside it is an international prestigious brand. The French prefer their Renaults and Peugeots, and the Germans like their Volkswagens and Mercedes.

The local environment plays a strong role in the perception of global brands and the values consumers attach to these brands. When the Berlin Wall fell in 1989, the first things eastern Europeans wanted were Western brands. But in 1995, local brands returned as a result of growing nationalism. Lower prices, improved quality, and nostalgia have made eastern European consumers return to their "good old" local brands. This is a slow but steady shift in consumer behavior. For a short time, values attached to a foreign or global brand may have a very strong appeal, but as time goes by, people return to their own values.

People increasingly prefer brands with a strong identity rooted in their own history, which can be national or regional. In Italy, there is no such thing as an Italian restaurant. There are restaurants focusing on the regional cuisines of Tuscany, Venice, Sardinia, or Umbria. The fragmentation of the German beer market has to do with historical and cultural issues, not with differences in consumer tastes.[9]

Nationalistic feelings can sometimes prevent further expansion of import brands. In August 1995, for example, as a response to the very successful McDonald's in that city, Moscow's mayor established by decree a successful competitive fast food restaurant called Russian Bistro, offering value-for-money, typical Russian fast food dishes.[10]

Global Branding Strategies

There are various strategies global companies can follow with respect to branding. First, there is the choice between different brand types, second the internationalization strategy.

Brand Types

Single-product brands or monobrands. An exclusive name is assigned to only one product. The brand's main purpose is to add value to the product. Examples are Lion, After Eight, Pepsodent, Club Med. The vast majority of existing brands were developed as single-product brands that were built to position products within national boundaries.[11]

Range brands or line brands. A group of products is ranged under one name, under one promise or positioning. The purpose is to give a product a place in a range of other products. An advantage of range brands is that products can share brand awareness and meaning. Examples are Schweppes (tonic, bitter lemon, soda water, ginger ale), Budweiser (light, dark), and Mercedes (C240, E500, S600).

Umbrella brands or corporate brands. Different products or brands are marketed under one name. The name can be the company name or an umbrella brand name. The corporate name can be used as an endorsement to indicate the source: Nestlé's name on the package of Nescafé, Maggi, or Dairy Crunch means it endorses the quality. GM endorses Pontiac, Buick, Oldsmobile, Cadillac, and Chevrolet. The L'Oréal company has a full range of personal care products under the corporate L'Oréal umbrella. Other examples of corporate brands are Benetton (clothes, perfume), Mitsubishi (banks, cars, domestic appliances), Philips (hi-fi, television, light bulbs, electric razors), Braun (razors, coffee machines, kitchen machines), Sony (television, audio, video), and Canon (cameras, photocopiers, office equipment). Examples of umbrella brand names that are different from the company name are Nivea (Beiersdorf) soap, facial products, body milk, deodorant; Knorr (Unilever Bestfoods) soups and sauces; and Sanex (Sara Lee) personal care products.

Brand Strategies

There are basically six strategies companies use for internationalization:

1. Cultivate established local brands. Develop a national brand into an international brand, transporting brand value and strategy to more countries. Products or brands may have characteristics (real or imaginary) that also appeal to consumers of other nations (but not necessarily to all). Coca-Cola is the best example of an originally local, American brand that became global. Timotei shampoo, which originated in Scandinavia, is another example: Its formula as well as its nature-based imagery seems to appeal to Asians.

2. Global concept, local adaptations. Develop one formula, a concept for the world that can carry local products with local values. This strategy is followed by McDonald's.

3. Create new brands. Recognize a global need or want and develop a new product for it. There are few successful examples of truly global needs and wants, so this is a very risky strategy. Recent technology brands can serve as an example: Nokia, Google, and the Nintendo Gameboy.

4. Purchase local brands and internationalize. This is a strategy used by such major packaged food companies as Unilever, Danone, Kraft, and Nestlé. The purpose of most mergers and acquisitions has been to become owners of a company's brands in order to thrive on local brands first, then add international brand names or harmonize local brands with international brand portfolios. This has been the strategy of large multinationals like Unilever and Procter & Gamble.

5. Develop brand extensions. Extend a brand name to other, related categories. Gillette offers, in addition to razors, shaving foam, aftershave, and deodorants. L'Oréal started in 1907 with hair care and expanded their corporate brand name to cosmetics, skin care, sun care, and bath and shower products. The German company Beiersdorf started with an all-purpose cream called Nivea in 1911 and extended the Nivea brand across a wide range of personal care products. Since 1913, Clorox extended from a liquid bleach product into household cleaning products, disinfectant wipes, laundry care, and toilet care. Gerber extended its baby care product line to the categories personal care, food, beverages, confectionary, and health care. The Cartier watchmaker extended its brand into the wider luxury goods market with leather goods, pens, and perfume. An advantage of brand extension is reaping the benefits of global promotion programs. The investment in global sports or event sponsorship is so enormous that trying to catch more products as extensions of one name is an appealing strategy.

6. Employ a multilocal strategy. Different strategies are developed for different countries for local recognition. The company name is often used as endorsement for quality guarantee ("Nestlé, the best of Australia").

Trends in International Branding Strategy

Since the early 1990s, there have been two main trends in international branding strategy.

1. From monobranding to endorsement branding. The cost of launching and developing new brands is so enormous that international companies increasingly choose endorsement strategies. Another likely reason is the popularity of corporate brands in Asia where the role of brands is different from that in the Western world (see Chapter 4). With growing Asian markets, global companies are inclined to adapt their strategies worldwide.

2. Brand rationalization or concentration on core brands. Brand rationalization means changing diverse multinational portfolios into a limited number of global brands. At the turn of the century, the 10 largest L'Oréal brands represented 90% of turnover. Nestlé, one of its largest brands, represented 40% of turnover. But the five largest Unilever brands represented only 5% of turnover, and 90% of turnover was represented by 400 brands. Unilever's target was to reduce 1,600 brands to 400 brands. At that time, Procter & Gamble had already advanced in the process. Compared with 10 years earlier, they had only one third of the product variations.

Rationalizing brand portfolios implies harmonizing brand names but also deleting local brands. Early examples of harmonizing brand names were the change of the Marathon candy bar into the Snickers bar, and Treets and Bonitos being replaced by M&Ms. Various brand names for household product Cif used to be Jif and Vim. There is some risk in deleting local brands as it leaves holes in the market for new entrants. It also means destroying capital investment of the past, as many of these brands were bought at a high price.

The Global-Local Dilemma

The core dilemma in global marketing is whether to sell an identical product (a global brand) throughout its sales area or to make whatever modifications are needed to account for local differences. A global brand can be a mass brand looking to satisfy a common product need in all countries, or it can be a niche brand targeted at common niche segments in every country. Conversely, a global product, via its advertising, can be loaded with local values to add local significance. In both global branding and global advertising, the choice has to be made between standardization or differentiation.

The ultimate form of standardization means offering identical products worldwide at identical prices via identical distribution channels, supported by identical sales and promotion programs. Assumed homogenization of needs across borders is the most frequently mentioned reason for standardization. Harvard Professor Ted Levitt,[12] in 1983, called it "the globalization of markets." The successful examples of fully standardized brands he mentioned were McDonald's, Coca-Cola, Revlon cosmetics, Sony television, and Levi's jeans—products that Levitt said could be bought to an identical design throughout the whole world. By standardization, companies could reap the benefits of economies of scale in procurement, logistics, production, and marketing, and also in the transfer of management expertise, all of which was eventually supposed to lead to lower prices. Standardization is also said to offer the possibility of building a uniform worldwide corporate image, a world brand or global brand with a global image. With a smaller portfolio of strong, global brands, companies expect to achieve greater marketing effectiveness. Proponents of the Levitt theory included the possibility of developing powerful advertising that crosses international boundaries, cutting across all lines of culture, nationality, race, religion, mores, values, and customs.

More than two decades later, many companies have learned that the standardized approach is not effective. Kenichi Ohmae, formerly of McKinsey,[13] said in 1989, "The lure of a universal product is a false allure," and that conclusion has been reached by many global companies such as Coca-Cola. Needs may be universal, but attitudes, motivations, and expressions of needs vary. Observation of Japanese people drinking Coca-Cola or eating at McDonald's in the Tokyo Ginza does not mean that Japanese core values are changing. The argument for global standardization is based on two assumptions: (a) the existence of global uniform segments, or global communities, and (b) convergence of consumer behavior.

Global Communities

One of the preconditions of standardization is the existence of homogeneous global segments across borders with similar values. Focus on similarities or marketing universals rather than the differences has led international marketers to search across countries for market segments of people with similar lifestyles and values that are called "global communities" or "global tribes." The assumptions are that an 18-year-old in Denmark has more in common with an 18-year-old in France than he has with his elders, or a young Japanese woman shopping in the Ginza has more in common with a young American woman strolling a Manhattan street than she has with her own parents. Business travelers and teenagers are most often cited as examples of such homogeneous groups. The European youth market is considered to be homogeneous because these people were reared on the same movies and global brands, like Coca-Cola and Levi's,[14] and watched MTV, all of which has supposedly encouraged the development of a global teenager with common norms and values. However, several value studies show that across countries young people vary as much as grown-ups. General evidence is the fact that cross-cultural psychologists who measure value differences across cultures tend to use students as subjects. Also, studies among parents and students in the United States, Japan, New Zealand, France, Germany, and Denmark demonstrate the strong influence of culture on the values of both parents and students. The values of parents and students within a culture are relatively similar, with the greatest similarity between Japanese students and parents.[15]

Youths from Stockholm to Seville may use the same type of mobile phone or computer, but they may have bought it for different reasons. A survey by the advertising agency Euro RSCG in 2001 showed that attitudes toward technology vary enormously among youth in the large European cities. For example, 16% of respondents in Amsterdam said entertainment was their primary reason for using technology, compared with 9% in Helsinki and London and only 4% in Milan.[16]

Western magazines suggest that Asian teens, in the way they behave and dress and express themselves, increasingly resemble American and European teens, but this behavior is not driven by Western values. Moreover, there is not one teenage culture in Asia; there is enormous diversity among Asian teenage lifestyles.[17] Young Japanese or Chinese may be typically Western on the surface, but traditional values like hard work remain in addition to aspiration toward money and display of success via branded goods.[18] If you take typical Indian teenagers in Bombay, Delhi, or Calcutta, they may be wearing a Lacoste shirt or Nike shoes, but they are very much Indian in their values. They respect their parents, live together in a family, and remove their Nike shoes before entering a place of religion.

A common misperception is that the values of youth worldwide are basically the same, that everywhere the young rebel against their elders as a universal aspect of adolescence. The way the young develop their identity, the way they relate to their elders, and the way they behave in school vary enormously across cultures because of the values with which they are raised. Indian adolescents show much less conflict than the adolescents of traditional American youth, who are involved in self-creation and integrating an identity. In traditional Indian society, adolescence is not the separate psychological state that it is in U.S. culture.[19] Westerners make a mistake when they think Japanese values are changing because students between 18 and 25 years old act in an extreme and revolutionary way. They have to realize that these years are the only free years a Japanese has in his or her entire life. With the advent of work comes conformance to the typical Japanese behavior. A study by ACNielsen in 1998 found that Indonesian youth increasingly like to use traditional Indonesian products, prefer advertisements that use Indonesian models, and when sick would rather use Indonesian medicine than Western medicine.[20]

Global homogeneous markets, like businesspeople, youth, or rich people, exist only in the minds of Western marketing managers and advertising people. Even people with similar lifestyles do not behave as a consistent group of purchasers because they do not share the same values. Yes, across countries there are young people and yuppies (young urban professionals), rich people, and graying populations that have economic and demographic aspects in common, but marketing communications cannot use similar motives and arguments because these groups do not have the same values across cultures. This is demonstrated by ownership of luxury products as measured by the European Media and Marketing Survey (EMS). The high-income European target, consisting of people who read international media, is not one homogeneous, cross-border target group for high-touch and high-tech luxury articles. Expenditures on expensive luxury articles by this high-income group in Europe vary enormously. The differences can only be explained by cultural variables.

Businesspeople are generally considered to be a "culture-free group" because of assumed rational decision making as compared with consumer decision making, but decision making by businesspeople is also culture-bound like many business habits. In 1999, to the question of where, outside the office, businesspeople would most like to discuss business with their most valuable customer, 49% of Spaniards opted for lunch at a restaurant or hotel, something favored by only 8% of Italians, who preferred a breakfast or dinner meeting. The favorite of Germans was a meeting at an airport or conference center. Asked about the use of new technology like e-mail, 94% of British managers said they used e-mail, whereas only 53% of French managers did so.[21]

The European Business Readership Survey (EBRS) has measured behavior of businesspeople in Europe since 1973. Data resulting from the 2000 survey demonstrated that in the past 25 years not a lot had changed in the world of the European business executive. In EBRS's 1975 survey, 11% of their universe was under the age of 35, and this figure was 10% in 2000. Both in 1975 and in 2000, 19% of top executives were over 55. The number of international flights made by European businesspeople had risen between 1980 and 1998, but not by a significant amount. Only 4% of EBRS respondents were nonnationals of the country in which they lived.[22]

Convergence and Divergence of Consumer Behavior

Industrialization, modernization, wealth, and technology are supposed to bring a universal civilization, including universal values and consumption patterns. This is a distinctive product of Western thinking.[23] As American advertising professor John Philip Jones[24] states, "Logic points to similar patterns emerging in other countries when their per capita income levels approach that of the United States." The consumption symbols of this assumed universal civilization are mainly American. As a result, global cultural homogeneity is also called "Americanization" or "cultural imperialism."

Indeed, in the developed world, technology and national wealth have converged to the extent that the majority of people have enough to eat and have additional income to invest in new technology and other durable goods. Countries are becoming similar with respect to penetration of such goods, not with respect to what people do with them or the motives for buying them. Technology has not brought a global village in which global consumers behave in the same way.

When the Canadian media philosopher Marshall McLuhan[25] coined the concept of the global village, he meant that the new electric media of his time, such as telephone and television, abolished the spatial dimension. By means of electricity, people everywhere could resume person-to-person relations, as if on the smallest village scale. Thus, McLuhan viewed the electronic media as extensions of human beings. They enhance people's activities; they do not change people. If you assume people are the same everywhere, global media extend homogeneity. If you realize that people are different, extensions reinforce the differences. McLuhan did not include cultural convergence in the concept of the global village. In fact, he said the opposite—that uniqueness and diversity could be fostered under electronic conditions as never before.

This is exactly what new technology has accomplished. People have embraced it to enhance current activities. In the cold climates where people used to preserve food in the snow, they have embraced deep-freeze technology most intensely. The colder the climate, the more deep freezers and the more ice cream consumed. The mobile phone penetrated fastest in countries that already had advanced fixed telecommunications infrastructures. The Internet was assumed to undermine authoritarian regimes, but it is used to strengthen them. The Internet has not changed people. It has reinforced existing habits that, instead of converging, tend to diverge.

Whatever convergence takes place is at *macro level*, convergence of demographic phenomena like national wealth or graying populations. If consumption converges, it also is only at macro level, and it follows economic development (i.e., household penetration of products like refrigerators, washing machines, or color television sets). Empirical evidence of convergence tends to be based on macrodata, such as the numbers of telephones, television sets, or passenger cars per 1,000 population.

There is increasing evidence that at *micro level* there is little convergence. U.S. sociologist Alex Inkeles[26] finds that macro-level data often mask diversity at micro level. Convergence at macro level—for example, convergence of GNI/capita (the new term for GNP/capita)—does not necessarily imply convergence of consumer choice. Countries similar economically are not necessarily similar in their consumption behavior, media usage, and availability patterns. There is no support for the argument that increased global mobility for business and vacations will cause people to homogenize. People do not travel to an extent that they are frequently confronted with other cultures. Even if all people were to have enough money to travel abroad, they would not all travel to the same extent. Of the high-income groups of Europe covered in 1997 by the European Media and Marketing Survey, 54.3% did not travel outside Europe. If these wealthy segments of European populations travel so little, what about the total population? Also, young people do not travel to an extent that induces them to adopt different habits and values. In 2001 in Europe, 44% of young people aged 15 to 24 had not visited another country in the last 2 years. This was the same percentage as in 1997. Of those who had visited other European countries in the last 2 years, 86% went on vacation.[27] White[28] adds that people on vacation are not in a mood that has much to do with their domestic purchasing behavior, so the relevance of any advertising they see is limited. Annually only 0.4% of Europeans (1.5 million) work in another EU state, compared with 2.4% of Americans who work in a state other than where they grew up. The percentage of people who *live and work* in another country is even lower: 0.1%, or 225,000 people.[29]

Differences in consumer behavior across countries are persistent. As people around the globe become well educated and more affluent, their tastes actually diverge. With increased wealth, people accord greater relevance to their civilizational identity.[30] At a certain level of economic development, in what I have called "post-scarcity"[31] societies, when people's stomachs are filled, when most people can afford proper housing and durable products such as cars and television sets, people reach a higher level of unsatisfied needs. That is the moment when cultural values become manifest, and these are reflected in the different choices of products and brands. At that level, countries tend to diverge. What people do with their incremental income, the extra money they have after they have bought the necessary durables to live a comfortable life, varies increasingly. This phenomenon is strongest in Europe where countries have converged most, economically.

If we look at a few specific examples of macro convergence and micro divergence, countries in Europe have converged for the total number of passenger cars per 1,000 population, but the distribution across populations, numbers owned per household, or type of car owned, diverge. If we look at daily TV viewing minutes, countries converged between 1991 and 1993 and diverged after 1993. Newspaper readership in Europe, measured by the question, "Did you read a newspaper yesterday?" diverged.[32]

In regions other than Europe, the trend is also toward divergence. Initially, with increased wealth, standards of living appear to converge, but a closer look makes clear that there are large differences. In Latin America, because of the large differences between rich and poor, the rich in each country have more in common with each other than with their poorer compatriots, but the middle-income people differ from one country to another. They vary in the use of their discretionary income. All Latin Americans use toothpaste and shampoo each day, but there are varying brand preferences. Although 25% of Latin Americans eat cold cereal for breakfast, the national figures vary from 48% in Central America to 11% in the Southern Cone.[33] Japan was the country that developed earliest and fastest of all Asian countries, and it was expected that development patterns of other countries in Asia would follow the pattern of Japan. This has not happened. The way other economies, such as Malaysia and Indonesia, are developing is totally different. Even the values gap of American and European elites has widened, according to studies conducted in 2002.[34]

Next to convergence or divergence, in many cases differences are stable in time. The Belgians drink 10 times as much mineral water as the British and 6 times as much as the Dutch, their neighbors in Europe. Although the quality of tap water has improved all over Europe, consumption of mineral water has increased in some areas and remained the same in others, and differences have remained similar since 1970 or have become larger. These differences cannot be explained by differences in national wealth, only by culture.

A difference that regardless of income has been consistent during the past 30 years is whether people prefer to buy their car new or secondhand. In 1999, according to EMS, 42.4% of the Italians, 33.8% of the Spanish, and 36.9% of the Belgians reported having bought their car new, as compared with only 7.5% of the Swedes and 13.6% of the Dutch. Differences in preferences are related to value differences.

The wealthier countries become, the more manifest is the influence of culture on consumption and consumer behavior. This phenomenon is reflected in many changes of the past decades, such as increased interest in local music and TV programs, which in turn resulted in localization of some of the international media such as MTV and CNN. More discretionary income gives people more freedom to express themselves, and that expression will be based in part on their national value system. Wealth brings choice. It enables people to choose leisure time or buy status products or devote free time to charitable work or to self-education.[35]

Global or Local? Factors That Influence Standardization

Because global companies have to be cost efficient, the discussion about which aspects of marketing to standardize will be ongoing. One more argument for standardization and a few factors that influence marketing standardization are presented after this. In addition to the false argument of converging consumer behavior, another argument is the existence of *international media*.

The availability and growing penetration of international media—especially satellite television—have led to high expectations. To use these media, an "international" campaign must be produced. But whether the media deliver to an international audience in any but a superficial sense seems highly questionable. Increased availability of cross-border television has not resulted in more cross-border campaigns. Different cultures demand different television programming reflecting national tastes, so the scope of pan-regional television programming is limited to only a few types of programs, such as sports.[36] Even these programs tend to be in the local language. There are very few truly international consumer magazines: Magazines such as *Elle* and *Cosmopolitan,* which used to be "exported" to other countries in the original format, have turned to local editions in most countries where they are sold.

Factors that influence the decision on standardization are the *product category,* the *product life cycle,* and the *culture of the company.*

A few product categories seem to follow a standardized marketing approach successfully. Examples are whisky and perfume, for which a standardized country-of-origin concept can be used (perfume from Paris). French cheese comes from France, Scotch whisky from Scotland. Finding that most advertising for French perfume is standardized should not lead to the conclusion that perfume is a culture-free product. Particularly with respect to perfume, people's tastes and motives vary widely. Also the substance of perfume varies from oil-based to alcohol-based according to local customs.

Logic points at technology products to have the greatest chance of standardization. A study by Reader's Digest[37] shows that a number of more or less standard global brands that are equally highly trusted in a large number of countries are in the technology area (Sony, Nokia, Canon, IBM). These brands have remained strong by offering consistent high quality.

The phase of the product in the product life cycle defines the possibility of standardization. New products or brands and marketing communications for these products are easier to standardize than mature products (see also Chapter 10). Yet by selling one single product worldwide and not adapting to usage and attitude differences that become apparent sometime after introduction, manufacturers will run the risk of finding a mass market in one culture and a niche market in another. A product may be in different phases of its life cycle in different markets, with the consequent need for different advertising approaches. Established brands in different markets may have different brand images, making it difficult to move the product to a global approach.

The degree of standardization also depends on a company's corporate culture, or the vision of its management. It depends heavily on how important advertising managers think cultural differences are. The culture of a company's country of origin strongly influences the vision of its managers. Some American companies have universalistic philosophies about people's values, assuming that their own values are valid for the whole world. French companies, too, because they are used to centralized governance, may also be inclined to impose one central idea on the world.

The Role of Advertising in Global Branding

Some global brands have become strong because of global advertising. When discussing global advertising strategies and the effectiveness of global standardized advertising, time and again brands like Levi's, Nike, and Coca-Cola are used as examples of successful global advertising. For these brands, however, it was not only advertising that has been the cause of success. A very important marketing mix instrument is distribution. Many brands have become global because of successful distribution. Nivea already was sold worldwide before the existence of television. The cause of Coca-Cola's success was the formula and intensive distribution. They controlled the bottlers and were able to claim to be available always, everywhere, when people are thirsty. This product benefit has been the core of the Coca-Cola concept. Their distribution system is visible everywhere. (Illustrations 2.4 and 2.5 show Coca-Cola delivery vans in the U.S. and in India).

Illustration 2.4   Coca-Cola Distribution USA

Coca-Cola has always been one of the first to penetrate into developing markets and to create strong positions in these markets. Early in the twenty-first century, they were the largest investor in the Ukraine, a country they entered right after it opened up to Western companies. Illustration 2.6 shows outdoor advertising for Coca-Cola in 1996. Coca-Cola is often called the definitive global brand, as it was one of the leaders in the globalization process. But its prototypical global commercial, "I'd like to teach the world to sing in perfect harmony," dates from the 1970s when it was a different world. Since then, much of Coke's advertising has been adapted to local circumstances.

Illustration 2.5   Coca-Cola Distribution India

In the dialogue on the standardization of advertising, three misconceptions are common: (a) that advertising concepts based on strong visual cues are able to cross borders more easily than campaigns based on copy; (b) that if the associative values are universal, image strategies can be used cross-culturally; and (c) that advertising themes or concepts can be standardized and only the execution may need adaptation.

Because the most described problem of international

Illustration 2.6   Coca-Cola Outdoor Advertising Ukraine

advertising is the translation problem, it is often suggested that using mainly visuals will make effective global advertising. Visuals, however, are as strongly culture-bound as language. Advertising themes and concepts are based on buying motives and only adjusting the execution won't do. The motives used in advertising, the form, and the communication style are all culture-bound, as will be described in Chapter 7.

The issue of standardized advertising is particularly relevant to the discussion about advertising overkill and irritation. Bland advertising, based on the lowest common denominator, is not appealing to anybody and can even cause irritation. One single message cannot be appropriate for everyone.

The Importance of Culture for Global Advertising

In advertising and marketing literature, influences of culture on consumer behavior and perception of advertising are at most anecdotal. They focus on the expressions of culture and little on the differences in values that are the cause of behavior and communication styles. Why do the British use so much humor in advertising? Why is it that comparative advertising works well in the United States but is not accepted in Japan? Why do people prefer different types of promotions? Saving stamps, for instance, are more popular in the Netherlands than in the United Kingdom.

Even when products are accepted in more than one culture, advertising will have to be culture-relevant, and that means more than translating a central message. Differences among languages go far beyond mere translation problems. Some concepts are not translatable; also, between cultures that speak similar languages, cultural differences are found. Even between English-speaking countries, adaptations are often necessary, both for copy and for visuals. A simple example is that in Australia, diapers are "nappies" as they are in Britain. The type of humor found in some Australian commercials might be considered in bad taste outside the Australian market.

Much of the standardization debate has concerned itself with the issue of standardizing the advertising stimulus, the message. Yet it is the response that counts. People process advertising messages in social and cultural contexts and then respond. Jeremy Bullmore,[38] with 33 years' experience at J. Walter Thompson, writes,

> Do not believe the old saying that good advertising speaks for itself. Good advertising speaks for itself only to those for whom it is intended. Much good advertising speaks quite deliberately in code, or uses a secret language, and excludes the rest of us. That's one of the reasons why it's good.

Taking into account cultural differences doesn't mean that all advertising must be local to be effective. Countries can be clustered according to similar values that are relevant for a product category in order to reach consumers in each cluster with relevant values. This will be described in Chapters 7 and 8.

Global Branding Means Adding Value to Global Products

Successful global brands are made by adding values to products in the global marketplace.

A brand is more than a product with a name, a trademark, or a promise of performance. A brand is a network of associations in the mind of the consumer. A name that is not in one's memory is not a brand.[39] The association network notion of a brand is crucial for understanding advertising's role in developing global

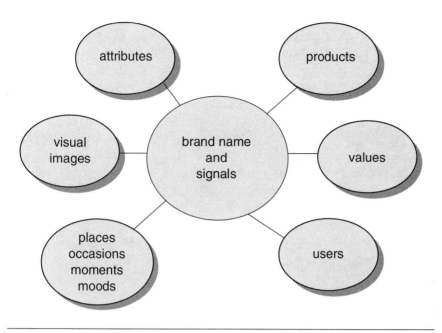

Figure 2.1   Elements Brand Association Network

SOURCE: Franzen (1993)

brands because it so clearly shows the link between consumers and brands as a result of advertising. The associations (meanings) that we attach to the objects of the material world influence our purchasing and decision processes.[40] It is the primary task of advertising to manipulate brand meanings. Advertising tries to attach meanings to brands, and these meanings are interpreted in the light of the target's motivations and aspirations. Association networks may vary across target groups, and the ultimate goal of advertisers will be to develop strong association networks for brands that fit the target's values and motivations. The associations in the consumer's mind will relate to a number of aspects of the brand (see Figure 2.1):

- The brand name and the brand's visual images: the package, logo, brand properties, and other recognizable aspects
- The product or products linked with the name (one product = monobrand; a number of products or extensions = range brand)
- Attributes: what the product is or has (characteristics, formula)
- Benefits or consequences: rewards for the buyer or user—what the product does for the buyer
- Places, occasions, moments, moods when using the product
- Users: users themselves or aspiration groups
- Values

Associations are structured in the human mind: Attributes and benefits will be linked with users and may be specific for the product category or for the brand. The

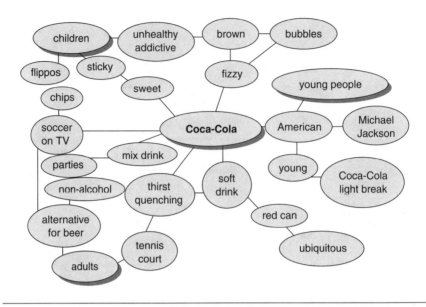

Figure 2.2   Associations With Coca-Cola

essence of the brand is the strength of associations among the product, its attributes, benefits, values, and user imagery.

An example is a simple association network or perceptual map for Coca-Cola (Figure 2.2) that I developed by conducting a number of interviews in my own environment in 1995. This association network is not representative for the Dutch and is only meant to serve as an example.

An important finding from a simple exercise like the one with Coca-Cola is the fact that associations included advertising properties of both Coca-Cola (Coca-Cola light break) and Pepsi-Cola (Michael Jackson). An explanation may be that both Coca-Cola and Pepsi-Cola used music marketing in the past. For the people I interviewed, the attribute "American" was indiscriminately linked with both Michael Jackson and Coca-Cola's advertising. New cola drink brands such as Virgin Cola or the Islamic brand Mecca-Cola could easily attack the positions of both Coca-Cola and Pepsi-Cola, not only by price differentiation but also on the undifferentiated values of both market leaders. Coca-Cola and Pepsi-Cola have the following attributes in common: soft drink, sweet tasting, thirst quenching, cola drink, and being "an American drink."

In our world of abundant brands and communications, differentiating a brand by its attributes or benefits is very difficult. It will only work if a product has unique attributes that distinguish it from the competition. Such distinctions usually do not last long, as they are copied quickly by the competition. Only a few strong global brands of large multinational companies have managed to consistently introduce innovative ingredients and consumer benefits (e.g., L'Oréal, Nivea, Dove, Colgate) and have communicated these in a distinctive and/or culturally relevant way.

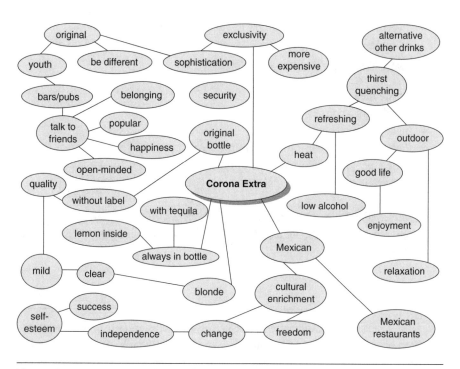

Figure 2.3   German and Spanish Associations With Corona Extra

If a brand is associated with meaningful and distinctive values, this distinctiveness can be transferred to other areas. The British brand Virgin, owned by Richard Branson, carries associations of adventure, rebellion, and nonconformism linked to the personality of its owner. These values are used for all products of Branson's company: the airline, records, cola drink, vodka. However, these values may not be meaningful for the whole world.

Another example of an association network is one for Corona Extra, a Mexican beer brand exported to many countries in the world. It distinguishes itself by its transparent white bottle with a long neck and the ritual of drinking from the bottle with a slice of lime pushed into the neck. A mixed group of Spanish and German students developed the association network presented in Figure 2.3. This association network includes attributes and benefits as well as values. Two clusters of values can be distinguished. Those of the Germans are success, self-esteem, independence, and freedom; those of the Spanish are belonging, happiness, and sophistication. In later chapters (4 and 5), we will see that these values are distinctive of German and Spanish culture.

The purpose of advertising is to turn products into brands by developing strong association networks in people's minds by adding value to products. The values selected to differentiate brands relate to the cultural mind-set of the strategist but should also relate to the cultural mind-sets of the target group. What makes advertising effective is the match between the values in the advertising message and the values of the receiver. A core problem in global advertising is a cultural mismatch between the advertisement and the target groups, which is rarely included in advertising tests. Although the large international companies try to measure the effectiveness of their advertising on a continuous basis, there is not much fundamental research on what makes advertising effective. There are, however, some rules of thumb.[41] To be effective, advertising must do the following:

- Create meaningful associations
- Be relevant and meaningful
- Be linked with people's values
- Reflect the role the product or brand plays in people's lives
- Reflect people's feelings and emotions
- Be instantaneously recognized

All these elements are influenced by the culture of both the advertiser and the audience. Effective advertising reflects culture, is a mirror of culture. This is a core topic of this book.

Conclusion

From the 1980s onward, the name of the game has been standardization because of assumed economies of scale. In reality, few successful global brands are fully standardized. The wish for global standard brands is in the mind of the producer, not in the mind of the consumer. Consumers don't care if the brand is global, and they increasingly prefer local brands or what they perceive as local brands.

In past decades, companies have learned that brands are their major assets, and a variety of branding strategies emerged. The major multinationals have at the same time learned their lessons about globalization. Many of them have restructured their organizations and harmonized their brand portfolios. Harmonization of brand portfolios was driven by the wish to create economies of scale in production, sales, marketing, and advertising. The core dilemma in this process has been choosing between a standardized product and marketing activities versus a differentiated approach (or some position between). Not all arguments for standardization have been equally valid. Some products can be standardized, but the role of advertising is different. Advertising adds value to products and thus makes them into brands. Advertising links products to people. Effective advertising reflects the values of the audiences it targets: The values included in advertising must match consumers' values in order to make advertising effective. This begs the question of whether one standardized advertisement can include the variety of values of all world populations. The question can be ignored if one global world culture is waiting around the corner. In order to understand the improbability of a global world culture, the concept of culture must be understood. That will be the topic of the next chapter.

Notes

1. The 100 Top Brands. (2004, August 9). *BusinessWeek* [special report], 68–71.

2. Data retrieved October 29, 2004, from Interbrand at www.brandchannel.com and 2003 Global Brands Scoreboard at http://bwnt.businessweek.com/brand/2003/index.asp

3. Reader's Digest conducts this study annually and publishes the results on the Internet [www.rdtrustedbrands.com] (see Appendix B).

4. Banerjee, A. (1994). Transnational advertising development and management: An account planning approach and a process framework. *International Journal of Advertising, 13,* 124.

5. Woesler de Panafleu, C. (1994, October). *Future identification values of brands.* Prague: ESOMAR Seminar on Building Successful Brands, p. 1.

6. Feldwick, P., & Bonnal, F. (1994, October). *Reports of the death of brands have been greatly exaggerated.* Prague: ESOMAR Seminar on Building Successful Brands, p. 23.

7. Mihailovic, P., & De Chernatony, L. (1995). The era of brand culling—Time for a global rethink? *Journal of Brand Management, 2,* 308–315.

8. This story is from the German brand consultant Klaus Brandmeyer.

9. Zambuni, R. (1993). Developing brands across borders. *Journal of Brand Management, 1,* 22–29.

10. Nijenhuis, H. (1995, August 16). Fast food per decreet in Moskou. *NRC Handelsblad.*

11. Macrae, C. (1993). Brand benchmarking applied to global branding processes. *Journal of Brand Management,* 289–302.

12. Levitt, T. (1983). The globalization of markets. *Harvard Business Review, 83*(3), 92–102.

13. Ohmae, K. (1989, May-June). Managing in a borderless world. *Harvard Business Review,* 152–161.

14. Berger, P. L. (2002). Introduction: The cultural dynamics of globalization. In P. L. Berger & S. P. Huntington (Eds.), *Many globalizations: Cultural diversity in the contemporary world.* Oxford, UK: Oxford University Press.

15. Rose, G. M. (1997). Cross-cultural values research: Implications for international advertising. In L. R. Kahle & L. Chiagouris (Eds.), *Values, lifestyles and psychographics.* Mahwah, NJ: Lawrence Erlbaum, p. 395.

16. Galloni, A. (2002, February). Marketers face divergent tech targets. *Marketing & Media,* 26.

17. Lau, S. (2001, March). I want my MTV, but in Mandarin, please. *Admap,* 34.

18. Cooper, P. (1997, October). Western at the weekends. *Admap,* 18–21.

19. Roland, A. (1988). *In search of self in India and Japan.* Princeton, NJ: Princeton University Press, p. 236.

20. ACNielsen Insights. (1998, November). p. 8.

21. There was a German, a Belgian and a Spaniard. (1999, January 23). *Economist,* 68.

22. Hicks, R. (2000, November). The unusual business suspects. *M&M Europe,* 56–57.

23. Huntington, S. P. (1996). *The clash of civilizations and the remaking of world order.* New York: Simon & Schuster, p. 58.

24. Jones, J. P. (2000). Introduction: The vicissitudes of international advertising. In J. P. Jones (Ed.), *International advertising: Realities and myths.* Thousand Oaks, CA: Sage, p. 5.

25. McLuhan, M. (1964). *Understanding media: The extensions of man.* New York: McGraw-Hill, pp. 225, 268, and 276.

26. Inkeles, A. (1998). *One world emerging? Convergence and divergence in industrial societies.* Boulder, CO: Westview, pp. 20–23.

27. *Young Europeans in 2001.* (2001). Eurobarometer report 151 (see Appendix B). Retrieved October 29, 2004, from http://europa.eu.int/comm/public_opinion/archives/special.htm.

28. White, R. (1998). International advertising: How far can it fly? In J. P. Jones (Ed.), *International advertising.* Thousand Oaks, CA: Sage, p. 34.

29. Theil, S. (2004, November 1). Not made for walking. *Newsweek,* 36–37.

30. Huntington, S. P. (1996). The goals of development. In A. Inkeles & M. Sasaki (Eds.), *Comparing nations and cultures.* Englewood Cliffs, NJ: Prentice Hall.

31.   De Mooij, M. (2003). *Consumer behavior and culture: Consequences for global Marketing and Advertising.* Thousand Oaks, CA: Sage, p. 71.

32.   An explanation of the calculations can be found in de Mooij, 2003, 56–65.

33.   Allman, J. (1997, January). Variety is the spice of Latin life. *M&M Europe,* 49–50.

34.   Living with a superpower. (2003, January 4). *Economist,* 18–20.

35.   Madsen, H. (2001). The world in 2001. *Economist,* 150.

36.   Dibb, S., Simkin, L., & Yuen, R. (1994). Pan-European advertising: Think Europe—Act local. *International Journal of Advertising, 13,* 125–135.

37.   Reader's Digest Trusted Brands. Retrieved October 29, 2004, from www.rdtrusted-brands.com

38.   Bullmore, J. (1991). *Behind the scenes in advertising.* Henley-on-Thames, Oxfordshire, UK: NTC Publications, pp. 79–82.

39.   Franzen, G. (personal communication, Branding Seminars BBDO College, 1993), former president of FHV/BBDO in the Netherlands and Professor of Advertising at the University of Amsterdam.

40.   Duckworth, G. (1995, January). New angles on how advertising works. *Admap,* 41–43.

41.   Franzen, G. (1994). *Advertising effectiveness.* Henley-on-Thames, Oxfordshire, UK: NTC Publications.

THREE

Culture

The global-local paradox points out the need to understand the consequences of culture. Most elements of consumer behavior are culture-bound, and so are the marketing strategies that marketers develop. Advertising is a cultural artifact. In order to build relationships between consumers and brands, advertising must reflect people's values. For most people, culture is viewed as something abstract and intangible. The purpose of this chapter and the next is to make culture more concrete so that it is easier to deal with. This chapter explains what culture is.

Culture Defined

In the English language, as in many others, *culture* is a complicated word. It is used to describe high art (classical music, theater, painting, and sculpture), and it is often used to contrast these forms with popular art. It is used by biologists who produce cultures of bacteria; it is used in agriculture and horticulture. In advertising, cultural differences usually refer to the expressions of culture.

Culture is the glue that binds groups together. Without cultural patterns—organized systems of significant symbols—people would have difficulty living together. Culture is what defines a human community, its individuals, and social organizations. The anthropologist Clifford Geertz[1] views culture as a set of control mechanisms—plans, recipes, rules, instructions (what computer engineers call "programs")—for the governing of behavior. People are dependent on the control mechanisms of culture for ordering their behavior. In line with this, Hofstede[2] defines culture as "the collective mental programming of the people in an environment. Culture is not a characteristic of individuals; it encompasses a number of people who were conditioned by the same education and life experience."

Individuals are products of their culture; they are conditioned by their sociocultural environment to act in certain manners. Culture includes the things that have "worked" in the past. It includes shared beliefs, attitudes, norms, roles, and values found among speakers of a particular language who live during the same historical period in a specific geographic region. These shared elements of subjective culture are usually transferred from generation to generation. Language, time, and place help define culture.[3] Culture is to society what memory is to individuals.

The term *culture* may apply to ethnic or national groups, or to groups within a society, at different levels: a country, an age-group, a profession, or a social class. The cultural programming of an individual depends on the groups or categories to which he or she belongs. The expressions of culture belonging to a certain level of cultural programming will differ: Eating habits may differ by country, dress habits by profession, and gender roles by both country and social class. When discussing "culture," it is important to be specific about the level, whether "national culture," "corporate culture," or "age culture," in order not to create confusion. What is true at one level need not apply to another.

Geertz[4] suggests that there is no such thing as a human nature independent of culture. Without interaction with culture, and thus the guidance provided by systems of significant symbols, our central nervous system would be incapable of directing our behavior. We are incomplete or unfinished animals who complete or finish ourselves through culture. Conclusions from psychoanalytic work in India, Japan, and the United States by the cross-cultural psychologist Roland are in accord with Geertz's statement. From Roland's[5] psychoanalytical work, it is apparent that the kinds of personalities persons actually develop, how they function and communicate in society, what their mode of being and experience is in the world and within themselves, and what their ideals and actualities of individuation are depend overwhelmingly on the given culture and society to which they belong.

Our ideas, our values, our acts, and our emotions are cultural products. We are individuals under the guidance of cultural patterns, historically created systems of meaning.

Advertising reflects these wider systems of meaning: It reflects the way people think, what moves them, how they relate to each other, how they live, eat, relax, and enjoy themselves. All manifestations of culture, at different levels, are reflected in advertising. In order to analyze advertising as a manifestation of culture at the broader level, it must be understood that culture is expressed in several ways.

Cultural Universals

Although people are not the same, Western marketing and advertising professionals tend to perceive them to be the same, which is led by wishful thinking: They want people to be the same, to have the same needs and aspirations. This leads to cultural blindness: both perceptual and conceptual blindness. As a result, many international marketers embrace the idea that there are cultural universals, modes of behavior that exist in all cultures. Textbooks on international marketing tend to mention the search for cultural universals as a valuable orientation, referring to, among others, Murdock's list of cultural universals,[6] modes of behavior existing in all cultures. Examples of universals are bodily adornment, cleanliness, training, and cooking and food taboos. Indeed, a basic, universal need is eating. But it is not just to eat, it is to prefer certain foods cooked in certain ways and to follow a rigid table etiquette in consuming them.[7] A universal need is to be healthy. But how we act to remain healthy is different. In the south of Europe, for example, people use more medication, whereas in the north people have a more active approach to health and exercise or play sports.

It is not to talk, it is to utter the appropriate words and phrases in the appropriate social situations in the appropriate tone of voice. Religion may be perceived as a cultural universal, but the belief in one god or more, people's relationships with their gods, and the rituals of worship are all part of culture and define the artifacts developed within a culture. Why are European cathedrals of a different structure than mosques or Hindu temples, or American churches? Because they serve different religious practices. The concept of divinity is a Western concept. Ruth Benedict,[8] in her classic study on Japanese culture, describes how, after World War II, Japan was to adopt modern values in which a concept of a divine monarch—as perceived through the eyes of the Americans—did not fit, and it was suggested to the Japanese emperor that he disavow his divinity. The emperor's reaction was said to be that it would be an embarrassment to strip himself of something he did not have.

Universals are always formulated in abstract terms, like happiness or love. But what makes people happy or how they express love not only varies by individual but even more by culture. The more values are formulated in an abstract way, the more universal they are. But in marketing and advertising, we'll have to express values and motives in a concrete way. Then most universality disappears.

Manifestations of Culture

Hofstede[9] distinguishes four manifestations of culture: symbols, rituals, heroes, and values. In Figure 3.1, these are depicted like the layers of an onion, indicating that symbols represent the most superficial and values the deepest manifestations of culture, with heroes and rituals falling somewhere in between.

Symbols are words, gestures, pictures, or objects that carry a particular meaning recognized only by those who share a culture. The words of a language or a particular kind of jargon belong in this category, as do dress, hairstyles, flags, status symbols, and brands like Coca-Cola. New symbols are easily developed and old ones quickly disappear; symbols from one cultural group are regularly copied by others. This is why symbols are shown in the outer, most superficial layer in Figure 3.1. Coca-Cola, Pepsi-Cola, Marlboro, and Nike are examples of brands that have become global symbols. Yet they may include different associations in America, the country of origin of the brands, than they do for the Chinese.

Heroes are persons—alive or dead, real or imaginary—who possess characteristics that are highly prized in a society, and who thus serve as role models for behavior. Even fantasy or cartoon figures, like Batman or Charley Brown in the United States and Astérix in France, can serve as cultural heroes. In the television age,

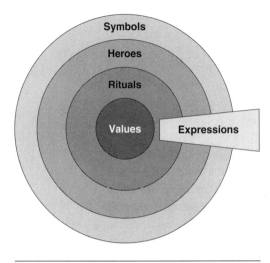

Figure 3.1   Culture as an Onion

SOURCE: Hofstede (1991)

outward appearances have become more important in choosing heroes than they were before. Fantasy heroes can become globally known, but the stories in which they play a part often are local. Astérix behaves in a different way than Donald Duck. The educational programs of *Sesame Street* are developed locally in order to fit into a country's education system. Topics vary among European countries.

Rituals are the collective activities considered socially essential within a culture: They are carried out for their own sake. Examples include ways of greeting, ways of paying respect to others, and social and religious ceremonies. Business and political meetings organized for seemingly rational reasons often serve mainly ritual purposes: for example, to allow the leaders to assert themselves. Sporting events are rituals for both the players and the spectators. The rituals around American football are very different from those around European football. In particular, the phenomenon of cheerleaders is nonexistent in Europe.

In Figure 3.1, symbols, heroes, and rituals are included in the term *expressions of culture*. They are visible to an outside observer. Their cultural meaning is invisible, however; it lies in the way the expressions are interpreted by the insiders of the culture. Brands are part of a ritual, and advertising helps make the ritual. Manufacturers use and create rituals around their products to differentiate them from competitive products. The beer brand Corona Extra distinguishes itself from others by the suggestion that it should be consumed by drinking from the bottle after having pushed a piece of lime into the long neck of the bottle. Advertising displays the rituals around products and brands found in the executional aspects of advertising. Examples of executional aspects are how people look, the color of their skin, how they are dressed, their language, their eating habits, and what their houses look like. These elements are the expressions or artifacts of culture that express "How we do things here."

At the core of culture lie values. Values are defined as "broad tendencies to prefer a certain state of affairs over others." Values are among the first things children learn, not consciously but implicitly. Developmental psychologists believe that by the age of 10 most children have their basic value system firmly in place and that after this age changes are difficult to obtain. People are not consciously aware of the values they hold, so it is difficult to discuss or observe them.

Researchers try to describe values by asking people to state a preference among alternatives. One of the difficulties in researching values is interpreting what people say. There is a distinction between the desirable and the desired: how people think the world ought to be versus what people want for themselves. Language is another problem: Values don't translate easily because words expressing values have abstract meaning. They must be seen as labels of values. A word may serve as a label of a value in one culture but be the label of a different value in another culture. This explains the difficulty of translating advertising copy into languages other than the one in which it is conceived. This issue will be further discussed in Chapter 5.

A so-called global culture refers to the expressions of culture, the symbols, converging eating habits, and global heroes, particularly those who appeal to the young. Nike and Coca-Cola have become global symbols. Fast food, and particularly the Big Mac or pizzas, have become a global ritual. Yet the core or central values have not become global; they vary across cultures and are not likely to change during our lifetime. This stability of core values is not well understood by advertising people, who are particularly fond of "trends." Linking new products and services to "new" habits and lifestyles can be a profitable activity. Lifestyles are the expressions of culture. Trends labeled as "changing values" or "global trends" might better be scrutinized before applying them. The core values of culture are stable, and often what is presented as a new "trend" is merely a new expression format of existing values.

Selective Perception

Perception is the process by which each individual selects, organizes, and evaluates stimuli from the external environment to provide meaningful experiences for him- or herself.[10] Selective perception means that people focus on certain features of their environment to the exclusion of others. This phenomenon plays a role in the discussion of an emerging *global culture.* Most of the discourse on this is by Anglo-Americans. Usually the examples and illustrations accompanying the discourse are American brands like Coca-Cola, McDonald's, and Starbucks. The authors' selective perception mechanism makes them see what they are used to in their own country, more than the much larger numbers of local regional brands in other continents that dominate more than American brands. In their eyes, the pizza is American, not Italian. The selective perception phenomenon also has strong consequences for advertising in an age in which the growing discrepancy between communication supply and consumption has led to the phenomenon of communication overload—that is, the share of communication supply that is not consumed. Communication overload in developed economies such as the United States and Japan is estimated at an average of 97%.[11] Consumers are increasingly selective in what receives their attention. Culture reinforces this selective process. No two national groups see the world in exactly the same way. Medical studies of blind adults given sight through corrective surgery show that we have to be taught the "rules of seeing." These rules of seeing are not universal principles but are formed by the natural and social environments that teach us both what to look at and how to see it.[12] What people see is a function of what they have been trained or have learned to see in the course of growing up. Perceptual patterns are learned and culturally determined. You see what you want to see, and you don't see what you cannot see because it does not fit with your experience, your prior learning. We perceive what we expect to perceive. We perceive things according to our cultural map.[13] We become confused when things appear to be different from what we expected, and we may draw the wrong conclusions. Expecting guests at 8 but having them arrive at 9 will lead some of us to conclude that our guests are polite, others of us that they are impolite. Others, arriving at our house at dinner time without invitation, may expect food because of their perception of hospitality. One reaction will be sharing whatever food there is, the other is embarrassment and waiting with dinner until the visitors have left. Some people nod their heads when they say "yes," but that may mean "no" in quite a few other countries. We expect and see things from our own cultural frame of mind. We are prisoners of our own culture. Consumers are, and so are creative directors who follow their own cultural automatic pilot when developing advertising. This phenomenon enables them to develop effective advertising for their own culture, but it limits their ability to develop effective advertising ideas, including meaningful values, for other cultures. Advertising in which the values do not match those of the culture of the receiver will be less noted or misunderstood and thus less effective.

Stereotyping

Stereotyping means mentally placing people in categories. Stereotypes can be functional or dysfunctional. Stereotyping is functional when we accept it as a natural process to guide our expectations. Stereotyping is dysfunctional if we use it to judge individuals incorrectly, seeing them only as part of a group. An example of a functional stereotype is that the Germans are punctual, which is correct. On average, they are more punctual than many other peoples. Certainly the Italians and the Spanish have a different concept of time. For the Spanish, knowledge of this aspect of the German culture means that they can adapt their behavior: When they are expected for dinner, 8 o'clock means 8 o'clock, and not 9 or 10 as it does in Spain. An example of a dysfunctional stereotype is the British saying that the French are dirty, oversexed, and ludicrously obsessed with their culture, and the French saying that the British are cold, uncultivated, hypocritical, and unreliable.[14] Yes, the British are more reserved in the eyes of the French, the Italians generally more chaotic in the eyes of the Germans, and the Germans rigid as perceived by the British. It is important to realize that culture is relative: Stereotypes are in the eyes of the beholder's culture. Because culture is stable, stereotypes can be found in literature from early times on. An example is the way the Dutch have become part of the English language: "Going Dutch," "a Dutch treat," and "a Dutch uncle" are expressions that reflect characteristics of the Dutch as observed by the English. Similar expressions do not occur in the German and French languages.

Advertising depends on the use of effective stereotypes because it must attract attention and create instant recognition. Advertising simplifies reality and thus has to use stereotypes. Advertising messages are generally short, and if audiences do not immediately recognize what the message is about, it is lost. Culture interferes. When we perceive or depict people of other cultures, we do so from the perspective of our own culture. Different cultures have different stereotypes of other

La gente la mira y sonríe.
Por fin todos entienden el humor alemán.

New Beetle

Illustration 3.1
Volkswagen, Spain

cultures. What are the characteristics of the stereotyped French? The Germans think the French are resourceful; the British think they are humorless and short-tempered. The Dutch think the French are not very serious; the Spanish think they are cold and distant. The Finns think they are romantic, yet superficial. The Americans think they are pleasant and intelligent, yet pretentious. Asians think they are indiscreet.[15]

From this example, it is obvious that it is particularly dangerous to use strong national stereotypes in international advertising. The creative director's stereotyped perception may be different from the stereotyped perception of audiences in countries other than his own. There are some stereotypes that are shared by several cultures in Europe, for example the stereotype of the German sense of humor not being understandable to others. The Spanish advertisement for Volkswagen (see Illustration 3.1) ties into that stereotype by saying, "People see this and smile. At last they understand German humor."

Thinking Patterns and Intellectual Styles

There is not just one way of logical thinking. Linear, externalized logic is part of Western philosophy and science and different from other cultures' "logic," such as the more inward-looking Buddhist philosophies. Digital thinking and decision making is a characteristic of the North American communication system. The Japanese are more inclined toward the analog. North Americans are structural and analytical; they lack the dynamics of the Chinese yin-yang, the European dialectic (the process aimed at abolishing differences of opinion), or the Japanese holistic pattern recognition approach that involves recognizing the feeling of the overall situation before looking at the details. The North American approach works toward extremes in order to facilitate decision making. In continental European cultures, the emphasis is on making an analysis in order to generate ideological and theoretical arguments.

The way in which arguments are supported also varies across cultures. Some tend to rely on facts, some on ideology or dogma, and others on tradition or emotion. For the Japanese, the *kimochi*, or feeling, has to be right; logic is cold. The Saudis seem to be intuitive in approach and avoid persuasion based primarily on empirical reasoning. The French have a philosophy; Americans want data and proof of hypotheses. Usunier[16] distinguishes four different intellectual styles: the "Gallic" (French), the "Teutonic" (German), the "Saxonic" (English and American), and the "Nipponic" (Japanese). Saxons prefer to look for facts and evidence. Teutonic and Gallic styles tend to place theoretical arguments at the center of their intellectual process. Data and facts are there to illustrate what is said rather than to demonstrate it. The Teutonic style includes a preference for reasoning and deduction. The Gallic style is less occupied with deduction; it is directed more toward the use of persuasive strength of words and speeches in an aesthetically perfect way. The Nipponic intellectual style favors a more modest, global, and provisional approach: Thinking and knowledge are conceived of as being in a temporary state, avoiding absolute, categorical statements.

Americans categorize virtually everything. Duality, a way of categorizing, is implicitly and explicitly part of American culture: concrete versus abstract, present versus past, new versus old, past versus future, harmony versus conflict, inner-directed versus outer-directed.[17] Japanese thought is not logical, but intuitive.[18] The Japanese are not familiar with polar thinking. Two-dimensional maps used to structure values or wants or for positioning brands are not very popular in Japan, where people are not used to responding on bipolar scales.

How people learn influences their thinking and response. "Western" learning methods are largely based on critical thinking and analysis. Asian learning systems are very much based on memorizing. Different cultures teach different ways of gathering and weighing evidence, of presenting viewpoints and reaching conclusions. Particularly in the United States, if there are no facts to support an opinion, the opinion will not be considered legitimate or valid. There is an expression in the American language that expresses this: "the point," as in "Let's get right to the point," or "What's the point of all this?" Writers and speakers are supposed to "make their points clear," meaning that they are supposed to say or write explicitly the idea or piece of information they wish to convey. The directness associated with "the point" is not part of Chinese or Japanese languages.[19]

Language

There are two ways of looking at the language-culture relationship: Language influences culture, or language is an expression of culture. Edward Sapir and Benjamin Lee Whorf hypothesized that the structure of language has a significant influence on perception and categorization.[20] The latter would imply that the worldview of people depends on the structure and characteristics of the language they speak. Users of markedly different grammars are led by their grammars toward different types of observations and different evaluations of similar acts of observation. According to this viewpoint, language is not only an instrument for describing events, it also shapes events. Observers using different languages will posit different facts under the same circumstances, or they will arrange similar facts in different ways. The other viewpoint is that language reflects culture. The approach is to realize that only the ability to speak is universal for humankind. Which language a person speaks is part of the culture in which she or he grows up. The language reflects all manifestations of culture, the expressions and the values. Language illustrates culture. Expressions of culture are particularly recognizable in the use of metaphors. Examples are expressions like "he is a team player," "he drives me up the wall," a "ballpark estimate," all derived from American baseball in the American language, whereas British English has a number of expressions relating to cricket. The elements used in metaphors will vary. In Egypt, for example, the sun is perceived as cruel, so a girl will not be described as "my sunshine," but may be compared with moonlight.[21] "Moonlighting" in English means having a second job in the evening.

It is the cultural environment that explains why some languages have more words for one thing than for others. Some languages have more different words for the different substances of ice or rain than others. The Norwegian language reflects a historic seafaring nation, having one strong word for "wind in your favor": *bør*. Some languages have words that do not exist in others. The English *pith*, the archaic word for marrow, refers to the white under the skin of oranges and other citrus fruit. This seems to be directly linked with the British "marmalade culture." There is no equivalent in the Dutch language for the English *to fudge* (empty talk, refusing to commit oneself). The Dutch are not inclined to fudge, which may explain their image of being blunt.

Some culture-specific words migrate to other languages if they express something unique. Examples of such words are *management, computer, apartheid, machismo, perestroika, geisha, sauna, Mafia,* and *kamikaze*.[22] Often, these words reflect the specific values of a culture. They cannot easily be translated into words of other cultures, or they have been borrowed from another culture from the start. The English language does not have its own words for *cousin* and *nephew*. These were borrowed from French (*cousin* and *neveu*). The way a person describes kin is closely connected with the way he or she thinks about them. In extended families, a father and a father's brother may both be termed "father." The Hungarians differentiate between a younger sister (*húg*) and an older sister (*növér*). The Russian language has different names for the four different brothers-in-law. In Indonesian, *besan* is the word for "parents of the children who are married to each other."[23]

The Dutch language shows frequent use of diminutives; so does the Spanish language. In both languages, use of the diminutive suffix reflects something positive, whereas using the enlargement suffix turns it into something negative.

The English language reflects the way Anglo-Saxons deal with action and time. They have a rich vocabulary expressing this, such as "down to earth," "feedback," "deadline." The English word *upset* expresses the way the English handle their emotions, with self-constraint. *Upset* is not translatable into most other languages. The English concept of sharing includes more values than a translation in other European languages can include. It includes "generosity," "participating," "caring for fellow people," "not totally concerned with the self," and "communicating positive things." It includes showing "how good you are" and "achievement." It covers both the German *teilen* and *mitteilen* or the Dutch *delen* and *mededelen* and more than that.

The Dutch and the Scandinavians have words for "togetherness" that express much more than "being together" and that do not exist in the Anglo-Saxon world. The words are *gezellig* (Dutch), *hyggelig* (Danish), *mysigt* (Swedish), and *kodikas* (Finnish). The Danes use it even in combinations like *hyggetime* ("together time") and *hyggemad* ("together food").[24] It means sharing your feelings and philosophies in a very personal way while being together in a small group. An Englishman living in the Netherlands, when asked his opinion about it, will shiver and say: "It is so intrusive." The concept means preferring a dinner party for four people to a larger group, whereas a small group is not considered to be a dinner party by the British or the Americans, who tend to apologize if there are not more than two couples for dinner. For the Dutch and the Scandinavians, the concept can be used very effectively in advertising for the type of product used during such meetings, such as coffee, sweets, and drinks. The concept will not be understood by members of other cultures. The coffee company Sara Lee/Douwe Egberts has used it very effectively for advertising their coffee in Holland during the past century and has earned a substantial market share through its use.

German examples include the word *Reinheit*, which has a wider meaning than the word *purity*. The word *ergiebig* is another example, meaning delivering quality and efficiency, or more for the same money. The Spanish word *placer* means much more than the translation *pleasure*. It includes pleasure while eating, enjoyment, sharing a social event, softness, warmth, the good life, contentment, and satisfaction. Some words represent interpersonal relations of one culture that do not exist in others. The French notions of *savoir faire* and *savoir vivre* include a vast array of values specific to French culture and cannot be properly translated. The Japanese expression for "computer graphics" carries the meaning of a picture, a drawing, and illustration or sketch, but not of a graph. Another example is the Japanese word for "animation," which in translation carries the meaning of "comics" or "cartoons."[25] In Japan, the word for "heart" associates with "warmth," not necessarily with "love," as love is not expressed the same as in the Western world. There are no proper equivalents to the words *identity* and *personality* in the Japanese language, as the concept of personality separate from the social environment is alien to the Japanese people.

Untranslatable concepts often are so meaningful to members of a specific culture that they are effective elements of advertising copy. They refer to collective memory. This implies that words that are labels of culturally meaningful concepts are too ambiguous to use in international campaigns. A European campaign for the KitKat candy bar was based on the concept of the "break": "Take a break, take a KitKat." The break was an English institution: the 11 o'clock morning tea break, when working people had their morning tea, and brought a KitKat as a snack. Because of this, KitKat in the United Kingdom was called "Elevenses." This type of break did not exist in any other country in Europe, so the break concept had to be "translated" in a different way for the other countries. Continental Europeans do not have the same "break" memory as do the British.

Illustration 3.2   CA International

Language is much more important than many international advertisers realize. It is common knowledge among those who are bi- or trilingual that copy carrying cultural values is difficult to translate. Monolingual people generally do not understand this. If translations are needed, particularly for research purposes, the best system is translating and back-translating the questions to be sure that at least the questions have the same meaning. Yet the values included in the words cannot be translated, and often conceptual equivalence cannot be attained.

Although English is the most spoken second language in the world, fluency varies widely, and advertisers have to understand that even in countries where most people seem to be able to understand English, this knowledge often is only superficial. Certainly colloquial English or American expressions will not be understood. The advertisement for Computer Associates (Illustration 3.2) uses the word *schmortal*, which is not understandable for Europeans who speak English. Yet the ad was in the European edition of *BusinessWeek*.

Signs, Symbols, and Body Language

Peirce,[26] one of the founders of semiotics as a discipline, distinguishes three basic types of sign: icon, index, and symbol. An *icon* bears a resemblance to its object. An *index* is a sign with a direct existential connection with its object—smoke is an index of fire. A *symbol* is a sign whose connection with its object is a matter of convention, agreement, or rule. Words and numbers are symbols; so is the red cross. Globalization has led to increased use of icons. Airports, stations, and other places frequented by international travelers use icons because they are not linked with language. They also help with faster information processing. Other examples are the use of diagrams such as bar or pie charts in reports and presentations. Icons, indexes, and symbols are part of the fundamental semiotic instruments used for advertising. Language codes, signs, symbols, and gestures are all rituals of culture and define cultural groups. *Culture* is the shared ability to recognize, decode, and produce signs and symbols, so culture also is a combination of semiotic habits. Differences in semiotic habits delineate cultures.

Semiotics, the study of signs and symbols, is in many countries an integral part of advertising theory, although used more in some countries (France, eastern Europe) than in others. Some cultures use more symbols in advertising than do others. This is related to writing and language. The Japanese and other Asians using the kanji script seem to have a greater ability to perceive and use symbols. Experience with Japanese students in a non-Japanese learning environment shows that, compared with Western students, they tend to be more comfortable with pictures and symbols than with language, particularly if the language is not their native language.

Signs and symbols are an important part of association networks in our memory: package, color, letters, signs. Color can have a particularly strong cultural meaning. Black is the color of mourning in the Western world. In China, white symbolizes mourning. Gold has a strong symbolic meaning for the Chinese, but not combined with black, a combination used by Benson and Hedges cigarettes in their global campaign. IKEA uses the colors blue and yellow internationally, the colors of the Swedish flag, but not in Denmark, a country that in the past was occupied by the Swedes. Those colors still have too negative a connotation for the Danes. Because of this, IKEA uses the combination of red and white in Denmark, the colors of the Danish flag. For

Illustration 3.3   Cigarette Brand 555, Cambodia

some cultures, symbolic language is much more important than verbal language. In Asia, numbers have significance unknown to Western cultures. Numbers can be particularly meaningful. An example is the 555 cigarette brand in Asia. Illustration 3.3 shows this brand in Cambodia.

Gestures are important cultural signs: Gestures that in one culture have a positive meaning can be embarrassing to members of another culture. A Russian gesture meaning "friendship" means "winning" in the United States. Germans raise their eyebrows in recognition of a clever idea. The same expression in Britain and the Netherlands is a sign of skepticism. The Hungarian gesture, as shown in outdoor advertising for Pepsi in Illustration 3.4, is

Illustration 3.4   Pepsi, Hungary

perceived as obscene, not only in West European countries but also in Bulgaria, close to Hungary. The U.S. OK sign means "zero" in France and Hungary, "money" in Japan. The thumbs-up gesture is used by pilots the world over, but in some countries, it is not so accepted. The V sign means "victory" for the English if the palm and fingers face outward; if the palm and fingers face inward, it means, "up yours."

Putting your feet up on your desk, as in the advertisement for Glenfiddich (Illustration 3.5), may demonstrate relaxation or a "Friday feeling" in the United States, but showing the soles of your shoes or feet is offensive in most other parts of the world, in particular in Asia and the Arab world. Showing your tongue to other people in Europe is a sign of contempt, but for children it is a sign of challenging other children. In Asia, it is impolite, even for children. For the Maoris in New Zealand, it is a sign of great respect.

The Friday Scotch

Making mistakes is easy, as every seasoned traveler will have discovered. What is considered polite in one culture may be considered obscene in another. What is friendly here is hostile there. A comprehensive guide to the meaning of gestures was developed by Desmond Morris,[27] who adds the note that signaling by gesture is a predominantly masculine pursuit. In one country, it is so exclusively masculine that a female researcher had to withdraw before the local men would even discuss the subject.

Proxemics, the study of people's use of space as a cultural artifact,[28] deals with the degree to which people want to be close to other people or to touch others. It is an aspect of body language and an expression of culture. When someone from the south of Europe makes a motion to a northern European to link arms while walking in the street, the latter may not know how to react, as touching in public is not something universal in Europe. Northern Europeans don't like to be close to other people. Observance of people's behavior in elevators will show that when the crowd in an elevator dissolves, the French will stay where they are, yet the British will quickly increase space between each other.

The anthropologist Edward Hall,[29] in particular, has studied differences in proxemics in various cultures. In the United States, there is a commonly accepted invisible boundary around any two or three people in conversation that separates them from others. Distance alone serves to isolate, give privacy. Someone can be in a room with other people without disturbing their "privacy." When a person stands still or sits down even in a public place, a small sphere of privacy balloons around him or her, which is considered inviolate. Anyone who enters this zone and stays there is intruding. For the Germans, there is no such thing as being in the room without being inside the zone of intrusion of the other party present, no matter how far away. When an American wants to be alone, she or he goes into a room and shuts the door. The English have internalized a set of barriers that they erect and that others are supposed to recognize. For the French or the Spanish, proxemics are very different. Mediterranean use of space can be seen in the crowded trains, buses, sidewalks, and cafés. These cultures are characterized by high sensory involvement, expressed in the way they eat, entertain, and crowd together in cafés. Isolating oneself is seen as an insult to others. Anglo-Saxons tend to go into their room and shut the door when they want to be alone. The Spanish don't do this. American students studying in Spain and living with families tend to become confused when their families show concern every time they are alone in their rooms with the door shut. Another example is how professors and students relate. Spanish professors and students socialize outside class. They go to bars, dance, and touch. This is seen as inappropriate in the United States, where professors can even be accused of sexual harassment if the interaction is between people of different sexes. Differences between Arabs and Americans or Europeans are even stronger. Arabs do not like enclosed space. Muslims have particularly strong rules for space between men and women. In advertisements, if showing men and women together is allowed at all, the distance must be carefully observed.

The American home compartmentalizes the family, so children grow up leading separate lives. This has consequences for media behavior. Americans are not used to watching television in groups, as are the Spanish.

When comparing cultures, it is important to learn which are the signs and symbols used by a culture and how they are recognized.

Imagery and Music

Imagery, or the use of pictures, symbols, or metaphors as a way of conveying meaning, is based on pictorial conventions. Pictorial conventions are not self-evident but formed for the purpose of representation. There are significant cross-cultural differences in pictorial perception and the construction of pictures. The selection of style, of point of view shown in a picture, is based on the cultural learning of a photographer or creative director, with the cultural learning of the audience in mind. Audiences (consumers) use their learned vocabulary of pictorial skills in the response.

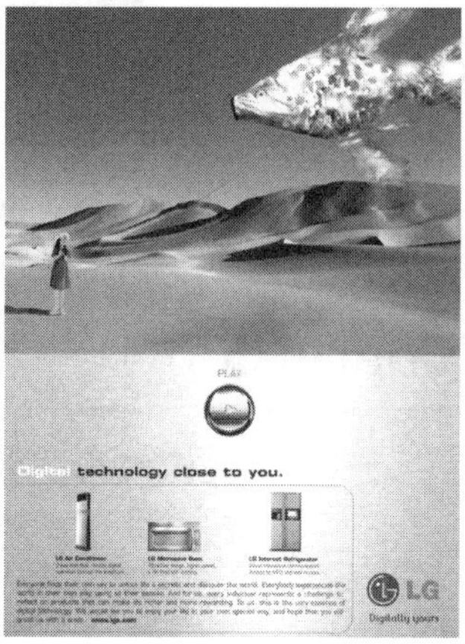

Western people tend to think of the interpretation of pictures as a process occurring in time: the sequence of information processing as a function of visual layout. But not all cultures have a sequential thinking pattern. The concept of time varies, as well as the direction of viewing (left to right or right to left). Preferences for symbols or verbal expression and for movement or stills vary so much that art directors should think twice before developing an international campaign based on visuals. Yet the statement that visuals travel better than words is still often heard. Pictures, just like verbal language, have to be translated into the pictorial language of other cultures.

Illustration 3.6
LG, International

Metaphors, in particular, represent cultural artifacts. The advertisements for LG (Illustration 3.6) and Infonet (Illustration 3.7), both from *Newsweek,* represent metaphors that will not be understood universally. Korean LG uses a fish, symbolizing prosperity in Asia, but which is not understood in most of the Western world.

**Break
the spell,
communicate
globally**

Whatever you wish for your global communications,
solutions from Infonet make it come true.

infonet
www.infonet.com

Illustration 3.7   Infonet,
International

Infonet refers to an originally German fairy tale written by the brothers Grimm, which may not be well understood in all countries in the world.

Music is another aspect of culture. Although many types of music have proved able to travel (classical music, jazz, pop music), cultures tend to have their own rhythm. A people's music is inseparable from their lives, and songs represent an important part of their identity. Music represents a sort of rhythmic consensus, a consensus of the core culture. Technically, little is known about what human synchrony is, but rhythm is basic to synchrony. Being in sync with the core culture must be more effective than being out of sync.[30] Language has a rhythm, too. Those who have learned to speak a foreign language well, according to grammar and idiom, know that they will not be understood if they have not learned the music and rhythm of that language.

Global Culture

Because of the ubiquity of a few global symbols, like Coca-Cola, Levi's, and Nike, people think that eventually there will be one global world culture, also with respect to values, created by large global companies. Global communication has, indeed, influenced the relationships among some people worldwide, resulting in several "global cultures," such as corporate cultures and professional cultures. These exist, however, at the level of practices and expressions of culture, the heroes and rituals. Large multinationals tend to shape a corporate culture with shared practices: ways of dressing, meeting, communicating, and presenting, all overriding the multitude of national cultures. This is useful to give cohesion to the worldwide group of employees and to give identity to the company.

National, historically defined cultures have strong emotional connotations for those who belong to them. These connotations define their identity, which means the subjective feelings and values of a population sharing cultural characteristics, a shared "memory," a "history." Global or cosmopolitan cultures cannot refer to such a common identity. Unlike national cultures, a global culture is essentially "memoryless."

Conclusion

Cultural values determine the way people think and behave. International marketing and advertising people must understand these differences because they influence the way advertising is made and perceived. Cultural universals exist only when formulated in abstract terms. When we are dealing with people of cultures other than our own, stereotyping and selective perception can inhibit our proper understanding of people's behavior. Because language is a reflection of culture, some words that are meaningful to people in one culture cannot be translated into the language of another culture.

This supports the advice that it is better to have local copywriters write texts from a central brief than to translate a copywriter's text from one culture into another. This advice is of even greater importance with respect to public relations (PR) work when often difficult messages have to be transferred from one culture into another.

The art of advertising is to develop symbols or advertising properties that must be understood by a target audience. In international advertising, these signs or symbols usually have originated in one culture and cannot be decoded the same way by members of other cultures. Understanding the concept of culture and the consequences of cultural differences will make marketing and advertising people realize that one message, whether verbal or visual, can never reach one global audience, because there is not one global culture composed of people with identical values. Worldwide, there is a great variety of values. The problem is that we have to be able to recognize and to vocalize the differences. Models for understanding this variety will be described in Chapter 4.

Notes

1. Geertz, C. (1973). *The interpretation of cultures.* New York: Basic Books, p. 44.

2. Hofstede, G. (1991). *Cultures and organizations: Software of the mind.* London: McGraw-Hill, p. 5.

3. Triandis, H. (1995). *Individualism and collectivism.* Boulder, CO: Westview Press.

4. Geertz, 1973, 49.

5. Roland, A. (1988). *In search of self in India and Japan.* Princeton, NJ: Princeton University Press, p. 324.

6. Murdock, G. P. (1945). The common denominator of culture. In R. Linton (Ed.), *The science of man in the world crisis.* New York: Columbia University Press.

7. Geertz, 1973, 53.

8. Benedict, R. (1974). *The chrysanthemum and the sword: Patterns of Japanese culture.* Rutland, VT: Charles E. Tuttle, p. 301. (Original work published 1946)

9. This draws on Hofstede, 1991, 9. With permission.

10. Adler, N. J. (1991). *International dimensions of organizational behavior* (2nd ed.). Belmont, CA: Wadsworth, p. 63.

11. Franzen, G. (1994). *Advertising effectiveness: Findings from empirical research.* Henley-on-Thames, Oxfordshire, UK: NTC, pp. 17–24.

12. Scott, L. (1994). Images in advertising: The need for a theory of visual rhetoric. *Journal of Consumer Research, 21,* 260.

13. Adler, 1991.

14. Platt, P. (1989, January). An entente cordiale mired in stereotypes. *International Management,* 50.

15. Usunier, J. C. (1993). *International marketing: A cultural approach.* Englewood Cliffs, NJ: Prentice Hall.

16. Usunier, 1993, 71.

17. Hall, E. T. (1984). *The dance of life.* Garden City, NY: Doubleday/Anchor, p. 135.

18. Doi, T. (1973). *The anatomy of dependence.* Tokyo: Kodansha International.

19. Althen, G. (1988). *American ways.* Yarmouth, ME: Intercultural Press, pp. 30–31.

20. As cited in Usunier, 1993, 99.

21. Hofstede, G. (personal communication, 1996).

22. Hofstede, 1991, 213.

23. Burger, P. (1996, June). Gaten in de taal. *Onze Taal,* 293.

24. Burger, 1996.

25. Miracle, G. E., Bang, H. K., & Chang, K. Y. (1992, March 20). *Achieving reliable and valid cross-cultural research results.* Working paper panel of Cross-Cultural Research Design, National Conference of the American Academy of Advertising, San Antonio, TX.

26. Peirce, C. S. (1990). Collected papers [1931–1958]. In J. Fiske (Ed.), *Introduction to communication studies* (2nd ed., pp. 47–48). New York: Routledge.

27. Morris, D. (1994). *Bodytalk: A world guide to gestures.* London: Jonathan Cape.

28. Hall, 1984, 7.

29. Hall, E. T. (1969). *The hidden dimension.* Garden City, NY: Doubleday/Anchor, pp. 131–157.

30. Hall, 1984, 190–191.

FOUR

Dimensions of Culture

onsumers and advertising professionals alike know very well when "something does not fit," when "something is not right" in international communications. But this has to by vocalized to make people of other cultures
understand why the "something" does not fit; one has to be able to explain and
convince.

Without systems for understanding and classifying cultural differences, objec-
tions to an imposed brand position or advertising concept from another culture
can too easily be labeled as the "not-invented-here syndrome." Cultural differences
have to be measured and documented.

Comparing Cultures

The study of culture can be characterized by the dispute between those stressing the
unique aspects of culture and those stressing the comparable aspects. A difficulty in
comparing cultures is ethnocentrism. Because our own culture works as an automatic pilot and we are all more or less prisoners of our own culture, it is difficult to
exclude our own cultural value pattern from the way we perceive and classify other
cultures. In a more extreme sense, *ethnocentrism* refers to a tendency to feel that the
home-country people are superior to people of other countries, that they are more
intelligent, more capable, or more reliable than people of other countries. Usually,
ethnocentrism is more attributable to inexperience or lack of knowledge about
foreign cultures than to prejudice.[1]

There are basically two approaches to comparing cultures, from the emic or
from the etic point of view. *Etic* refers to what is general in cultures, *emic* to what is
specific in one or more cultures. The usefulness of culture as an explanatory variable depends on our ability to "unpackage" the culture concept. To do so, the etic
approach must be used, and cultural values must be arrayed along interpretable

dimensions. Differences in the locations of cultures along these dimensions can then be used to explain variance of behavior patterns, norms, attitudes, and personality variables.

Cross-cultural value surveys follow the etic approach, and similar questionnaires are used. Questions about values must be translatable, and meanings must have conceptual equivalence across all cultures. Some values that are specific for certain cultures alone cannot be measured directly by the etic method but only by interpreting the values included in the various etic scales. For culture-specific values, there are often no linguistic or conceptual equivalents. An example is the concept of competitiveness linked with individuals. In the English language, one can say about an individual that he or she is "a competitive person." The Dutch language does not link competitiveness to a person.

Comparing Nations

A point of discussion is the delineation of cultural groups by national boundaries, although there is much diversity within national borders. Many nations, however, are historically developed wholes that usually share one dominant language, mass media, a national education system, and national markets for products and services.[2] Because of the availability of national statistics, collected by national governments, companies generally compare nations with respect to demographics and GNI/capita. National-level culture data add value to these comparisons. Yet with respect to values, some nations are more homogeneous than others, although differences between nations are substantially larger than differences within nations. Cross-cultural psychologist Shalom Schwartz[3] assessed cultural unity within nations by comparing the cultural distance between samples within countries with the cultural distance between samples from seven different countries. The cultural distance between samples from different countries was almost always greater than the distance between samples from the same country. Between-country distances were greater in 183 of 187 comparisons. This implies that the similarity of cultural value orientations within nations, when viewed against the background of cultural distance between nations, is considerable. Comparisons of, for example, younger and older subcultures yielded similar relative national scores.

Cross-cultural consultant Arne Maas used regional data from the European Social Survey[4] to calculate a measure of cultural cohesion by cluster analysis of 21 value questions that were answered by people from all provinces in a country. The questions measured value preferences such as the importance of having friends, family, equality, the importance of work, or of being rich. These are not representative of the total value system of countries, but variety gives an indication of the degree of coherence of countries. The coherence measure found for 19 countries ranged from 1.4 for Norway to 14.9 for Spain, indicating that of these 19 countries, Norway is most homogeneous and Spain most heterogeneous. The score for the whole region, comprising the 19 countries, was 27.

The northern European countries are evidently culturally coherent. Their measures ranged from 1.4 for Norway to 2.4 for Sweden. Only Denmark appears to be

Table 4.1   Measures of Coherence for 19 Countries

1. Norway	1.4	11. Austria	5.7
2. Finland	1.9	12. Netherlands	5.7
3. Sweden	2.4	13. United Kingdom	7.0
4. Hungary	2.9	14. Switzerland	7.2
5. Slovenia	3.0	15. Israel	7.5
6. Belgium	3.6	16. Portugal	8.3
7. Ireland	3.6	17. Germany	8.5
8. Poland	4.5	18. Greece	12.2
9. Czech Republic	5.0	19. Spain	14.9
10. Denmark	5.3	20. All 19 countries	27.0

less coherent with a measure of 5.3. The United Kingdom seems to be somewhere in the middle with 7.0, but this changes dramatically when Northern Ireland is left out of the analysis, and the measure changes from 7.0 to 1.6. A similar change occurs in Switzerland (coherence = 7.2) when Ticino, the Italian part of Switzerland, is left out. The figure then drops to 2.6. Spain is the least culturally coherent of all countries measured. It has a score of 14.9, the highest of all 19 countries. This is not so strange for a country with at least three regions with different languages and histories (Castilia, Cataluña, and Pais Vasco). Also, Greece is not very coherent (12.2), although the regions within Greece have more in common with other Greek regions than with regions in other countries. This means that Greek culture is quite different from other European cultures.

A third country that is culturally not very cohesive is Germany (8.5). It is interesting to see that the differences are especially large in former Western Germany (13.7) and that the former DDR is quite cohesive (4.3). Some southern German regions cluster with Austria and Switzerland rather than with other German regions. Also, Hamburg is quite different from the rest of Germany. Table 4.1 provides the measures for the 19 countries.

The consequences of heterogeneity of countries is that companies, when testing products or advertising, have to be careful which region to select as a test market in a particular country if it is a heterogeneous one. For international research, using a too homogeneous or too heterogeneous country as a test market is risky.

Classifying Cultures

Cultures can be described according to *descriptive characteristics* or classified into *value categories* or *dimensions* of national culture. Examples of descriptive characteristics are by Gannon and by Harris and Moran. Gannon[5] describes cultures by identifying metaphors that members of given societies view as very important, if not critical. He focuses mostly on the expressions of culture, among others religion, family structure, small-group behavior, public behavior, leisure pursuits and interests, greeting behavior, humor, language and body language, sports, educational system, food and eating behavior, and social class structure. He provides a description of 16 cultures according to the following metaphors: the traditional British house, the Italian opera, the German symphony, French wine, the Swedish *stuga,* the Russian ballet, Belgian lace, the Spanish bullfight, Irish conversations, the Turkish coffeehouse, the Israeli kibbutzim and moshavim, the Nigerian marketplace, the Japanese garden, the Shiva's dance of India, American football, and the Chinese family altar. These metaphors provide good insight into the expressions of culture, but they are less useful for analyzing cultures and predicting people's behavior.

Cultural characteristics distinguishing countries described by international management consultants Harris and Moran[6] are sense of self and space, communication and languages, food and feeding habits, time consciousness, values and norms, beliefs and attitudes, and work habits and practices. These characteristics are based on observations, and many of these are also found in dimensional models derived from large surveys.

The advantage of dimensions over descriptions is the empirical base. Dimensions are generally developed from large numbers of variables by statistical data-reduction methods (e.g., factor analysis) and provide scales on which countries are scored. Dimensions that order cultures meaningfully must be empirically verifiable and more or less independent.

The most common dimension used for ordering societies is their degree of economic evolution or modernity, ordering societies from traditional to modern. One of two dimensions used by U.S. political scientist Ronald Inglehart,[7] who leads the World Values Survey, follows this order of societies. Inglehart arranges world values in two broad categories. The first is "traditional" versus "secular-rational," and the second looks at "quality of life" attributes ranging from "survival" to "well-being," the latter including so-called postmaterialist values. Increasingly more complex models are developed. Most of them define patterns of basic problems that are common to all societies and that have consequences for the functioning of groups and individuals. Few are true dimensions in the sense of being statistically independent. Such categories are better called *value orientations* or *value categories.*

The idea that basic common problems exist is not new. An early analysis was by Alex Inkeles and Daniel Levinson,[8] who suggested that the following issues qualify as common basic problems worldwide: (a) relation to authority; (b) the conception of self, including ego identity; and (c) primary dilemmas of conflict and dealing with them. These basic problems have been found in many later studies. American anthropologists Kluckhohn and Strodtbeck[9] proposed five value orientations on the basis of their investigations of small communities in the southwestern United States: (a) perception of human nature (good/evil); (b) relationship of man to his environment (subjugation-mastery); (c) time orientation (past-present); (d) orientation toward the environment (being and doing); and (e) orientation toward human relationships (hierarchical-individualistic). Differences between cultures with respect to the relationship between man and his environment (nature) still are viewed as rather unique, so one section in this chapter will describe the various nature orientations.

The five value orientations are recognized in later studies, for example by Fons Trompenaars,[10] who applied these orientations to countries and presented seven categories of work-related values. These are universalism-particularism, achievement-ascription, individualism-collectivism, emotional-neutral, specific-diffuse, time orientation, and orientation to nature. Trompenaars's concept of culture is defined as a way in which a group of people solves problems. Trompenaars's database was analyzed by the British psychologist Peter Smith,[11] who only found two independent dimensions in the data that basically measured various intercorrelated flavors of Hofstede's dimension individualism. Trompenaars's dimensions are not statistically independent, and he produced no country scores, so his findings are not useful for marketing as they cannot be used to analyze consumption data.

The anthropologist Edward Hall[12] distinguished patterns of culture according to context, space, time, and information flow. In particular, the context concept is useful for understanding consumer behavior and advertising across cultures. Also, Hall did not develop country scores, but the context orientation is related to individualism-collectivism, one of Hofstede's dimensions. A separate section in this chapter will be dedicated to the context and time orientations.

Only a few dimensional models provide country scores that can be used as independent variables for the analysis of consumption and other aspects of consumer behavior across cultures. These are the models by Geert Hofstede and by Shalom Schwartz. The Dutch scholar Geert Hofstede developed five independent dimensions of national culture, which will be described comprehensively in this chapter with examples of how the dimensions can be used to analyze consumption and consumer behavior.[13]

The Israeli psychologist Shalom Schwartz[14] developed an alternative conceptual and operational approach for deriving cultural dimensions of work-related values in a study of value priorities among teachers and students from 41 cultural groups in 38 nations. Originally Schwartz and Bilsky searched for a theory of a universal psychological structure of human values. Individual-level value types were distinguished that were extended to the culture level. From 10 value types at the individual level, seven value types were distinguished for use across cultures. The seven value types (or motivational domains, not dimensions, as they are not statistically independent) are labeled *conservatism, intellectual autonomy, and affective autonomy, hierarchy, mastery, egalitarian commitment,* and *harmony.*

Both models describe similar basic value orientations of countries and are based on large quantitative surveys. Further similarities are (a) focus on the etic in comparisons, (b) the perspective of values being at the core of culture, and (c) the notion of culture being located within national boundaries.

The models are different with respect to the level of analysis (individual versus culture level) and the dimension structure. Schwartz's dimension structure is very complicated because he uses two-poled categorizations (e.g., self-enhancement versus self-transcendence) and each dimension has relationships with more or less adjacent other dimensions. Except harmony, they correlate significantly with GNI/capita[15] and to various degrees with the Hofstede dimensions. For marketing purposes, the Schwartz dimensions are not as useful, first because the model covers fewer countries and second because they do not show results that are as consistent as the Hofstede dimensions, which may be caused by conceptual and methodological differences between the models.[16]

Correlations of the Schwartz value categories with several consumption data suggest that the seven value types by Schwartz are basically one dimension, opposing an active versus a passive attitude to life, which is similar to Hofstede's individualism-collectivism dimension.

A reason for widespread adoption of Hofstede's classification of culture lies in the simplicity of his dimensions, which are straightforward and appealing to both academic researchers and business readers across disciplines. In this chapter, the Hofstede model is described in detail. First, context, the time concepts, and nature are described.

High-Context and Low-Context Cultures

Hall[17] distinguishes cultures according to the degree of context in their communication systems. In a high-context communication or message, most of the information is part of the context or internalized in the person; very little is made explicit as part of the message. The information in a low-context message is carried in the explicit code of the message. In general, high-context communication is economical, fast, and efficient. However, time must be devoted to programming. If this programming does not take place, the communication is incomplete. To the observer, an unknown high-context culture can be completely mystifying, because symbols that are not known to the observer play such an important role. Thus, high-context communication can also be defined as inaccessible. Low-context cultures are characterized by explicit verbal messages. Effective verbal communication is expected to be direct and unambiguous. Low-context cultures demonstrate high value and positive attitudes toward words. The Western world has had a long tradition of rhetoric, a tradition that places central importance on the delivery of verbal messages.[18] In advertising, argumentation and rhetoric are found more in low-context cultures, whereas advertising in high-context cultures is characterized by symbolism or indirect verbal expression. An important consequence of context is that words and sentences as well as pictures have different meanings depending on the context in which they are embedded.

Hofstede suggested a correlation between collectivism and high context in cultures. In collectivistic cultures, information flows more easily between members of the group, and there is less need for explicit communication than in individualistic cultures.

Cultures are on a sliding scale with respect to context. Most Asian cultures are high context, whereas most Western cultures are low-context cultures, the extremes being Japan and China (high-context) and Germany, Switzerland, and the United States (low-context cultures).

Americans, in particular, need data to evaluate things. For foreigners, the quantity of numbers and statistics encountered in the media and in daily conversations in the United States is stunning.[19] As Hall[20] says, "Many Americans don't seem to be able to evaluate the performance of anything unless they can attach a number to it."

How differences in communication and advertising styles can be explained by the distinction between high- and low-context cultures will be further described in Chapter 7.

Dimensions of Time

Time is more than what the clock reads. Different cultures have different concepts of time. Western advertisers tend to use clocks in their international advertising to symbolize efficiency. Clocks are not recognized as symbols of efficiency in cultures where people have a different sense of time. Time is a core system of cultural, social, and personal life. Each culture has its own unique time frame. Hall's[21] important study of time as an expression of culture provides an explanation of differences in behavior and language. He distinguishes different types of time, among others biological time (light-dark/day-night, hot-cold/summer-winter), personal time (how time is experienced), and sync time (each culture has its own beat). Hall developed his theories during his stay with Native Americans, discovering how differently they dealt with time than did Anglo-Americans. Different concepts of time can explain significant differences in behavior. A few aspects of time that are relevant to consumer behavior are summarized in the following sections: closure; past, present, and future orientation; linear versus circular time; monochronic versus polychronic time; and cause and effect.

Closure

Americans are driven to achieve what psychologists call "closure," meaning that a task must be completed or it is perceived as "wasted." What Hall saw as characteristic of Hopi (Native Americans of the Southwest) villages was the proliferation of unfinished houses. The same can be seen in Turkey, in southern Europe, and in other collectivistic cultures where additional rooms will only be built when family needs arise. American novels or films always have a "happy ending," including solutions to problems, which are rare in Japanese novels.

Time Orientation Toward the Past, Present, or Future

North Americans tend to be future oriented; the future is a guide to present action, although the time horizon is short-term. The old is easily discarded and the new embraced. Most things are disposable, from ideas, trends, and management fads to marriage partners. Even the "old" is treated as new. Many Europeans are past oriented; they believe in preserving history and continuing past traditions.[22] Japan has a very long-term future time horizon, as have the Chinese, but they look to the past for inspiration. The Chinese tend to combine both the past and the future in one holistic view of life, including reverence for their forefathers and long-term responsibility for future generations, but have no respect for cultural history. African time is said to be composed of a series of events that are experienced. The future is of little meaning because future events have not yet occurred.[23] Destiny as an aspect of time and referring to a future is part of the Indian magic-cosmic world that the Western world has regarded as superstition and ignorance.[24] In the sense of destiny, time becomes extremely complicated. There are premonitions as to what will happen in the future, what part one will have, and what part one can play.

Time Is Linear or Circular

Time can be conceived as a line of sequential events or as cyclical and repetitive, compressing past, present, and future by what these have in common: seasons and rhythms. The latter time orientation is linked with Asian culture; the former is the Western time orientation. The linear time concept causes people to see time as compartmentalized, schedule dominated. Americans have a linear time conccpt with clear structures, such as beginning, turning point, climax, and end. Time is used as a measuring instrument and a means of controlling human behavior by setting deadlines and objectives. Time is tangible, like an object; it can be saved, spent, found, lost, and wasted. Temporal terms such as *summer* and *winter* are nouns; they are treated as objects. For Native Americans, summer is a condition: hot. The term is used as an adverb, not related to time but to the senses.

In Japan, time is circular and is related to the special meaning of seasons. Japanese time thinking is not in terms of today, tomorrow, or the day after tomorrow. The seasons form an automatic, upward spiral; everything returns automatically. Saying "back to the old values" in Japan does not imply a step backward but a step forward. It means progressing through an upward spiral, using what was good in the past for progress.

Monochronic and Polychronic Time

Another distinction by Hall[25] of how people handle time is between monochronic (M-time) and polychronic (P-time) cultures. People from monochronic cultures tend to do one thing at a time; they are organized and methodical, and their workdays are structured to allow them to complete one task after another. Polychronic people, on the other hand, tend to do many things simultaneously. Their workday is not a chain of isolated, successive blocks; time is more like a vast, never-ending ocean extending in every direction. The Germans adhere to the more rigid and compartmentalized way of dealing with time. To people who do many things at the same time, however, such as the Spanish, Arabs, Pakistanis, or South Americans, punctuality is nice, but by no means an absolute necessity in the middle of a hectic day. In monochronic cultures, time spent on the Internet takes time from other activities, such as TV viewing. In polychronic cultures, people do both at the same time.

When two people of different time cultures meet, they may easily offend each other because they have different expectations of time. In particular, the fact that in polychronic cultures people interfere during meetings is very annoying to people of monochronic cultures. Not all M-time cultures are the same, however. In Japan, tight M-time is for business, and P-time is for private life.

Cause and Effect

Time also relates to the concept of cause and effect used to explain the sequence of events. The cause-effect paradigm appears particularly in North American decision-making culture. Things don't just happen. Something makes them happen. Symbolic and mystical explanations of events are not accepted. Preference is given to concrete and measurable causes that precede the consequence or effect. With the Chinese, on the other hand, causes and results do not have to follow each other. They often happen simultaneously. One event can be explained by another unrelated event that is happening at the same time.[26] The American way of decision making often leads to suboptimization due to the too simplified cause-and-effect model they use. The Japanese use a holistic cause-and-effect model that takes into account a multitude of causes that have a joint effect.[27]

Relationship of Man With Nature

There are basically three types of relationships between humanity and nature: *mastery over nature* (man is to conquer nature), *harmony with nature* (man is to live in harmony with nature), and *subjugation to nature* (man is dominated by nature).[28]

In the Western world, humanity is viewed as separate from nature. In particular, the North American relationship to nature is that it should be conquered, controlled. Nature and the physical environment can be and should be controlled for human convenience. To most North Americans, the expression "to move a mountain" is not a metaphor symbolizing the impossible but rather an optimistic challenge based on past experience. The outlook of U.S. culture is that it is the person's responsibility to overcome obstacles that may stand in his or her way. The harmony-with-nature orientation draws no distinction between or among human life, nature, and the supernatural; each is an extension of the others. The Japanese experience of nature is one of communion, of exchange, characterized by a subtle intimacy. It is an experience of identification with nature. Westerners tend to explain the Asian reverence for nature as a relationship with God that involves living in harmony with the world of nature. Takeo Doi,[29] a Japanese psychiatrist, says that in Japan, God as a creator is absent and human beings therefore seek comfort by attempting to immerse themselves completely in nature. Other cultures, such as many African cultures, see people as dominated by nature, and supernatural forces play a dominant role in religion. This subjugation to nature involves the belief that nothing can be done to control nature.

Hofstede's Five Dimensions of National Culture

Geert Hofstede[30] developed a model of five dimensions of national culture that helps to explain basic value differences. This model distinguishes cultures according to five dimensions: *power distance, individualism/collectivism, masculinity/ femininity, uncertainty avoidance, and long-term orientation.* The dimensions are measured on a scale from 0 to 100, for 75 countries and regions. Although the model is most used to explain differences in work-related values, I have applied it to consumption-related values and motives. This was validated in two ways: (a) by content analysis of television commercials and print advertisements and (b) by linking the Hofstede data to secondary data on consumption, attitudes, and behavior. Much product data and data on related behavior appear to correlate with culture. Hofstede's dimensions are increasingly used as independent variables for comparative cross-cultural studies and provide many useful explanations of cross-cultural differences in consumer behavior. Although his country scores originally were produced in the early 1970s, many replications of Hofstede's study on different matched or nonmatched samples have proved that his data are still valid. In the second edition of his book *Culture's Consequences* (2001), Hofstede describes over 200 external comparative studies and replications that have supported his indexes. A list of country scores is in Appendix A.

Power Distance (PDI)

The power distance dimension can be defined as *the extent to which less powerful members of a society accept and expect that power is distributed unequally.* It is reflected in the values of both the less powerful and more powerful members of society. In large power distance cultures, everyone has his or her rightful place in a social hierarchy, and as a result acceptance and giving of authority is something that comes naturally. To the Japanese, behavior that recognizes hierarchy is as natural as breathing. It means, "everything in its place."[31] In Japan, every greeting, every contact must indicate the kind and degree of social distance between individuals. In cultures scoring lower on the power distance index, authority can have a negative connotation, as focus is on equality in rights and opportunity and independence is highly valued.

In large power distance cultures, one's social status must be clear so that others can show proper respect. Global brands serve that purpose. In continental Europe, some luxury alcoholic drinks have such social status value in the high power distance cultures. There is a significant correlation between power distance and consumption of Scotch whisky. Figure 4.1 illustrates this relationship.

The rightful place concept implies that in high power distance cultures, being the "number one" brand is important. A brand that has entered markets early and is viewed as the number one brand will remain such more easily than it would in low power distance cultures where challengers are favored with a "we try harder" approach.

In high power distance cultures, older people are important because of respect for old age. In cultures of small power distance, powerful people try to look less powerful; older people try to look younger.

Dependency is an element of hierarchical relationships between people: Someone who becomes dependent immediately reinforces the other as superior in

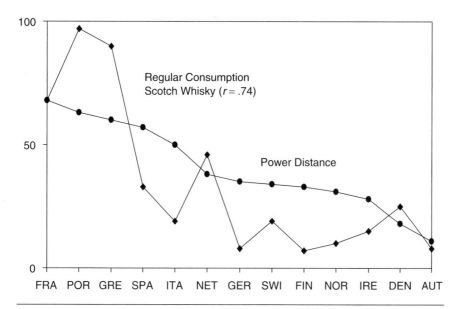

Figure 4.1   Social Status and Scotch Whiskey

SOURCE: Data from Hofstede (2001) (see Appendix A); European Media and Marketing Survey (EMS) (1999) (see Appendix B)

the hierarchical relationship, thus enhancing the latter's inner esteem by giving a sense of being needed and of being idealized.[32] In large power distance cultures, there are strong dependency relationships between parents and children, bosses and subordinates, professors and students, masters and learners. In small power distance cultures, children are raised to be independent at a young age. Americans will avoid becoming dependent on others, and they do not want others, with the possible exception of immediate family members, to be dependent on them.

Relationships between parents and children vary with power distance. In low power distance cultures, parents play with their children as equals, whereas in high power distance cultures children play more with each other, and adults and children live in different worlds. This explains why the Danish Lego (toys, building blocks) did not sell as well in France as in Denmark. The concept is based on parents and children constructing buildings together.

The degree of power distance tends to decrease with increased levels of education. As a result, it is expected that improved education worldwide will lead toward decreased power distance, but relative differences between countries are not expected to change.

Individualism/Collectivism (IDV)

The individualism/collectivism contrast can be defined as "people looking after themselves and their immediate family only, versus people belonging to in-groups that look after them in exchange for loyalty." In individualistic cultures, one's identity is in the person. People are "I"-conscious and express private opinions, and self-actualization is important; individual decisions are valued more highly than group decisions. Individualistic cultures are low-context cultures with explicit verbal communication. In collectivistic cultures, people are "we"-conscious. Their identity is based on the social system to which they belong, and avoiding loss of face is important. Collectivistic cultures are "shame" societies. Having or losing "face" is the expression used by people of collectivistic cultures. When one has done something wrong, it reflects not on oneself but on the group to which one belongs, and one therefore feels shame. Collectivistic cultures are high-context cultures. In individualistic cultures, people give priority to the task; in collectivistic cultures, priority is given to relationships with people.

The roots of individualism are in England. In early English society, as early as the thirteenth century, children at the age of 7 or 9 years—both males and females— did not grow up in an extended family but were put out to hard service in the houses of other people.[33]

Between 70% and 80% of the world's population is more or less collectivistic. All of Asia, Africa, and Latin America are collectivistic. In Italy, the data were collected in the north where people appeared to be highly individualistic. Other studies[34] indicate that the Italians as a whole are collectivistic.

Members of collectivistic cultures emphasize goals, needs, and the views of the in-group over those of the individual; the social norms of the in-group are favored over individual pleasure and shared in-group beliefs over unique individual beliefs.[35] They draw sharp distinctions between members of in-groups and out-groups. The type and rank-order of importance of in-groups vary from the extended family (whether members live in joint or unitary households is not relevant, with neighborhood and school friends absorbed into the extended family) to the larger community such as the Indian *jati* or Spanish *barrio* or the occupational unit such as in Japan.[36] Some put kinship organizations (family) ahead of all other in-groups whereas others put their companies ahead of other in-groups. Modernization in Japan has made the occupational unit more important than kinship links.

The group defines the identity of members of collectivistic cultures. Members of individualistic cultures belong to many specific in-groups that they join willingly. Because they are joined willingly, these in-groups have less influence than in-groups do in collectivistic cultures. Members of the collectivistic in-group are implicitly what in individualistic cultures are called one's "friends." Members of individualistic cultures have to invest time in friendship. Although many Americans have close friends to whom they feel special attachments and strong obligations, such friendships are small in number. Many other people are called "friends," but there is no element of mutual obligation, something that comes so naturally in the collectivistic in-group.

In individualistic cultures, there is a strict division between private time and work time and between private space and the public domain. In collectivistic cultures, there is no such strict division. This is illustrated by the fact that in collectivistic cultures people have relatively few private gardens and prefer to socialize in public places. Within Europe, there is a correlation between individualism and ownership of private gardens, as illustrated in Figure 4.2, which presents the correlations

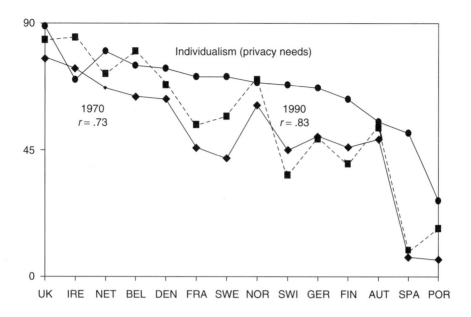

Figure 4.2   Private Gardens and Individualism

SOURCE: Data from Hofstede (2001) (see Appendix A); Reader's Digest Surveys (1970, 1991) (see Appendix B)

between individualism and ownership of private gardens in 1970 and 1990 from two Reader's Digest surveys. In these 20 years, the correlation has become more significant. Although increasingly one-family houses are being built also in the south of Europe, many of these have communal gardens, a phenomenon that would be unthinkable in individualistic cultures like those of the United Kingdom and the Netherlands.

The merging of private and work time in collectivistic cultures explains differences in use of technology such as personal computers or the Internet. In Japan, the penetration of personal computers has lagged because there was no incentive to have a computer at home. People prefer to continue working in the office with their colleagues instead of going home and finishing whatever work is left on their PCs. How and where people access the Internet also varies by culture. In Europe, the way people access the Internet is related to the private-public domain distinction. Figure 4.3 illustrates the way people access the Internet in different places in individualistic and collectivistic cultures. In the latter, people are used to doing all sorts of activities in the public domain, both in the streets and in bars or cafés, as reflected in the numbers of cafés per 10,000 people. Because of these habits, people also have no problems accessing the Internet in the cyber café, whereas in individualistic cultures people will not want to access the Internet outside the home.

Individualistic cultures are universalistic cultures, whereas collectivistic cultures are particularistic. People from individualistic cultures tend to believe that there are universal values that should be shared by all. People from collectivistic cultures, on the other hand, accept that different groups have different values. Being individualistic,

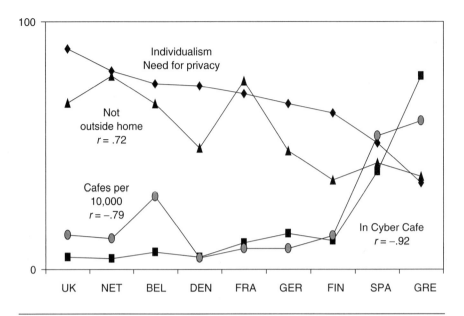

Figure 4.3   Internet Access Inside or Outside Home, Europe

SOURCE: Data from Hofstede (2001) (see Appendix A); Eurostat (2001) (see Appendix B); Hotrec data on numbers of cafés per 1,000 people (1997) (www.hotrec.com)

most North Americans believe that democracy, especially North American democracy, should ideally be shared by all. People from collectivistic cultures find such a view hard to understand.[37] Hall[38] observes, "Americans, more than most, seem dominated by the need to shape other people in their own image." This is particularly reflected in American marketing and advertising philosophies. A statement by Cristina Martinez, Latin American regional account director for Eastman Kodak at J. Walter Thompson Co., Miami, reflected this attitude: "We're finding that teen-agers are teen-agers everywhere and they tend to emulate U.S. teen-agers."[39] The Japanese, the Chinese, and other Asians feel so unique that they cannot and will not imagine that Westerners will ever be able to adopt their values and behavior.

Individualism is increasing worldwide because it is linked with wealth, but it remains a relative concept. If it is said that Japanese society is individualizing, that does not mean Japanese values will come close to American values. The relative difference is expected to remain. Japanese words with respect to individualism carry different meanings. What the Japanese call collectivism is conformance to the group. What they call individuality is a way to rebel against overly strong conformance to the group, which limits their competitiveness.

In the sales process in individualistic cultures, parties want to get to the point fast, whereas in collectivistic cultures it is necessary to first build a relationship and trust between parties. This difference is also reflected in the different roles of advertising (see Chapter 7). In collectivistic cultures, corporate brands are favored over product brands. You can build a relationship between a company and consumers better than between (abstract) brands and consumers. In collectivistic cultures, people are more interested in concrete product features than in abstract brands. Individualists tend to see brands as unique human personalities. In the extremely individualistic United States, even children have been named after big brands, such as L'Oréal, Chevrolet, and Armani.

Masculinity/Femininity (MAS)

The masculinity dimension can be defined as follows: *The dominant values in a masculine society are achievement and success; the dominant values in a feminine society are caring for others and quality of life.* In masculine societies, performance and achievement are important; and achievement must be demonstrated, so status brands are important to show one's success. There is a tendency to polarize: Big and fast are beautiful. Feminine societies, those scoring low on the masculinity index, are more people oriented, and small is beautiful. There is a tendency to strive for consensus. Quality of life is more important than winning. The need to show one's success in masculine cultures is reflected in the relationship between masculinity and sales of real jewelry (gold and diamonds). Figure 4.4 illustrates this relationship. There is no relationship with national wealth, only with culture.

Being a "winner" is positive in masculine societies and is negative in feminine societies. In masculine cultures, children learn to admire the strong. In feminine cultures, children learn sympathy for the underdog, the loser.

A core value of feminine cultures is modesty, not showing off. So, if one excels, it should not be shown. This is illustrated by Jante's law (*Janteloven*), 10 rules that give a fairly accurate depiction of the moral code in Sweden and Scandinavia today. Jante's law comes from the novel by nineteenth-century Dano-Norwegian author

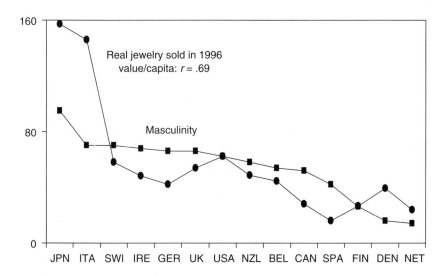

Figure 4.4   Sales of Real Jewelry Worldwide and Masculinity

SOURCE: Data from Hofstede (2001) (see Appendix A); Euromonitor (1997) (see Appendix B)

Aksel Sandemose entitled *"En flygtning krysser sitt spor"* *(A Refugee Crosses His Tracks)*. The 10 rules are the following:

Du skal ikke tro . . . (You should not "feel" that . . .)

du er noget (you are anything)

du er lige så meget som os (you are equal to us, i.e., at our level)

du er klogere end os (you are more clever than we are)

du er bedre end os (you are better than we are)

ved mere end os (you know more than we do)

er mere end os (you are more than we are)

at du du'r til noget (you are good at anything)

Du skal ikke le ad os (you must not make fun of us)

Du skal ikke tro . . . (you should not think . . .)

nogen bryder sig om dig (that anybody likes you)

at du kan lære os noget (or that you can teach us anything).[40]

Envy is a principal part of Jante's law. If you break the social code, it means that your neighbors will despise you for your uniqueness or an excess show of wealth. The desire of people of feminine cultures to not want to stand out in a crowd is reflected in the dislike of "employee of the month" schemes, which are effective human resource instruments in the United States. A U.S. TV commercial for Tylenol used this to demonstrate the effectiveness of the product. Carolina hears she has just been elected Employee of the Month for the 11th time, because she didn't use a single sick day (Illustration 4.1).

Illustration 4.1   Tylenol, USA

An important aspect of this dimension is role differentiation: small in feminine societies, large in masculine societies. In feminine cultures, males can take typically female jobs without being seen as "sissy." In Germany (high on masculinity), household work is less shared between husband and wife than in the Netherlands (low on masculinity).[41] In the feminine cultures, more men work part-time than in the masculine cultures because both partners want to share the task of raising the children.

In the masculine cultures of Latin America, men must be real men. In a Latin American survey across seven countries, the percentages of answers agreeing with the statement "Real men don't cry" correlated with masculinity.[42]

Japan is a very masculine society with strong role differentiation. This combined with collectivism can explain the way men and women relate. There is no such thing as the Western love relationship between men and women in marriage. "You are there, exist together, and you take each other for granted." Literally: You are like air for each other. Kumiko Hashimoto, the wife of former Japanese Prime Minister Ryutaro Hashimoto, was quoted as saying the following about her relationship with her husband: "I give way to him almost as if he were a feudal lord, with everything done as he wishes."[43]

The masculine/feminine dimension discriminates between cultures particularly with respect to values related to winning, success, and status, which are much used in advertising appeals. It is therefore an important dimension to understand differences in marketing-communication styles. Masculinity/femininity reflects the division between countries in which hype and the hard sell prevail versus countries where a soft-sell, more modest approach is successful.

U.S. researchers seem reluctant to use the masculinity dimension, possibly because of the label. Masculine/feminine can be misinterpreted as politically incorrect wording. At the time Hofstede labeled this dimension, there was no such thing as a political correctness movement. The problem can be solved by using the term "gender of nations, tough versus tender."

An interesting observation on the cultural homogeneity of the Scandinavian countries is that they are not only a cluster of feminine cultures but also similar with respect to the other dimensions. This cultural homogeneity of the region may have been the cause of Erik Elinder's statement in 1961[44] that cultural differences were decreasing. Elinder was a Swedish marketing executive who discovered that a campaign for a savings bank had identical results in all Scandinavian countries and concluded that the same campaign could easily be extended to Europe. At the time, he may not have realized the scale and scope of his remark, which has been quoted ever since, though it was based on an assumption valid only for Scandinavia, not for the rest of Europe. The Scandinavians are culturally very much alike and very different from the rest of Europe. Erik Elinder fell into the trap of extending the findings of one cluster of similar cultures to an entire region, assuming all would be similar.

Uncertainty Avoidance (UAI)

Uncertainty avoidance can be defined as *the extent to which people feel threatened by uncertainty and ambiguity and try to avoid these situations.* Life is unpredictable. Some people do not mind unpredictability or uncertainty whereas others hate uncertainty or ambiguity and try to cope with it by making rules and prescribing behavior. In cultures of strong uncertainty avoidance, there is a need for rules and formality to structure life. This translates into the search for truth and a belief in experts. Communication is more formal. Conflict and competition are threatening. People generally have a higher level of anxiety and tension, which must be released. This is done in various ways, by showing emotions, talking loudly, using hands while talking, driving cars more aggressively, and embracing more emotionally. Members of weak uncertainty avoidance cultures tend not to show their emotions (e.g., the British "stiff upper lip") and are more tolerant drivers. There should be as few rules as possible. They believe more in generalists and common sense, and there is less ritual behavior. Conflict and competition are not threatening.

The expert in strong uncertainty avoidance cultures must be a real expert with degrees in specialized areas in order to allow him- or herself to be called an expert. This is different in the United States, where anyone can become an expert because no one says what an expert is or must know. Americans can get themselves listed in the *Yearbook of Experts* for a few hundred U.S. dollars.[45] The combination of masculinity and weak uncertainty avoidance, which combines the wish to be a winner with relative freedom from anxiety, appears to be indicative of creativity and innovation. It may explain why a relatively large number of creative advertising awards are won by the British.

Members of high uncertainty avoidance cultures express in their behavior a need for purity related to several product categories, such as mineral water and washing powder. In Europe, with increased wealth and improved quality of the tap water, the correlation between mineral water consumption and uncertainty avoidance has become more significant over time. Figure 4.5 illustrates the correlation between bottled water consumption and uncertainty avoidance for 15 countries worldwide.

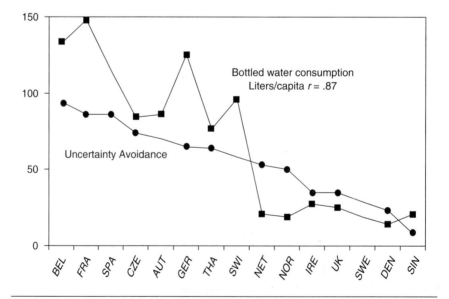

Figure 4.5   Bottled Water Consumption

SOURCE: Data from Hofstede (2001) (see Appendix A); Beverage Marketing Corporation (www.beveragemarketing.com) (2003)

In high uncertainty avoidance cultures, mineral water also tends to be advertised by its purity attribute, which is often symbolized by showing the brand in a nature setting. Illustration 4.2 shows TV images of mineral water brands from Spain, France, and Italy.

Illustration 4.2   Aquarel, Spain; Volvic, France/Germany; Allegra, Italy

Cultures of strong uncertainty avoidance feel the need to structure reality, but they will do this in different ways. Configuration with other dimensions will show differences in how reality is structured. If combined with individualism, the rules are explicit and written. Combined with collectivism, the rules are implicit and rooted in tradition. Combined with small power distance, the rules are internalized; one accepts the rules and that one has to abide by them. Combined with large power distance, one need not abide by the rules because they are externalized. Germans and French, both from strong uncertainty avoidance cultures, like rules; but the Germans use them to structure themselves, the French to structure others. In French culture, reality is structured through conceptualization. This difference explains the propensity for the conceptual or the "grand idea" of the French, which is so different from the German thinking model. When the artist Christo suggested wrapping the Pont Neuf in Paris, it did not take the French long to agree. When he suggested wrapping the Reichstag in Berlin, it took the Germans years to say yes.

Long-Term Orientation (LTO)

Because of the Western bias of researchers, no dimension was originally found that explained the economic success of a number of Asian countries. Michael Bond, together with a number of Chinese social scientists, developed the Chinese Value Survey, resulting in a fifth dimension that included some typical East Asian values of Confucian philosophy. Long-term orientation is *the extent to which a society exhibits a pragmatic future-oriented perspective rather than a conventional historic or short-term point of view.* Values included in long-term orientation are perseverance, ordering relationships by status and observing this order, thrift, and having a sense of shame. The opposite is short-term orientation, which includes personal steadiness and stability, respect for tradition and reciprocation of greetings, and favors and gifts.[46] Focus is on pursuit of happiness rather than on pursuit of peace of mind.

The combination of long-term orientation and collectivism results in family ties, long-term thinking, and other elements of Confucian philosophy such as filial piety and paternalism. This is reflected in the successful family entrepreneurship that makes East Asian development so different from Western development. Pragmatism is an important aspect of most East Asian cultures. They adapt to other cultures in such a way that Westerners are often fooled and think they are Westernizing.

The concept of truth, as it is experienced in the West, does not exist in East Asian cultures. The Western concept is supported by an axiom in Western logic that a statement excludes its opposite: If A is true, B, which is the opposite of A, must be false. Eastern logic does not have such an axiom. If A is true, its opposite B may also be true, and together they produce a wisdom that is superior to either A or B. Pragmatism makes people prefer what works over what is "true" or what is "right."

Something that is often perceived as paradoxical in the measurements on this index is the combination of strong respect for tradition and short-term orientation in a large part of the Western world, whereas respect for old age and ancestor worship are such strong elements of Asian value systems. This reflects the desirable versus the desired: Tradition is important, but it is innovativeness that is desired. Particularly in China, pragmatism tends to overrule respect for tradition. An example is the 10-year Cultural Revolution that destroyed a priceless cultural heritage. It is not the first time such a frenzy has happened. Mao Zedong, the instigator of the Cultural Revolution, was inspired by the first emperor, Shi Huangdi, who unified China in 220 B.C.[47] He had all books destroyed and 463 philosophers buried alive in an attempt to remove the traditional Confucian thought from the collective Chinese memory. It was in vain: The emperor died after 11 years, and the scriptures of Confucius and other philosophers, which had been memorized, were reissued.[48] Yet pragmatism in accepting foreign habits in China has a limitation; they must fit *guo qing*, or "the Chinese national context." Good ideas applicable to China must be promoted; corrupted and inapplicable ideas must be discarded.

A strong value in long-term orientation cultures is reverence for nature. This is also related to collectivism, so it is particularly in the configuration of long-term orientation and collectivism that harmony of man with nature plays such a strong role in people's lives. Nature and symbols of nature are important elements of advertising in Japan, China, and Chinese-related cultures.

Configurations of Dimensions

The cultural dimensions described in this chapter can be used to generalize the specific. Countries can be described according to a number of characteristics. As examples, we do this for three countries: the United States, the Netherlands, and Japan.

The United States

The cultural dimensions of the United States are as follows: an M-time culture, linear time pattern, low-context, below average on power distance, high on individualism, high on masculinity, relatively weak in uncertainty avoidance, and with a short-term orientation.

The United States shows the following cultural characteristics:

- Short-term thinking, which influences all aspects of American life: the bottom line, success now rather than in the future, extremely short-range schedules
- Obsession with change, "new" and "better"
- More a credit card than a debit card culture
- Linear thinking; time is compartmentalized
- Hype, persuasive communication, and rhetoric
- Education valued only if it allows the individual to compete more effectively
- Expression of private opinions
- Equal opportunity
- Independence
- Need for privacy, universalistic thinking, ethnocentrism
- Winning, power, success, and status are important
- Strong role differentiation
- Humor, innovativeness, creativity
- Man must conquer nature
- Education teaches students to "be critical," makes them think. Students ask "why?" not "how?"

The Netherlands

The cultural dimensions of the Netherlands (and the Scandinavian countries) are as follows: M-time culture, linear time concept, low-context, small power distance, high on individualism, low on masculinity, of relatively weak uncertainty avoidance, relatively long-term orientation.

The Netherlands shows the following cultural characteristics:

- Longer-term thinking
- More a debit card than a credit card culture
- Traditional; reverence for the past
- Linear thinking, rhetoric
- Time is compartmentalized
- Need for privacy
- Equality, not so much in opportunity as in freedom and care
- Independence
- Universalistic thinking, preachers
- Winning is OK, but not its display; status not important
- Small role differentiation
- Consensus seeking, jealousy
- Thrift, perseverance
- Caring rather than winning is the ideal
- Education beyond the basic ability to get a job

Japan

The cultural dimensions of Japan are as follows: a P-time culture, circular time concept, high-context, above average power distance, collectivistic, masculine, strong uncertainty avoidance, long-term orientation.

Japan shows the following cultural characteristics:

- Pressure on every Japanese person to know his or her place, to behave like his or her neighbors, not to shame his or her family, and to avoid jolting social harmony
- Dependence
- Private opinions not expressed
- Status is important to show power and success, but avoid standing out in a crowd: "the nail that sticks out will be hammered down"
- Long-term thinking
- A cash culture, not a credit card culture
- Thrift, perseverance
- Strong role differentiation
- Education is not based on teaching students to be critical: The very meaning of "to think" is differently understood. In Japanese culture, it means something like, "to find an answer that can be shared by others." Students ask "how?" instead of "why?"
- Education has an intrinsic value, which cannot be measured purely in terms of the labor market
- "New" is accepted as a collective necessity, but basically the Japanese do not like change
- Obsession with cleanliness, purity
- Harmony with nature rather than conquest over nature

Conclusion

For people concerned with global marketing and advertising, the most important aspect of culture is that it influences our perception—our own culture drives how we communicate and what we communicate.

Classification of cultures is necessary to differentiate marketing and advertising strategies across countries. Classifying cultures on dimensions has proved to be the most constructive method. It helps in vocalizing and labeling cultural differences and similarities. In the past decades, several classifications of culture have been developed that were reviewed in this chapter.

A broad classification is the degree to which cultures contextualize, which is reflected in the type of communication cultures use. The difference between high- and low-context communication cultures helps us understand why, for example, Japanese and American advertising styles are so different, why the Japanese prefer indirect verbal communication and symbolism over the direct assertive communication approaches used by Americans. Hofstede's model proves to be most useful for comparing cultures with respect to consumption-related values. As a result, it can explain the variety of values and motives used in marketing and advertising across cultures. This will be particularly useful for companies that want to develop global marketing and advertising strategies.

Further understanding our own values and the receiver's values and how they may or may not match will be the topic of Chapter 5.

Notes

1.   Miracle, G. E. (1982). Applying cross-cultural research findings to advertising practice and research. In A. D. Fletcher (Ed.), *Proceedings of the 1982 Conference of the American Academy of Advertising.* (Contact Robert King, AAA Executive Secretary, School of Business, University of Richmond, Richmond, VA 23173)

2.   Hofstede, G., & Hofstede, G.-J. (2004). *Cultures and organizations: Software of the mind* (2nd ed.). New York: McGraw Hill.

3.   Schwartz, S. H. (2004). Mapping and interpreting cultural differences. In H. Vinken, J. Soeters, & P. Ester (Eds.), *Comparing cultures: Dimensions of culture in a comparative perspective.* Leiden, The Netherlands: Brill.

4.   This study is conducted in cooperation between universities in Norway, the Netherlands, Belgium, and Germany and covers 23 mostly European countries: Austria, Belgium, Czechia, Denmark, Finland, France, Germany, Greece, Hungary, Ireland, Israel, Italy, Luxembourg, the Netherlands, Norway, Poland, Portugal, Slovenia, Spain, Sweden, Switzerland, Turkey, and the United Kingdom. It provides answers to value questions that can be isolated for the various provinces of the participating countries. At the time of writing this book, the full data file could be downloaded (http://ess.nsd.uib.no). In the cultural cohesion analysis, France and Italy could not be included, as the respondents hadn't answered the particular set of questions.

5.   Gannon, M. J. (1994). *Understanding global cultures.* Thousand Oaks, CA: Sage.

6.   Harris, P. R., & Moran, R. T. (1987). *Managing cultural differences.* Houston, TX: Gulf, pp. 190–195.

7.   Inglehart, R., Basañez, M., & Moreno, A. (1998). *Human values and beliefs.* Ann Arbor: University of Michigan Press.

8.   Inkeles, A. (1997). *National character.* New Brunswick, NJ: Transaction, pp. 45–50.

9.   Kluckhohn, C. (1952).Values and value orientations in the theory of action. In T. Parsons & E. A. Shils (Eds.), *Toward a general theory of action.* Cambridge, MA: Harvard University Press; Kluckhohn, F., & Strodtbeck, F. (1961). *Variations in value orientations.* Evanston, IL: Row, Peterson.

10.   Trompenaars, F. (1993). *Riding the waves of culture: Understanding cultural diversity in busines*s. London: Nicholas Brealy.

11.   Smith, P. B., Dugan, S., & Trompenaars, F. (1996). National culture and the values of organizational employees: A dimensional analysis across 43 nations. *Journal of Cross-Cultural Psychology, 27,* 231–264.

12.   Hall, E. (1984). *Beyond culture.* New York: Doubleday; Hall, E. (1994). *The dance of life.* New York: Doubleday, pp. 85–128.

13.   Throughout this book for correlation analysis, the Pearson product-moment correlation (r) coefficient is used. Correlation analysis is one-tailed. Significance levels are indicated by * $p < .05$; ** $p < .01$; and *** $p < .005$. When regression analysis is used, multiple linear regression analysis is done stepwise. The coefficient of determination or R^2 is the indicator of the percentage of variance explained.

14. Schwartz, S. H., & Bilsky, W. (1987). Toward a universal psychological structure of human values. *Journal of Personality and Social Psychology, 53,* 550–562; Schwartz, S. H., & Bilsky, W. (1990). Toward a theory of the universal content and structure of values: Extensions and cross-cultural replications. *Journal of Personality and Social Psychology, 58,* 878–891; Schwartz, S. H. (1994). Beyond individualism/collectivism. In U. Kim, H. C. Triandis, et al. (Eds.), *Individualism and collectivism: Theory, method, and applications: Vol. 18. Cross-cultural research and methodology.* Thousand Oaks, CA: Sage, pp. 85–119.63; Schwartz, 1994, 101–105.

15. Hofstede, G. (2001). *Culture's consequence* (2nd ed.). Thousand Oaks, CA: Sage, p. 265.

16. A more detailed comparative analysis of the two models can be found in De Mooij, M. (2003). *Consumer behavior and culture: Consequences for global marketing and advertising.* Thousand Oaks, CA: Sage, pp. 39–45.

17. Hall, 1994, 85–128.

18. Ferraro, G. P. (1994). *The cultural dimension of international business.* Englewood Cliffs, NJ: Prentice Hall, pp. 50–51.

19. Althen, G. (1988). *American ways.* Yarmouth, ME: Intercultural Press, p. 31.

20. Hall, 1984, 62.

21. Hall, 1984, 16–27, 32–34.

22. Adler, N. J. (1991). *International dimensions of organizational behavior.* Belmont, CA: Wadsworth, pp. 30–31.

23. Ferraro, 1994, 94.

24. Roland, A. (1988). *In search of self in India and Japan.* Princeton, NJ: Princeton University Press, p. 302.

25. Hall, 1984, 17–24.

26. De Mooij, M. (1994). *Advertising worldwide.* London: Prentice Hall International, pp. 135–136.

27. This is demonstrated by the cause-and-effect approach in the Ishikawa or fishbone diagram, in Oakland, J. S. (1989). *Total quality management* (2nd ed.). Oxford, UK: Butterworth Heinemann.

28. Kluckhohn, R., & Strodtbeck, F. L. (1961). *Variations in value orientation.* Evanston, IL: Row, Peterson.

29. Doi, T. (1985). *The anatomy of self.* Tokyo: Kodansha International, pp. 147–148.

30. The descriptions of the dimensions are summaries from Hofstede, G. (1991). *Cultures and organizations: Software of the mind.* London: McGraw-Hill, respectively from pp. 23–48 (power distance), 49–78 (individualism/collectivism), 79–108 (masculinity/femininity), 109–138 (uncertainty avoidance), and 159–174 (long-term orientation). More detailed information is in Hofstede, 2001.

31. Benedict, R. (1974). *The chrysanthemum and the sword: Patterns of Japanese culture.* Rutland, VT: Charles E. Tuttle, p. 47. (Original work published 1946)

32. Roland, 1988, 280.

33. Macfarlane, A. (1978). *The origins of English individualism.* Cambridge, MA: Blackwell, pp. 146, 174.

34. Michael Hoppe, a German American management educator, replicated the IBM study on a population of political and institutional elites and found that Italy is much more collectivistic than the IBM scores lead one to believe. Hoppe's study also found differences with respect to Finland, which may be more individualistic than the IBM scores indicate. Contradictory information about the level of individualism or collectivism in Italy is probably due to the fact that Italy is bicultural: The north is individualistic, but the rest of the country is collectivistic. Hofstede's IBM data were mainly collected in the north, and he found

strong individualism. Consumption and media behavior data are based on a country average; where these relate to individualism or collectivism, Italy tends to score similarly to Spain, which is much more collectivistic.

35.   Gudykunst, W. B., & Ting-Toomey, S. (1988). *Culture and interpersonal communication.* Thousand Oaks, CA: Sage, pp. 42–43.

36.   Roland, 1988, 134, 149.

37.   Adler, 1991, 47.

38.   Hall, 1984, 86.

39.   Malkin, E. (1994, October 17). X-ers. *Advertising Age International,* 1–15.

40.   Sandemose, A. (n.d.). *Jante's law.* (Personal communication, Donald Nekman).

41.   Bundesministerium für Familie, Frauen, Senioren und Jugend, 1991/1992. (1994, December 8). *NRC Handelsblad.*

42.   Soong, R. (2003, 23 December). Argentina, Brazil, Chile, Colombia, Ecuador, Mexico, and Peru. Message posted to TGI Latina (www.zonalatina.com/Zldata332.htm).

43.   Perspectives. (1996, April 22). *Newsweek,* 7.

44.   Elinder, E. (1965). How international can European advertising be? *Journal of Marketing, 29,* 7–11.

45.   Samuelson, R. J. (1995, June 5). A nation of experts: If you think you're one, well, maybe you are. *Newsweek,* 33.

46.   Hofstede, 1991, 159–171.

47.   Suyin, H. (1994). *Eldest son.* London: Jonathan Cape, p. 392.

48.   Ross, J. (1990). *The origin of Chinese people.* Petaling Jaya, Malaysia: Pelanduk (M) Sdn. Bhd. (Original work published 1916)

FIVE

Values and Marketing

In modern marketing and advertising, values are used to differentiate and position brands vis-à-vis competitive brands. Values are said to be the basis for segmentation and positioning decisions. In the previous chapter, we reviewed different value orientations of the inhabitants of different countries. Values of both consumers and marketers are defined by their culture and marketing, and advertising will only be effective if these values match. The old marketing paradigm, "markets are people," presupposes that marketing programs can only be successful when the marketing mix of the product is matched with the values of the consumer. This chapter will deal with the value concept as applied to marketing and advertising.

The Value Concept

A value is defined by Rokeach[1] as "an enduring belief that one mode of conduct or end-state of existence is preferable to an opposing mode of conduct or end-state of existence." A value system is "a learned organization of principles and rules to help one choose between alternatives, resolve conflicts, and make decisions." Preferred alternatives are clean, not dirty; happy, not sad; healthy, not sick. One can feel emotional over such preferences. Preferences can lead to action: change dirty into clean by washing. When expressed in an abstract way, these preferences seem to be universal. But priorities vary, and how we express our values varies. We all want to be clean, but to reach that goal, people use various methods. The Belgians use twice as much soap powder as their neighbors, the Dutch. We all want to be healthy, but how we remain healthy varies. In the south of Europe, more antibiotics are used than in the north.

Values are taught at an early age and in an absolute manner. They describe what people in general think the world ought to be in an absolute way: freedom, peace (not a little bit of peace or a little bit of freedom). This is the *desirable* as opposed to the *desired:* The desired is what you want for yourself. The desired is not necessarily the same as what one "ought" to do. This distinction between the desirable and the desired is particularly meaningful for advertising. It will be further discussed in Chapter 8.

Rokeach states that "a person prefers a particular mode or end-state not only when he compares it with its opposite but also when he compares it with other values within his value system. He prefers a particular mode or end-state to other modes or end-states that are lower down his value hierarchy."[2] Thus, values include opposites, and there are different types of values in a value system, which may have a different order of importance. Values are integrated in an organized system in which they are ordered in priority with respect to other values. Values can serve as standards that guide our choices, beliefs, attitudes, and actions.

Like other authors, Rokeach assumes (a) that the total number of values a person possesses is relatively small, (b) that all people everywhere possess the same values to different degrees, and (c) that the antecedents of human values can be traced to culture, society, and its institutions.

Rokeach distinguishes two levels of values: terminal values and instrumental values. *Terminal values* refer to desirable end-states of existence. *Instrumental values* refer to desirable modes of conduct. Instrumental values are motivators to reach end-states of existence. Table 5.1 shows Rokeach's instrumental and terminal values, alphabetically arranged.[3] This list is based on an inventory of American values of the 1960s.

Table 5.1   Rokeach's Terminal Values and Instrumental Values

Terminal Values	Instrumental Values
a comfortable life	ambitious
exciting life	broad-minded
a sense of accomplishment	capable
a world at peace	cheerful
a world of beauty	clean
equality	courageous
family security	forgiving
freedom	helpful
happiness	honest
inner harmony	imaginative
mature love	independent
national security	intellectual
pleasure	logical
salvation	loving
self-respect	obedient
social recognition	polite
true friendship	responsible
wisdom	self-controlled

SOURCE: Reprinted with the permission of The Free Press, a Division of Simon & Schuster Adult Publishing Group, from *THE NATURE OF HUMAN VALUES* by Milton Rokeach. Copyright © 1973 by The Free Press. All rights reserved.

These values can be recognized in much of American advertising. An example is a TV commercial for Tele King Communications Corporation that offers people the opportunity to be their own boss, independence, big money, and leisure time. (see Illustration 5.1). Being your own boss means independence and equality. The examples of leisure time reflect an exciting life (cruises, mountaineering) and pleasure. Earning big money reflects a comfortable life.

Illustration 5.1   Tele King, USA

What people refer to as central or core values are usually terminal values. Moral values, including the norms of people or society, refer to modes of behavior. Social norms, or what one "ought" to do, how one "ought" to behave, are requirements for behavior in a specific society and more related to the instrumental values than the terminal values of that society.

Values guide and determine attitudes and behavior. A value is a specific, single belief; it guides and determines actions, attitudes, and judgment. Whereas an attitude is an organization of several beliefs focused on a specific object or situation, a value is an enduring standard; an attitude is not a standard, but is object or situation oriented. Values are more stable than attitudes and occupy a more central position in a person's cognitive system.[4]

Values Are Enduring

Values are among the first things children learn, not consciously but implicitly. Developmental psychologists believe that by the age of 10, most children have their basic value systems firmly in place.

Yet marketing researchers regularly try to demonstrate that values change. What they usually find are changes in how people express their values, changes in the symbols and rituals of culture. Or one can be misled by the behavior of members of a subculture, such as youth or businesspeople. Roland[5] gives the example of how an Indian man at work may dress in Western clothes and disregard intercaste rules in eating and other rituals while strictly observing all of these codes and dressing traditionally at home.

The core values of national culture appear to be very stable. How enduring values are was demonstrated by Yankelovich,[6] who found that despite increased affluence and other changes, many of America's most important traditional values have remained firm and constant. Despite the transformations in America's lifestyles, a number of core values shared by virtually all Americans have endured unchanged:

- Freedom (valuing political liberty, free speech)
- Equality before the law
- Equality of opportunity (the practical expression of freedom and individualism in the marketplace)
- Fairness (placing a high value on people getting what they deserve as a consequence of their own individual actions)
- Achievement (a belief in the efficacy of individual effort: the view that education and hard work pay off)
- Patriotism (loyalty to the United States)
- Democracy (the belief that the judgment of the majority should form the basis of governance)
- American exceptionalism (a belief in the special moral status and mission of America)
- Caring beyond the self (concern for others, such as family or ethnic group)
- Religion (a reverence for some transcendental meaning)
- Luck (good fortune can happen to anyone at any time)

Yankelovich adds that this tiny cluster of values holds Americans together as a single people and nation; it is the unity amid the variety of American life.

Data from Eurobarometer surveys between 1973 and 2002 show that across countries the levels of satisfaction with life in general have remained more or less the same, and there are remarkable cross-cultural differences: Consistently, the Danish, Dutch, and British publics show a higher level of satisfaction than the Italian, French, and German. These differences have remained stable over time. An explanation of these differences can be given by Hofstede's cultural dimension uncertainty avoidance that correlates negatively with feelings of well-being, and this relationship remains stable over time. Figure 5.1 illustrates the stability of the differences as well as the consistently significant correlations with uncertainty avoidance. An important finding is that similar differences are found for young people 15 to 24 years old. At regular times, Eurobarometer asks young people in Europe to what degree they are satisfied with their lives, and, as the chart shows, this line runs parallel to the one of the general publics.

Value Shift

Although values are enduring, some values may change in the long term. Value shift can be caused by economic change, modernization, maturation and generation effects, Zeitgeist, and seniority effects.

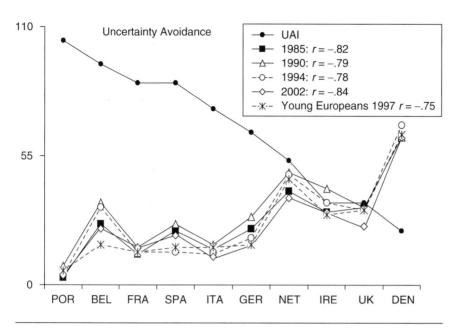

Figure 5.1   Values Are Stable: Satisfaction With Life

SOURCE: Data from Hofstede (2001) (see Appendix A); Eurobarometer (1985, 1990, 1994, 2002); Young Europeans (1997) (see Appendix B)

Wealth leads to individualism, and poverty leads to collectivism. With better education, the level of power distance goes down. Yet relative differences remain, and some differences may even become stronger. At face value, people tend to become more individualistic, but individuation follows different patterns. Modernization, including industrialization and urbanization, is assumed to turn collectivistic societies into individualistic societies. Although urbanization tends to break up the joint household of the extended family in favor of more nuclear households, this does not imply decreasing extended family values. Roland[7] states that the Indian family always remains an extended one. The extended family maintains strong family ties, gets together on holidays, makes mutual decisions on important matters, and sometimes maintains joint ownership. Indian society and culture modernize by traditionalizing various foreign innovations. A class society has formed, but classes do not predominate over caste. Instead, caste associations have been formed to provide assistance for jobs, marriages, or loans; and castes have participated in the political process. The Japanese remain enmeshed within traditional family and group hierarchical structures, although new skills and greater education have led to increased individuation. Modernization for the Japanese has reinforced the traditional Japanese ego-ideal into a total dedication to the task, which contributes to the good of the group. The system of structural hierarchy of unquestioned subordination in large power distance cultures may change, but dependency values included in a hierarchy by quality, deep respect for superiors, and reciprocal relationships remain.

Maturation[8] effects mean that people's values shift as they grow older. Stress, for example, is highest at middle age. Masculinity decreases with increasing age. Young people who want to make it in life generally adhere more to masculine values than do those who have already made it. Youngest and oldest age categories are less individualistic.

Generation effects occur when values are fixed in the young from a certain period and then stay with that age cohort over its lifetime. Drastic changes in the conditions of life during youth may lead to generations having different fixed values. The value shift of the generation of the 1960s in Europe and the United States is an example of a generation effect.

Zeitgeist effects occur when drastic systemwide changes in conditions cause everyone's values to shift, regardless of age. In times of recession, the degree of power distance may increase because equality is less functional, or it may lead to increased bureaucracy and shift to a stronger level of uncertainty avoidance. Seniority effects occur when the values of people who are more senior in an organization are measured. Seniority and age effects cannot be separated easily.

Cross-Cultural Value Research

The Rokeach Value Survey was one of the first to be used in marketing. A simpler approach to values, called List Of Values (LOV), was developed by Kahle and Goff Timmer.[9] LOV consists of nine values: a sense of belonging, excitement, fun and enjoyment in life, warm relationship with others, self-fulfillment, being well respected, a sense of accomplishment, security, and self-respect. The nine items of LOV became the basis for the development of a new measurement scheme of the U.S. Marketing Science Institute, called MILOV (Multi-Item List Of Values). The nine values resulting from MILOV are security, self-respect, being well respected, self-fulfillment, sense of belonging, excitement, fun and enjoyment, warm relationships, and sense of accomplishment. Both Rokeach's list and LOV have been used for value studies worldwide, also in marketing and advertising. At the time of Rokeach's value survey, he already realized that values vary by culture. Nevertheless, some research agencies keep using American lists of values for their own value studies in other cultures. Surveys developed in one environment and used to measure values of another environment will lead to irrelevant results. International value studies from the start should take into account the different value systems of the participating countries.

There are several cross-cultural value studies, the results of which are available in the public domain. A European cross-cultural value study is the European Values Study (EVS),[10] which has been extended to the World Values Survey (WVS) by Ronald Inglehart.[11] The data from the European Social Survey (ESS), another European value survey, can be downloaded from the Internet.[12] This is a valuable data source of European values. Some international media studies have included questions that measure value differences. Examples are surveys by the Reader's Digest and the European Media and Marketing Surveys (EMS).[13] There are several consequences of using lists of values developed in one culture for other cultures: Value priorities may vary; terminal values of one culture may serve as instrumental values in other cultures; and values that are relevant in one culture may not exist at all in another culture, and thus there are no linguistic or conceptual equivalents in other languages.

Value Priorities Vary

Some values may exist everywhere, but there is a difference in *rankings of priorities of values.* In an exercise to find cross-cultural differences among American, Australian, Israeli, and Canadian students, Rokeach found differences in the ranking of the importance of the values on his list.[14] The Israeli students, in particular, deviated. For example, they cared more about being capable than being ambitious, and they were less individualistic and more group oriented than the other students, all of whom were from Anglo-Saxon cultures (American, Australian, and Canadian). This supports Hofstede's findings on the Israeli culture, which is more collectivistic and of high uncertainty avoidance, resulting in a higher regard for competence than is found in U.S. culture. Low priority to being ambitious may be explained by the relatively low score of the Israelis on the masculinity index. Later studies by others confirmed that surveys in non-American cultures will find different rankings of the same values.

Grunert, Grunert, and Beatty[15] compared values for two age-groups in three countries (U.S., Germany, and Denmark) based on Kahle's LOV instrument and found that ratings varied, particularly with respect to the values fun and enjoyment and self-fulfillment. Danish respondents, independent of their age, rated fun and enjoyment much higher than both German and U.S. respondents. The latter, on the other hand, rated self-fulfillment higher.

Kamakura and Mazzon[16] found substantial differences between the United States and Brazil for the Rokeach terminal values. Although family security, world peace, and freedom have consistently been important values in the United States, true friendship, mature love, and happiness appear to be the most important values in Brazil. Comparison of rankings of 1971 and 1981 also showed that the ranking of values in the United States had been quite stable over time.

Mixing Terminal and Instrumental Values

Terminal values of one culture may be the instrumental values of another culture. Rokeach listed obedience, getting along well with others, and self-control as instrumental values.[17] In large power distance as well as in collectivistic cultures, however, obedience may well be a terminal value. Respect for elders, parents, or any higher-placed person is ingrained in these cultures. Similarly, if the division between terminal and instrumental values were used in Asian cultures, getting along with others, or harmony, might be a terminal value rather than an instrumental one. A Belgian value, listed as the first terminal value by the Belgian Patrick Vyncke,[18] is having one's own house, one's own place under the sun. The Dutch consider this to be an instrumental value. The house is the instrument of security or care. And, indeed, the Dutch are very different from the Belgians, not only with respect to this value. Specific to the Belgians is strong linkage to the soil of their birthplace, which is expressed by the saying "a stone in your belly." For practical reasons, in cross-cultural value studies the distinction between instrumental and terminal values is better avoided.

Culture-Specific Values

Some important values are culture-specific. Relevant values of one culture may not exist in another culture. For example, in Rokeach's list of values, two important Asian values are missing: perseverance and thrift. Relevant, culture-specific values can be found by looking at the important cultural concepts that appear to be untranslatable into any other language, or only translatable into the languages of similar cultures. Due to the fact that there are no linguistic or conceptual equivalents for some value-expressive words, using a single value list for cross-cultural research can cause errors. In the translation process, values can become incomprehensible or get a different loading.

Knowing that the Rokeach values are typical American values, one would expect that countries with different cultures would develop their own lists of values. This is only happening at a slow pace. Examples are lists of Belgian and Dutch values presented in this section. Another way of observing culture-specific values is by analyzing questions used for local psychographic or lifestyle research. The questions or statements used reflect culture-specific values, and cultural dimensions can be recognized in the questions. To demonstrate this, a few questions from an Indian and a Japanese survey are presented.

Belgian Values

A list of values developed by Belgian scholar Patrick Vyncke[19] shows values not found in Rokeach's list (see Table 5.2). The Belgian list includes individualistic values such as self-esteem, self-interest, and "doing your own thing." It reflects individualistic values as well as the masculine and high power distance values of success, status, and prestige. Most interesting is the fact that the first eight values all seem to be a reflection of strong uncertainty avoidance, which is a characteristic of Belgian culture. Owning your own house is a form of security; so are thrift, progeny, health, safety, being able to count on people, and being without pain. In particular, the statement "keep everything, all you have, as it is" reflects the reluctance to change that is characteristic of strong uncertainty avoidance cultures. The value progeny is reflected in the importance of children in Belgian society.

Dutch Values

Dutch Joke Oppenhuisen[20] found six dimensions of Dutch values that are summarized in Table 5.3. Each of the dimensions reflects the paradox that is typical of individualistic cultures that are also low on masculinity: freedom versus affiliation, which is also found in Scandinavian value studies. For each dimension, this paradox is related to different societal aspects: social relations, fellow human beings, society, security, family life, and dependence on approval by others. Each dimension consists

Table 5.2   List of Belgian Values

1. Having your own house, place "under the sun"
2. Thrift, frugality
3. Progeny, having descendants
4. Health, a healthy life
5. Safety, living in a safe world
6. Security, being able to count on people
7. Being without pain, fear, or misfortune
8. Keeping everything, all one has, as it is
9. Paying attention to oneself, self-interest
10. Romanticism, being in love, romantic love
11. Erotic love, sex, sensuality, seduction
12. A strong, intimate, and mature partner relationship
13. Love for children
14. Strong friendship, comradeship, "mateship"
15. Strong family ties, good family relationships
16. A better world for one's fellow man
17. A better environment, love of nature
18. Self-esteem, self-respect
19. Being respected by others
20. Being admired, having prestige, status, success
21. Leadership, power
22. Ability to be oneself as one is
23. Freedom, independence, doing one's own thing
24. Development of one's own abilities, creativity
25. Having one's own lifestyle
26. Being without stress, having peace, inner harmony
27. An active, exciting, adventurous life
28. Enjoying the simple things in life
29. Leading a prosperous, comfortable, luxurious life

SOURCE: Vyncke. (1992). *Imago-Management*. Used with permission of Mys & Breesch, Ghent, Belgium

of a set of 10 items. In Table 5.3, the first three of each dimension are presented. The study doesn't provide value priorities. Several values were similar to the Rokeach values, but additional values were found that do not occur on the Rokeach list.

Indian Values

In Indian culture, the values of the extended family are predominant, although individuality is richly developed in Indians, including a large degree of freedom in feeling, thinking, and cultivation of one's inner life. Competitive individualism, however, is severely frowned on in Indian society because it can disrupt relationships.[21]

Table 5.3   Dutch Values: Six Dimensions

Dimension 1		**Dimension 2**	
Affiliation	*Achievement*	*Social*	*Individual*
Cuddling	Ambition	Empathy	Enjoyment
Friendship	Fanatic	Understanding	Attractive
Love	Power	Helpful	Carefree

Dimension 3		**Dimension 4**	
Old values	*New values*	*Security*	*Challenge*
Patriotism	Hobbies	Tidy	Challenge
Respectable	Education	Rich	Spontaneous
Proud	Have time	Clean	Break new ground

Dimension 5		**Dimension 6**	
Family life	*Freedom*	*Conformist*	*Go it alone*
Be a mother	Freedom	Well-groomed	Go it alone
Have children	Ordinary	Attractive	Believe
Cuddling	Peace and quiet	Prestige	Rebel

SOURCE: Oppenhuisen (2000)

Other values that are typical of Indian culture can be derived from statements used in psychographic research. Examples of such statements are presented in Table 5.4, showing a list of 10 questions of a total of 74 used in an Indian survey.[22] To show how they rank in the total list, the table also provides (in parentheses) the original numbers of the questions in the survey.

India is a large power distance and medium collectivistic culture, masculine, and of relatively weak uncertainty avoidance. Large power distance is recognized in questions 1 and 4 (expressing respect for elders) and in question 10 (expressing

Table 5.4   Ten of 74 Questions Reflecting Indian Values

1. I do not wear clothes that are considered disrespectful in our society even though I would like to. (1)
2. I am uncomfortable chatting with men other than my immediate relatives. (8)
3. In today's world, it is important for a man and woman to get to know each other well before they get married. (9)
4. It is important that we obey our elders. (20)
5. I generally have my meals along with the rest of the family. (40)
6. I don't feel confident shopping alone except for groceries. (41)
7. I like the idea of staying in a joint family. (42)
8. Our lives are determined by what is written in our stars—we can do very little to change it. (54)
9. When we have visitors at home, I serve a variety of foods, even if it means a drain on my budget. (68)
10. I do not complain about products which do not meet my expectations. (74)

SOURCE: Shunglu and Sarkar (1995)

dependence). Collectivism is recognized in questions 5, 6, 7, and 9, reflecting the extended family, a preference for not being alone, and catering to visitors, even beyond one's financial means. Also, typically Indian historical values and practices are reflected, such as a segregated society and the arranged marriage.

Japanese Values

First we describe Japanese values that are also found in other East Asian cultures and that are frequently recognized in marketing and advertising: harmony with fellow human beings and harmony with nature. They are characteristic of the combination of long-term orientation and collectivism and, although here explained for Japanese culture, are applicable to many other East Asian cultures.

Harmony. One of the most important basic Japanese values is harmony (*wa*): walk together, think together, dine together. Related is empathy (understand and anticipate the feelings of others), respect for age, and honesty. Honesty cannot be related to the Western concept of truth. The Japanese concept of honesty is linked to respect. For example, government should not treat us as children, but as grown-ups.

Nature. When the Japanese speak of the providence of nature, they refer to a natural order that they believe to be the fountainhead of all existence. In the Christian world, God is the fountainhead of all existence, and humans seek comfort from God. In Japan, human beings seek comfort by attempting to immerse themselves in nature. Another explanation of the reverence for nature is that the Japanese turn to nature because there is something unsatisfying in the way they deal with human relations, where the surface is always glossed over and conflict is kept in the shadows. Living with the strong distinction between dealing with people in one's inner circle and one's outer circle can be very complicated and stressful. Nature does not have this distinction and can therefore be trusted completely.[23] Relating to nature is not as confusing as relating to human beings. Thus, nature has a relaxing function.

Other typical Japanese values can be recognized in a model developed by the late Kazuaki Ushikubo,[24] who studied people's wants in Japan and developed a model for structuring wants. This structure is based on 12 Japanese core values. From 1982 onward, he carried out an annual survey among 3,000 respondents, presenting them with 12 statements. Respondents received a number of stickers to distribute over the value statements to show their preference. This technique circumvents the problem of Asians not being able to think in opposites. Ushikubo found four clusters of basic values, which he named "Change," "Participation," "Freedom," and "Stability," as presented in Figure 5.2.

The 12 statements are as follows:

1. "To keep friends is very important." This relates to the element "family and friends" in the participation cluster. "Friends" in this statement applies to the members of the in-group. It does not relate to the Western concept of friendship, but to "correct behavior versus the others in your group."

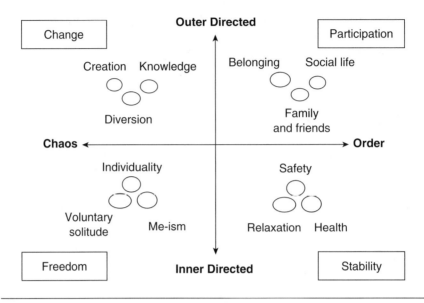

Figure 5.2   Japan (Ushikubo): "Freedom and Order"

SOURCE: Ushikubo (1986)

2. "Want to refresh from a tired brain or body." This statement is related to relaxation and is part of the stability cluster.

3. "Want to learn knowledge faster than other people." Values related to this statement are part of the change cluster.

4. "Identity of myself is important." This question relates to freedom and fits with the "individuality" trend. It is an example of a value that is emphasized because it is lacking in society.

5. "Have a happy time with friends and family." The Japanese word is *danran,* which has no equivalent in English, according to Ushikubo. It means having a happy time, enjoying open-hearted conversation with your family and good friends. It is part of the participation cluster.

6. "To live without fear—safety." This is included in the stability cluster.

7. "To create something and upgrade my ability." This is included in the change cluster. This reflects the Japanese value "continuous improvement."

8. "Live easy, I do not care about my surroundings." This me-ism, wanting to be yourself, outside the group, is included in the freedom cluster.

9. "Do well with all people around me." This relates to social life, included in the participation cluster.

10. "Want to be healthy." This is included in the stability cluster.

11. "To live in loneliness, have a lonely time." This means voluntary solitude, included in the freedom cluster.

12. "Want to have stimulation, change in my life, diversion, new things." This is included in the change cluster.

The freedom cluster, defining individuality (individuality, me-ism, and voluntary solitude) was indicated by only 10% of the respondents, which illustrates the different meaning of freedom in Japan: individuality, me-ism, thus escaping the (sometimes) stifling conformity of the group.

Important Values Don't Translate

Values have to be labeled, and if the labels are translated but the values are not comparable, they tend to represent different values. Thus, translation of values of American value lists into other languages can result in meaningless concepts or may even turn positive concepts into negative ones. A few examples of untranslatable words and concepts were given in Chapter 3. Such words and concepts are very important for advertising because in the specific culture they can communicate a message instantly. During the past century, the Dutch coffee producer Douwe Egberts (Sara Lee/DE) has built a high market share in the Netherlands by consistently connecting coffee with the typically Dutch togetherness concept, which could not be implanted in other parts of Europe except in the similar cultures of Scandinavia. Because American lists of values are so frequently used for cross-cultural studies, in this section the translation problems of a few of the typical Rokeach values are described.

Values like patriotism and nationalism are more meaningful in some countries than in others, often depending on their histories. For countries that have always had open borders, such as the Netherlands, these values are neither meaningful nor important. If someone in the Netherlands were to declare himself ready to die for his country, people would start laughing. Feelings of nationality also vary between individualistic and collectivistic cultures. For the former, a "nation" is the abstract ultimate unit to which one chooses to belong. For Americans, it is loyalty to the "stars and stripes," not to the current president. For members of collectivistic cultures, one is more implicitly part of a "grand family" in which a good ruler has the role of the benevolent father, and loyalty is to the ruler. This explains how in Japan, a culture based on personal ties, the emperor was and still is a symbol of loyalty far surpassing a flag.[25] Also, in Europe the degree to which people feel attached to their town or region (not the nation) is much stronger in collectivistic cultures than in individualistic cultures, according to a Eurobarometer[26] survey of 2001 that asked the degree of attachment to town or region in 14 west European countries. Collectivism explained 62% of variance of the answers "feeling attached to one's region" and 43% of variance of the answers "feeling attached to one's town."

Happiness is one of the most important American values. Yet the idea that the pursuit of happiness is a serious life goal by which the state and family are judged is unthinkable to the Japanese. To the Japanese, the supreme task in life is fulfilling one's obligations. Pleasure or happiness is a relaxation that can easily be given up in order to fulfill one's obligations.[27] Advertisers often present happiness as a universal value, but the above makes clear that the priority of importance varies. Next to that, what makes people happy varies even more.

Another Western value, romantic love, is underplayed by the Chinese but is cultivated by the Japanese. Erotic pleasure, on the other hand, is a moral issue or even a taboo to the Americans, whereas the Japanese see no need to be moralistic about sex pleasures. In Indian culture, too, the erotic is accepted and expressed.[28]

Salvation, an American value, when translated into Dutch seems to be irrelevant. The literal translation is the same word as delivering a baby. In the Dutch value study, it was listed as problem solving. All concepts related to religion or to belief in higher beings are culture-bound. The Japanese cannot cope with concepts relating to God at all. For them, the concept of salvation is nonexistent. When they seek comfort, they seek it in nature.

Belonging is an important end-goal for individualistic cultures: Being "by yourself" or "going it alone" is part of the individualistic value system, but not always desirable, so one has to make an effort to be with others. For collectivistic cultures, belonging is part of existence: The individual exists only as part of the group.

Achievement is a value complex that has high priority in Anglo-Saxon cultures that score high on masculinity (importance of visible results) and low on uncertainty avoidance (willingness to run risks). This combination is the recipe for the economic success of Anglo-Saxon culture, as it is a component of entrepreneurial activity. Other cultures show different components of success. The French, Swedes, Dutch, and Japanese will either not use the word or will change its meaning into something with better culture-fit. Thus, in Japanese it has become "inner harmony, personal attainment."

The word *freedom* has different connotations across cultures. The concept of freedom as described by U.S. students means "free enterprise." Dutch students tend to describe *freedom* as "freedom to express your feelings, to be yourself." In 1996, Russian students from western Siberia associated the word *freedom* primarily with "not being in prison" and secondarily with freedom from pollution and freedom of speech.[29] To the Japanese, *freedom* means "to behave as you please, to transcend the group." It is experienced as "having individual ideas, escape from spiritual bondage," which is not the same as the Western individualistic notion of freedom that serves as a basis for asserting the precedence of the individual over the group, which is not seen as desirable in Japanese society. The Japanese word used to translate the English word *freedom* (*jiyu*) is of Chinese origin. It means to behave as one pleases, without considering others, which for a collectivistic society basically means disharmony and thus is negative. As liberty and freedom in the West signify respect for the human being, the concept has become ambiguous, to say the least, to the Japanese.[30]

The Rokeach value "a comfortable life" is linked with material prosperity. To the Japanese it means to be rich, not in money, but spiritually, to be without fear, have stability, no change, good relations, a good house. In the Dutch value study, it was listed as enjoyment.

The Rokeach values "self-respect" and "self-esteem" are related to the concept of "self" of an individualistic culture as will be described in more detail in Chapter 6. *Self-respect* (*jicho*) in Japan means restraint, which is the opposite of the American value, which includes values like character, reputation, and prestige. A major dimension of Japanese self-esteem relates to reflecting well on the family and work group through high performance, thus gaining their respect. Indians' inner feelings of esteem are deeply tied up with family reputation.[31]

Asking people of different cultures to define a word like *pleasure* leads to long sentences and explanations, which suggests that it has different connotations in different cultures. Because it is frequently used in advertising, understanding its meaning and connotations in other cultures is important. In Japan, *pleasure* is a personal feeling of pleasure, related only to the inner circle. The Spanish concept of *placer* reflects a wide variety of feelings of social and inner enjoyment.

The concept of friendship is ambiguous. It does not exist in Japanese society. It is known and used because it is an often encountered American word, but those whom you call your friends are basically members of the inner circle. True friendship is made to mean "understanding how to communicate." This is very different from the North American concept of friendship, in which you can make friends and lose friends (see also Chapter 4, under Individualism/Collectivism). In the Japanese outer circle, you have no friends. Rarely might you find a new friend in your work. As a result, asking Japanese respondents to choose the degree of importance of true friendship is a nonsense question. Japanese cannot express the importance of true friendship. This also holds true in China and in other collectivistic cultures, though more strongly in some than in others.

Americans call people friends who are merely acquaintances in the European context. In continental Europe, only close friends are on a first-name basis. Dealing with everybody on a first-name basis, as the Americans do, confuses the friendship concept. It is particularly confusing to Germans, for whom the wider usage of the word friendship is too ambiguous, as is illustrated by the reaction to a *Newsweek* article about service:[32]

> Germans, like most Europeans, are more distant with customers than Americans are used to, but can hardly be summed up as unfriendly. The artificial friendliness commonly practiced by shop assistants and restaurant staff in America would be off-putting to Germans. Who wants to be on a first-name basis with a waiter who'll be forgotten promptly after the meal?

Many Western, abstract concepts are beyond understanding to the Japanese and other Asian cultures. In particular, those that are remote from daily life, such as a "world at peace" or striving for "quality of life," are concepts they have difficulty coping with. Most East Asians can better handle pragmatic, down-to-earth thinking. This implies that even the basic notion of a "concept" is not familiar to their way of thinking. Peace, not the large concept of peace, but peace nearby, means health, safety, and having good people around you.

Value and Lifestyle Research

Lifestyle research for marketing aims to group people according to their value systems as expressed by their lifestyle. In the early days of consumer behavior research, there was great interest in explaining consumer choices based on psychological personality measurements. Lifestyle research grew out of this. Working with AIO variables (attitudes, interests, and opinions), segments were identified such as "the happy housewife" or the "price-conscious shopper." This work had limited success in explaining consumer choices, particularly at brand level, and the segments did not seem to be very stable over time. In the late 1970s and early 1980s, researchers began to work with more general values in an attempt to identify variables that could explain consumer behavior and that at the same time were relatively stable over time.[33] The Stanford Research Institute's values and lifestyles (VALS) program was one of the first applications of a psychographic classification of consumer behavior. VALS, developed by SRI International, Menlo Park, California,[34] is based on the Rokeach value system. It uses a questionnaire asking motivations and demographic characteristics that are seen as predictors of consumer preferences. Later, a parallel system called RISC International (after the International Research Center for Social Change in Paris) emerged in Europe. In several other countries, such studies were developed.

The common aspect of these studies is the use of two-dimensional space in which consumption, respondents, and values are placed. The primary dimensions of VALS are motivations and resources. The three primary motivations are ideals, achievement, and self-expression. Six basic segments are defined for each motivation and for high and low resources.[35] RISC distinguished three dimensions: "expansion-stability" (openness to new ideas vs. resistance to change), "enjoyment-responsibility," and "flexibility-structure."[36] The VALS segmentation system was developed in the United States, and the values included are typical for the United States. Nevertheless, international research and advertising agencies apply it to other cultures.

Usually the responses to value questions are submitted to factor analysis, and the resulting factors are given labels that cover the factor items, as interpreted by the creators of the studies. As a result, the labels will reflect the culture of the developers of the study. This leads to labels like "strivers," "devouts," or "fun seekers" if the study is directed by Americans, or to labels like "mythical" or "emotional" by French researchers, whereas British researchers tend to include class-based segment labels. Both concepts and dimensions used in value studies reflect the culture of the home country and cannot be extended to other cultures without losing meaning. A few examples follow.

CCA, a French system developed in the 1990s, worked with the dimensions "progressive-conservative" and "material-spiritual." Like the RISC dimension expansion-stability, the first dimension reflects the paradox of high power distance and high uncertainty avoidance cultures where people want progress and innovation, but the need for stability makes them conservative.

The Belgian market research agency Censydiam uses theories by the psychoanalyst Adler, who saw in fear of inferiority and the tension that results from it a powerful source of energy from which the individual can draw added value for his or her existential being. Censydiam follows the philosophy that "eventually behavior is nothing else than energy directed at the release of tension (such as unsatisfied needs or unrealized motives), and fear of inferiority or anxiety."[37] According to this theory, consumers develop basic strategies for the management of tension. This focus on anxiety reflects the high score of Belgium on uncertainty avoidance. The dimensions found among Belgian subjects of the study are "social affirmation-social integration" and "expression of emotions" versus "control of emotions." These are dimensions that are typical for a culture of the configuration of high power distance and high uncertainty avoidance. The results of such studies are often presented without saying that the findings are based on a study among Belgians and are not applicable to, for example, Dutch subjects that are of a totally different culture.[38]

A commercial segmentation system developed by Gallup in Scandinavia, Kompas, works with the dimensions "modern" versus "traditional" and "individual" versus "social" values.[39] The latter dimension is similar to the Dutch freedom-affiliation paradox: expressing one's individuality is important, but affiliation needs are even more important and can be conflicting.

A Japanese model developed by Dentsu[40] uses the dimensions "achiever" versus "membership dependent" and "group merit" versus "intelligent, nonconformist" that both reflect the individualism-collectivism paradox.

Sometimes studies of different countries use similar English-language labels for different typologies or classification cues that can be misleading. One example is the difference between the group "achievers" in VALS and in the Japanese lifestyle study by Dentsu. The achievers in VALS have goal-oriented lifestyles that center on family and career. They avoid situations that encourage a high degree of stimulation or change. They prefer premium products that demonstrate success to their peers. Hiroe Suzuki of Dentsu's information technology center distinguished four life models in Dentsu's lifestyle study:[41] "Achiever," "Intelligent," "Group Merit," and "Membership Dependent." Key words in the description of the achiever in this study were "enterprising," "importance of individuality," and "importance of human relationships." The achiever was described as practicing innovative consumption, which is a reflection of an enterprising personality whose aim is a Japanese-style society of successful people.

Value and Lifestyle Studies for Global Marketing

Global and pan-European lifestyle studies aim at identifying similar lifestyle segments across borders, assuming that national and cultural influences on consumption patterns are less significant than modern lifestyle patterns. Most describe typologies and focus on changes in people's lifestyles to apply to new-product development, new-product introduction, and the positioning of brands.

These studies generally are centrally driven and organized. Value statements are collected that are assumed to be valid in all cultures. Studies that segment world populations in terms of global values end up in rough descriptions of consumers that are appealing but not very practical because significant links between such global values and actual product or brand behavior are rare. Generally, the sellers of such studies do not provide much information about the way the data are manipulated. It is difficult to assess the value of such studies as they are proprietary and often little information is provided about the methods used. Varying methods and questions can lead to different results. Some studies ask for the desirable, others ask for the desired, so they measure different things. A global value study by Roper Starch[42] asks consumers to respond to statements representing "the guiding principles in their lives." Other studies, such as by RISC, measure actual behavior.

Usually lifestyle groups that are given one label across countries are very different as to content. The British TGI (Target Group Index),[43] for example, categorizes age categories of women and labels the 15- to 24-year-old group as the "@ generation." What members of this group have in common is that they are mostly single women. Young Italian and Spanish women, however, mostly live at home with their parents, whereas young Germans start to live as a couple early on. All spend money on pleasure articles: CDs, makeup, sportswear, or snack products. Italians and Spaniards, however—probably because they live at home and have more spending power—spend more on personal and luxury goods and going out. They live in larger households and share products and brands, so brands must address the collective, not the individual. Italian and British women are more involved in appearance. Snack consumption is high among this age-group, but snacks are consumed in different situations. In Britain, potato chips are an around-the-clock, individual snack product, but in Spain they are used as tapas, when people are socializing.

The advertising agency Young & Rubicam, who originally worked with VALS, offers a consumer value segmentation study titled *Cross-Cultural Consumer Characterization,* which measures consumer lifestyles in seven European countries and suggests the existence of seven sets of fundamental values that describe types of consumers and that exist worldwide: "Succeeder," "Mainstream," "Resigned," "Reformer," "Explorer," "Aspirer," and "Struggler."[44]

Some commercial studies have found meaningful dimensions that explain cultural differences and that can be linked to specific consumer preferences, media behavior, or people's relationships with brands.

Two studies serve as examples: The Semiometrie study by the international research agency Taylor Nelson Sofrès and the Crocus study by the joint venture of the European advertising agency Interpartners and the French research agency chain EuroNet.

Semiometrie

Originally the French agency Sofrès started this study by using 210 words that together reflected people's value patterns. The international agency Taylor Nelson Sofrès extended it to four other European countries: Germany, the United Kingdom, Spain, and Italy. For the cross-cultural application, 20 words could not be used because these words had entirely different associations in different languages. According to the researchers, the connotations of freedom, for example, in France date back to the French revolution, whereas in the United Kingdom, it has more recent associations with Thatcherite "freedom of choice" in the 1980s.[45] The five countries involved in the study had four factors in common that are typical of western Europe. Surveys conducted in the Middle East and North Africa brought out very different divisions. What the five European countries had in common are four dimensions that reflect the value paradoxes of western Europe:

1. *Duty* versus *Pleasure:* To abide by the rules *or* to satisfy one's own immediate desires.

2. *Community* versus *Singularity:* To create bonds *or* to call attention to oneself.

3. *Materialism* versus *Culture:* To look for earthly goods *or* to look for spiritual nourishment, culture.

4. *Idealism* versus *Pragmatism:* To look for an embellished reality *or* to be pragmatic.

Next to these common dichotomies, specific national values (called mentalities) were found. For example, specific for Spain are love, family, idealism, desire to learn and innovate, and moderation. Specific for Italy are social interaction, imagination, art-orientation, and sense of rules. Specific for France is quality of life. Specific for Germany are pragmatism, pleasure, and success. Specific for the United Kingdom are strong individualism, refusal to create bonds, singularity, and eccentricity next to a sense of duty. In the four factors, several values of the Hofstede dimensions can be recognized. "Duty-Pleasure," for example, is similar to the dependence-freedom paradox, as it includes values like respect for authority and social conventions versus freedom. The "Community-Singularity" dichotomy is like the value paradox of individualistic cultures: On the one hand individualists want to do it their way, but they also want to belong (see also Chapter 8). The latter paradox is found in many other European value studies. Semiometrie is used as a media planning instrument by adding an extra dimension to basic consumption and lifestyle data. It helps to understand brand users and the context in which to create and place effective advertising.

Crocus

Crocus (Cross-Cultural Solutions)[46] is a cross-cultural study that measures brand value (called "brand pull") and provides a cultural explanation of strong or weak brand value in different countries. The findings help to develop effective cross-cultural brand positioning and advertising. The study was conducted in 2003 among Internet users in 17 countries: the United States, Turkey, Russia, and Ukraine, as well as 13 western European countries. A set of value questions was combined with questions that measure consumers' relationships with brands as well as buying intentions and brand characteristics attributed to a large number of brands, both local and global. Factor analysis of the data resulting from the value questions delivered four robust and meaningful cultural factors explaining differences in consumer relations with international brands across countries. These factors are related to Hofstede's dimensions. The four dimensions were labelled "Dependence," "Conformance," "Passion," and "Security." The descriptions of the four dimensions summarize important characteristics of consumers and their match with brand characteristics. Dependence measures the degree to which people are dependent on brands to demonstrate their social position versus independence and self-reliance.

It correlates with power distance ($r = .54$). Conformance measures the degree to which people use brands to conform to others versus using brands to stand out as a unique individual. This dimension correlates negatively with individualism ($r = -.58$). Passion measures the degree to which people are achievement oriented and use brands to show off. On the one end, you find *self-enhancement,* and on the other end *modesty.* This dimension correlates with masculinity ($r = .65$). Security measures the inclination to seek security through high-quality brands versus innovation and modernity. Security correlates with uncertainty avoidance ($r = .56$). The 17 countries each have a score on the dimension scales, and thus countries can be clustered according to the importance of various brand characteristics.

Typical brand characteristics like "trustworthiness" or "friendliness" appeared to be culture-specific. Trustworthiness is most appealing to consumers in high security cultures. Friendliness is most appealing to consumers in low dependence and high passion cultures. Some characteristics were found in two dimensions, but they had different functions. For example, in high dependence cultures, "modern" and "international" add to prestige, whereas in high conformance cultures they add to the need to belong to a wider world. This implies that dimensions clustered in a two-dimensional map reinforce each other. For example, for a country like Turkey, ranking high in terms of dependence and security, trustworthiness and prestige are of great importance for international brands.

One of the important conclusions was that strong international brands appear to have different and culturally relevant positions in the different culture clusters.

The Value Concept in International Marketing and Advertising Strategy

In marketing, the value concept refers to people and to objects. A brand will be a strong brand if people's values match the values of the brand. "Branding" means adding values to products, and advertising is an important instrument for achieving this.

Values play an important role in consumer behavior because they influence choice. They provide consumers with standards for making comparisons among alternatives. Consumers' value systems can be divided into three groups:[47]

1. Central values: the core values of the individual's value system

2. Domain-specific values: values acquired in specific situations or domains of activities

3. Product-specific values: evaluations of product attributes

Examples of different domains include economy, religion, politics, work, and consumption. In using values to evaluate products and brands, the values of interest are product-specific values applied to product categories or specific brands. Examples are purity for mineral water or detergents, pleasure or security for automobiles, and self-respect (in the Western sense) or beauty/aesthetics for cosmetics.

Western advertising strategy development includes (a) selecting values or end-states to emphasize in advertising, (b) determining how advertising will connect the product to key end-states, and (c) developing advertisements connecting the product to the end value. Values offer an opportunity to differentiate brands by going beyond attributes and benefits or the deliverance of higher-level consequences to consumers. Adding values creates association networks that distinguish the brand vis-à-vis the competitive brands in the category and thus can help build strong positions for brands.

Value Structure Maps

A tool for strategy is the *value structure map* (VSM), which describes how a particular group of subjects tends to perceive or think about a specific product or brand.[48] A value structure map links the product's attributes and benefits to values.

Attributes can be concrete or abstract; benefits can be functional or psychosocial consequences of the product's attributes. Value structure maps provide a structure of people's associations with a brand at the three levels: attributes, benefits, and values. They show how the types of associations that people make between a specific attribute of a product and its subsequent benefits and values are connected. This connection, developed by Gutman,[49] was presented as the means-end chain model. Gutman formulated the essence as follows: Means are objects (products) or activities in which people engage; ends are valued states of being such as happiness, security, accomplishment. A *means-end chain* is a model that seeks to explain how the choice of a product or service facilitates the achievement of desired end-states. Such a model consists of elements that represent the major consumer processes that link values to behavior. Rokeach's distinction of instrumental and terminal values compares with the means and ends.

The technique used to develop means-end chains is *laddering,* an in-depth, one-on-one interviewing technique used to develop an understanding of how consumers translate the attributes of products into meaningful associations with respect to the self.[50] By using this laddering technique, sets of linkages can be determined between perceptual elements, which are then represented at different levels of abstraction. Figure 5.3 shows three levels of associations for toothpaste, and Figure 5.4 shows six levels of (hypothetical) associations for Coca-Cola. An example of a value structure map is one for automobiles in Figure 5.5, including a number of Rokeach's terminal and instrumental values as well as one Asian value, harmony with nature.

Advertisers who want to differentiate a brand can follow different routes via attributes and benefits to reach end values. In this system, the product attributes may be the same worldwide, yet different end values may be connected to the attributes (to be found through research), reflecting different cultures. An example of a route in the VSM for automobiles is selecting, for example, one attribute, a Strong Motor, and one end value, Pleasure, and following the route Fast Acceleration → Imaginative, Daring → Personal Enjoyment → Independence to Pleasure. Another route takes the same

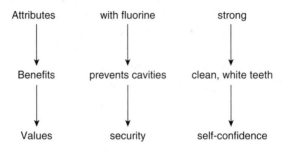

Example: toothpaste

Attributes	with fluorine	strong
Benefits	prevents cavities	clean, white teeth
Values	security	self-confidence

Figure 5.3   Levels of Communication (VSM, Laddering)

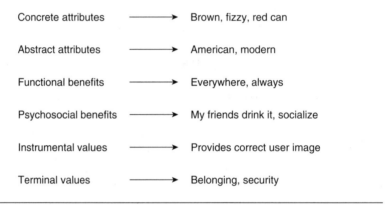

Concrete attributes	→	Brown, fizzy, red can
Abstract attributes	→	American, modern
Functional benefits	→	Everywhere, always
Psychosocial benefits	→	My friends drink it, socialize
Instrumental values	→	Provides correct user image
Terminal values	→	Belonging, security

Figures 5.4   Levels of Communication: Coca-Cola

attribute as a starting point but continues via Safe → Protects Family & Myself → Responsible → Love/Care to Family Security. This could be an example of a route for a feminine culture. Volvo has used this route from the attribute "Strong Body." A route for cultures of the configuration collectivist/high power distance/high uncertainty avoidance would be Design/Colors → Modern Sophistication/Good Taste → Authority/Power to Social Status. Different routes can be followed, depending on the target group, the culture, and the competition. In a multinational campaign targeted at countries that are similar with respect to one or more dimensions, it may be possible to select one route with values that the different countries have in common. Two other examples are VSMs in Figures 5.6 and 5.7.

These VSMs were developed by a group of Spanish and German students who, in casework, had to develop a common strategy for Spain and Germany for the beer

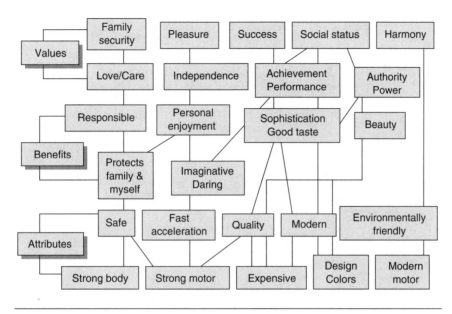

Figure 5.5   Value Structure Map: Automobiles

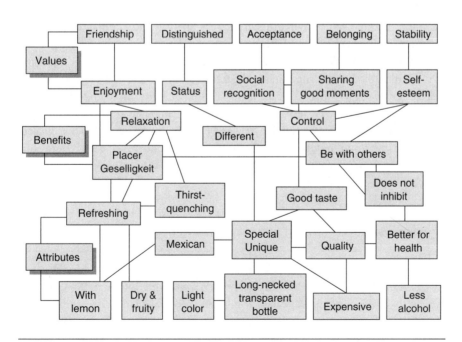

Figure 5.6   Value Structure Map: Corona Extra, Spain

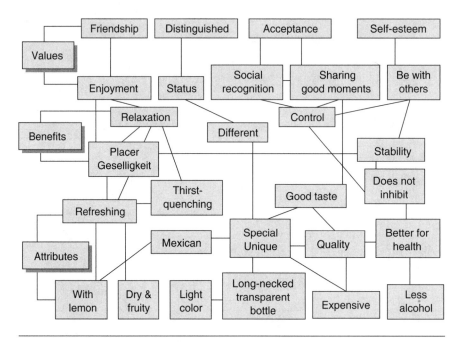

Figure 5.7   Value Structure Map: Corona Extra, Germany

brand Corona Extra. First they selected the attributes, and then they tried to find common terminal values. What they found the Spanish and German cultures had in common were Friendship, Distinguished, and Acceptance. The Spanish found Belonging and Stability to be important terminal values with Self-Esteem and Being With Others as instrumental to the terminal values. The Germans found that Self-Esteem was a terminal value for them and that Stability and Being With Others were instrumental to the terminal value Self-Esteem. They concluded that only the two routes leading toward Belonging and Stability for Spain and to Self-Esteem for Germany could not be used for a common strategy, whereas Friendship, Distinguished, and Acceptance, which they formulated as terminal values, could be shared and used for one common strategy.

Conclusion

This chapter described how values are used in marketing. Value and lifestyle stud-ies based on the Rokeach Value Survey are used worldwide, although the values are typical for American culture. When translated into other languages, some values become meaningless, and meaningful values of other cultures are overlooked. Values are also stable, which means that the core values of a culture either do not change or change only over longer periods of time—not within the lifetime of current marketing and advertising people. This seems to be paradoxical, as the marketing and advertising world shows a preoccupation with change and is in continuous pursuit of new trends and changing lifestyles. Those who are involved in value and lifestyle research have to be aware of the fact that new lifestyles generally concern the expressions of culture. They are not based on new values but are usually a new format of existing values. Core values, so useful for differentiating brands at a higher level, are stable. Transplanting surveys developed in one environment to another that differs significantly cannot lead to an effective strategy. People's values vary by culture, and researchers' values differ as well. If there is no match between the culture reflected in a research model and the culture of the country where it is applied, the outcome will not be meaningful. Using axes of one culture to position brands in another culture is an interesting but not very efficient exercise. Understanding that the values of one culture cannot be used indiscriminately in another culture should lead toward more refined value studies for developing effective global marketing and advertising strategies. Several new models are being developed that measure brand-related cultural values that can help international advertisers. Value structure maps are valuable tools that enable companies to develop global products and differentiate them by using the core values of national culture.

Notes

1. Rokeach, M. (1973). *The nature of human values.* New York: Free Press, p. 5.

2. Rokeach, 1973, 10.

3. Rokeach, 1973, 28.

4. Herche, J. (1994). *Measuring social values: A multi-item adaptation to the list of values* (MSI Report Summary, Report No. 94–101). Marketing Science Institute, 1000 Massachusetts Ave., Cambridge, MA 02138; tel. (617) 491–2060.

5. Roland, A. (1988). *In search of self in India and Japan.* Princeton, NJ: Princeton University Press, p. 94.

6. Yankelovich, D. (1994). How changes in the economy are reshaping American values. In H. J. Aaron, T. E. Mann, & T. Taylor (Eds.), *Values and public policy.* Washington, DC: Brookings Institution, pp. 23–24.

7. Roland, 1988, 90–93, 102–103, 131.

8. Hofstede, G. (1984). *Culture's consequences: International differences in work-related values.* Beverly Hills, CA: Sage, pp. 232–251.

9. Kahle, L. R., & Goff Timmer, S. (1983). *A theory and method for studying values and social change: Adaptation to life in America.* New York: Praeger.

10. Halman, L. (2001). *The European Values Study: A third wave.* WORC Tilburg University. PO Box 90153, 5000 LE Tilburg, The Netherlands. E-mail evs@kub.nl.

11. Inglehart, R., Basañez, M., & Moreno, A. (1998). *Human values and beliefs.* Ann Arbor: University of Michigan Press.

12. This study covers 23 mostly European countries: Austria, Belgium, Czechia, Denmark, Finland, France, Germany, Greece, Hungary, Ireland, Israel, Italy, Luxembourg, the Netherlands, Norway, Poland, Portugal, Slovenia, Spain, Sweden, Switzerland, Turkey, and the United Kingdom. (http://ess.nsd.uib.no)

13. Reader's Digest Surveys: A Survey of Europe Today, 1970; Eurodata, 1991; Reader's Digest Surveys: Trusted Brands, 2001, 2002, 2003, 2004; European Media and Marketing Surveys (EMS), 1995, 1997, 1999 (see Appendix B).

14. Rokeach, 1973, 90.

15. Grunert, K. G., Grunert, S. C., & Beatty, S. E. (1989, February). Cross-cultural research on consumer values. *Marketing and Research Today,* 30–39.

16. Kamakura, W. A., & Mazzon, J. A. (1991). Value segmentation: A model for the measurement of values and value systems. *Journal of Consumer Research, 18,* 208–218.

17. Rokeach, 1973, 15.

18. Vyncke, P. (1992). *Imago-Management: Handboek voor Reclamestrategen.* Ghent, Belgium: Mys & Breesch, Uitgevers & College Uitgevers, p. 134.

19. Vyncke, 1992, 133–135.

20. Oppenhuisen, J. (2000). *Een schaap in de bus? Een onderzoek naar waarden van de Nederlander* [A sheep in the bus? A study of Dutch values]. Unpublished doctoral dissertation, University of Amsterdam, The Netherlands.

21. Roland, 1988, 240.

22. Shunglu, S., & Sarkar, M. (1995, May). Researching the consumer. *Marketing and Research Today,* 124.

23. Doi, T. (1985). *The anatomy of self.* Tokyo: Kodansha International, pp. 147–156.

24. Kazuaki Ushikubo was president of Research and Development, Inc., Japan. He developed a model describing Japanese values that is described in Ushikubo, K. (1986). A method of structure analysis for developing product concepts and its applications. *European Research, 18,* 174–184. Quotes in this chapter are from a conversation I had with Mr. Ushikubo in November 1995. Research and Development gave permission to use Mr. Ushikubo's statements and model with the note that the text only partially represents the total concept of CORE, R&D's proprietary lifestyle analysis.

25. Benedict, R. (1974). *The chrysanthemum and the sword: Patterns of Japanese culture.* Rutland, VT: Charles E. Tuttle, p. 129.

26. Eurobarometer Survey no. 55, 2001 (see Appendix B).

27. Benedict, 1974, 192.

28. Benedict, 1974, 183; Roland, 1988, 109–110, 262.

29. Students' answers during a seminar on marketing and culture for Russian students from western Siberia, organized by the Finnish Marketing Institute, Brussels, October 2, 1996.

30. Doi, 1985, 84–86.

31. Roland, 1988, 131, 203; Benedict, 1974, 290.

32. Letters: A failing role model? [Letter from Mike Dunn of Bamberg, Germany] (1996, April 16). *Newsweek.*

33. Hansen, F. (1998). From life style to value systems to simplicity. *Advances in Consumer Research, 25,* 181–195.

34. Holman, R. H. (1984). A values and lifestyles perspective on human behavior. In R. E. Pitts, Jr., & A. G. Woodside (Eds.), *Personal values and consumer psychology* (pp. 35–54). Lexington, MA: Lexington Books, D. C. Heath.

35. www.sric-bi.com/VALS August 8, 2004

36. RISC International. (1995). *Why people buy* [Brochure]. Paris (www.risc-int.com).

37. Callebaut, J., Janssens, M., Lorré, D., & Hendrickx, H. (1994). *The naked consumer: The secret of motivational research in global marketing.* Antwerp: Censydiam Institute, p. 106.

38. Wijman, E. (2001, June). *Autostudies van Censydiam gaan alleen over Belgen: Turnhout is geen Tilburg* [Car studies by Censydiam are about Belgians only: Turnhout is not Tilburg]. *Adformatie, 28,* 36–38.

39. Hansen, 1998.

40. De Mooij, M. (1994). *Advertising worldwide* (2nd ed.). London: Prentice Hall International, pp. 178–183.

41. Received from Hiroe Suzuki, November 1995. Earlier description in Suzuki, H. (1998, June 18–20). *Japanese lifestyle, life models and applications to creative concepts.* Paper presented at a meeting of the ESOMAR Conference on America, Japan and EC '92: The Prospects for Marketing, Advertising and Research. Venice.

42. The Public Pulse. (1997, October/November). Roper Reports Worldwide Survey.

43. *TGI, European women report.* (n.d.). Retrieved November 4, 2004, from www.bmrb.co.uk.womensreportch2.htm

44. Information about Young & Rubicam's study retrieved July 25, 2004, from www.4Cs.yr.com

45. Marks, R., & Evans, C. (2001, July/August). Probing the subconscious using Semiometrie. *Admap*, 25.

46. The author of this book contributed to this study by providing value questions and conducting the cultural analysis. For more information contact Marieke de Mooij at info@mariekedemooij.com

47. Vinson, D. E., Scott, J. E., & Lamont, L. M. (1977, April). The role of personal values in marketing and consumer behavior. *Journal of Marketing, 41,* 44–50.

48. Olson, J. C., & Reynolds, T. J. (1983). Understanding consumers' cognitive structures: Implications for advertising strategy. In L. Perry & A. G. Woodside (Eds.), *Advertising and consumer psychology.* Lexington, MA: Lexington Books.

49. Gutman, J. A. (1982). Means-end chain model based on consumer categorization processes. *Journal of Marketing, 46,* 60–72.

50. Reynolds, T. J., & Gutman, J. (1988, February-March). Laddering theory, method, analysis, and interpretation. *Journal of Advertising Research,* 29–37.

SIX

Culture and Consumer Behavior

How people behave and what motivates them is largely a matter of culture. How they perceive themselves and relate to each other, whether their decisions are individual decisions or group decisions, how they process information, all are influenced by the culture to which they belong. Consequently, theories of consumer behavior are not culture-free. U.S. concepts of marketing and consumer behavior, when used in other cultures, should be adapted. This chapter provides an overview of consumer behavior theory and will point out the influences of culture.

Consumer Behavior

Consumer behavior can be defined[1] as the study of the processes involved when people select, purchase, use, or dispose of products, services, ideas, or experiences to satisfy needs and desires. In this definition, consumer behavior is viewed as a process that includes the issues that influence the consumer before, during, and after a purchase. Various components of human behavior are involved in this process. These can be summarized as *what people are* ("who am I"), the self and personality, defined by people's attributes and traits ("what sort of person am I"), *how people feel, how people think and learn,* and *what people do.* The terms of the social sciences for feeling, thinking, and doing are "affect," "cognition," and "behavior."

The model presented in Figure 6.1[2] structures the cultural components of the person in terms of *consumer attributes* and *processes,* and the cultural components of behavior in terms of *consumer behavior domains.* Income interferes. If there is no income, there is little or no consumption, so income is placed in a separate box. The attributes of the person refer to *what people are* and the processes refer to *what*

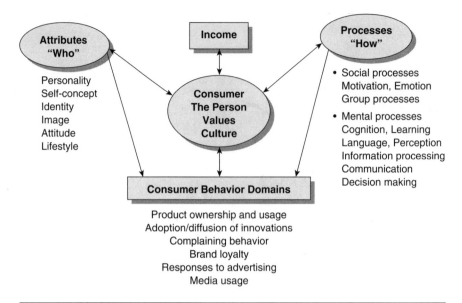

Figure 6.1   Cross-Cultural Consumer Behavior Framework

SOURCE: Adapted from Manrai and Manrai (1996)

moves people—the *who* and the *how*. The central question is "Who am I?" and in what terms people describe themselves and others—their personality traits and identity. Related to the *who* are attitudes and lifestyle because they are a central part of the person. How people think, and perceive, and what motivates them—*how* the aspects of "me" process into behavior—are viewed as processes.

Consumer Attributes

One aspect of Western marketing is the focus on product attributes—benefits or values that are to distinguish the user's self from others. Another aspect is the distinction between the actual self and the ideal self. People will buy products that are compatible with their self-concept, or rather that enhance their "ideal self"–image. In that sense, our self-concept is the image we carry in our mind of the type of person we are and who we desire to be. Frequently mentioned drives related to the ideal self are self-esteem, self-respect, and self-actualization. The concepts of self, the ideal self—personality, identity, and image—are all typical of Anglo-Saxon and northwest European culture and not applicable to other cultures without modification.

The Concept of Self

The concept of self, as used in consumer psychology, is based on Western-centric psychoanalytic theory of the self and personality, which is rooted in individualism. It includes the following ideas about a person. A person is an *autonomous entity* with a distinctive set of attributes, qualities, or processes. The configuration of these internal attributes or processes causes behavior. People's individual behavior varies, and this distinctiveness is good. People's attributes and processes should be expressed consistently in behavior across situations, and this consistency is good. Behavior that changes with the situation is viewed as hypocritical or pathological.

In the collectivistic model of the self, persons are fundamentally interdependent with one another. The self cannot be separated from others and the surrounding social context. This concept of self is characteristic of Asia, South America, Russia, the Middle East, Africa, and the south of Europe. The interdependent view of human nature includes the following ideas about a person. A person is an *interdependent entity* who is part of an encompassing social relationship. Behavior is a consequence of being responsive to the others with whom one is interdependent, and behavior originates in relationships. Individual behavior is situational; it varies from one situation to another and from one time to another. This sensitivity to social context is good.[3]

In individualistic cultures, a youth has to develop an identity that enables him or her to function independently in a variety of social groups apart from the family. Failing to do so can cause an identity crisis. In collectivistic cultures, youth development is based on encouragement of dependency needs in complex familial hierarchical relationships, and the group ideal is being like others, not being different.[4]

For individualists, the norms are self-reliance, self-assertion, and self-actualization and a high degree of verbal self-expression. Members of collectivistic cultures conceive of the self as part of the group to which they belong. As a result, for members of collectivistic cultures self-esteem, if used as a concept, is not linked to the individual but to relationships with others. The self is not defined as a set of abstract unique characteristics but defined through a web of social and personal relationships. In Japan, "respecting yourself" means always showing yourself to be the careful player; it does not mean, as in English usage, consciously conforming to a worthy standard of conduct. In India, "we"-self-regard means that feelings of inner regard or esteem are experienced not only around oneself but equally around the "we" of the extended family, particular community (*jati*), and other groups to which one belongs.[5] These are called in-groups, or inner circle, as opposed to out-groups or outer circle.

Next to individualism, masculinity explains variation of the self-concept. A relationship orientation, including family values, is not only specific of collectivistic cultures but is also found in individualistic cultures that are also feminine.[6] Whereas in feminine cultures modesty and relations are important characteristics, in masculine cultures self-enhancement leads to self-esteem, which is a valid barometer of psychological health. In cultures of the configuration individualism/ masculinity (all Anglo-Saxon cultures), self-enhancement, or ego-boosting, is most pronounced. It can be recognized in a TV commercial for Discover Card, pictured in Illustration 6.1. The card is used to buy Christmas decorations. Whatever the actor buys, the neighbor has more. The actor cannot stand having less. In the end, his whole house is illuminated, all bought with the card.

The influence of masculinity can also be recognized in answers to a question in the European Social Survey[7] that asks respondents across western and eastern European

Illustration 6.1　Discover Card, USA

countries to mark the importance of getting respect from others. Collectivism explains 47% of variance, and masculinity explains an additional 13% of variance. The relationship between respect from others and collectivism is illustrated in Figure 6.2, which also shows that feminine cultures such as Sweden, Norway, and Finland score lower than masculine cultures such as Ireland, Switzerland, and Poland.

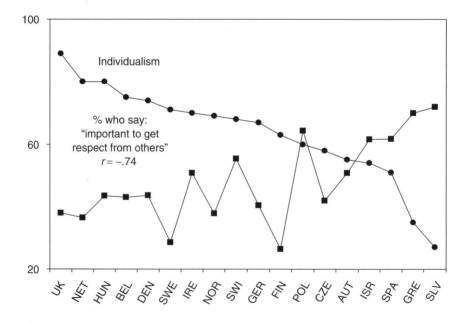

Figure 6.2　Importance of Getting Respect From Others

SOURCE: Data from Hofstede (2001) (see Appendix A); *European Social Survey 2002/2003* (see Appendix B)

Next to the term "interdependent" self in collectivistic cultures, the term "familial"[8] self is used. It is a "we" self, relational in different contexts. It includes a private self and a public self. The *private self* operates in interdependence with others of a person's in-group. There is emotional connectedness, empathy, and receptivity to others. It is through the *public self* that the social etiquette of relationships with the outer group is maintained in varying interpersonal contexts.

Understanding the cultural aspects of the self should make marketers careful with extending the Western concept of self to other cultures. Examples are personal drives such as self-esteem, self-confirmation, self-consistency, self-actualization, recognition, exhibition, dominance, independence, and the need for achievement.

Personality

Broadly defined, *personality* is the sum of the qualities and characteristics of being a person in individualistic cultures where the person is defined as an "independent self-contained, autonomous entity who comprises a unique configuration of internal attributes (e.g., traits, abilities, motives, and values) and who behaves primarily as consequence of these internal attributes."[9] This personality is unique and cross-situationally consistent; that is, people are assumed to behave in a consistent way in different situations. Personality is usually described in terms of traits such as autonomy or sociability. This concept of personality as an autonomous entity separate from the social environment includes the characteristics of an independent self of individualistic cultures. In collectivistic cultures, people's ideal characteristics vary by social role. East Asian thinking does not make a sharp person-situation distinction and has a more holistic notion of the person without a boundary between the person and the situation. Easterners believe in the continuous shaping of personality traits by situational influences.[10]

In Japan, people do not ascribe integrated personalities to fellow human beings. Behavior is relative to the circle within which it appears. It is related to context; thus personality is contextual. Western personality means consistency, acting in character. Men and women picture themselves as acting as particular kinds of persons, not as different persons in different situations or contexts.[11]

Personality Traits

The Western habit of describing oneself and others in terms of abstract characteristics has led to the development of characterization systems of personal traits. Examples of such traits are "nervous," "enthusiastic," or "original." Although there are thousands of trait-descriptive adjectives in English, there are only a few major groups of traits. The most used set of traits is called the Five-Factor Model, the most recent version being named the Revised NEO Personality Inventory (NEO-PI-R), by Costa and McCrae.[12] This model consists of five factors labeled "Neuroticism" (N), "Extraversion" (E), "Openness to experience" (O), "Agreeableness" (A), and "Conscientiousness" (C). Each factor is defined by six specific traits or facets. For example, conscientiousness is represented by competence, order, dutifulness, achievement striving, self-discipline, and deliberation. Psychologists have found evidence that our personality traits are partly biologically inherited, partly shaped by culture. The relationship with culture was found by correlating Hofstede's cultural variables with culture-level means of individual-level scores on the five factors for 36 cultures. All five factors were related to one or more cultural dimensions. For example, neuroticism scores are higher in cultures of strong uncertainty avoidance and high masculinity. Extraversion scores are higher in individualistic cultures where autonomy and variety are valued more highly than duty and security.

Identity and Image

Identity is the idea one has about oneself, one's characteristic properties, one's own body, and the values one considers to be important. *Image* is how others see and judge a person.[13] Definitions of identity refer to an independent individualistic self. Identity among collectivists is defined by relationships and group memberships whereas individualists base identity on what they own and their experiences. When persons are asked what their identity is, they can categorize themselves in terms of desirable values ("I believe that . . ."), as members of social groups (a father, a student), or by personality traits (ambitious, cheerful.)[14]

The importance of a unique identity for individualists emerges from a Eurobarometer survey asking respondents to what degree people believe in a shared cultural identity.[15] The percentages of respondents who agreed correlated negatively with individualism whereas the percentages disagreeing correlated positively with individualism. Figure 6.3 illustrates this relationship for 12 countries in Europe.

In most Western cultures, people tend to assess the identity of self and others based on personality traits, on other individual characteristics such as age and occupation, and on material symbols.[16] In collectivistic cultures, people are not used to doing so. They will assess themselves in terms of their ability to maintain harmonious relationships with others.

Individuals can be pleased with personality traits that form a part of their *real* identity, or they may want to change them as a function of an image they would like to have. This produces an identity that reflects what psychoanalysts have termed the "ideal self." If these two aspects of identity are far apart from each other, efforts are usually made to reduce the gap, and in individualistic cultures material possessions can serve this purpose. Whereas in individualistic cultures brands can contribute to an ideal and unique identity, in collectivistic cultures brands serve the need to conform to others in order to preserve harmony.

Personality and Identity in Marketing

In Western marketing practice and theory, identity and personality are used as metaphors to define brand positions. The concepts of brand personality and brand

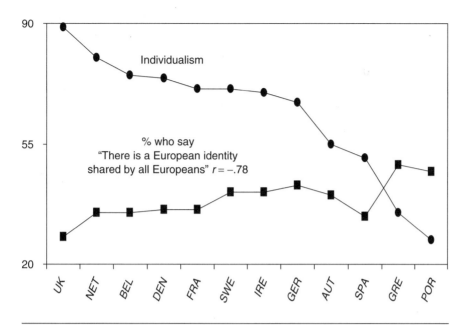

Figure 6.3   Identity and Culture

SOURCE: Data from Hofstede (2001) (see Appendix A); Eurobarometer Report *How Europeans See Themselves* (2000) (see Appendix B)

identity are metaphors from individualistic cultures that are less understandable and less useful to collectivistic cultures.

Words for the concepts *identity* and *personality* do not even exist in the Chinese and Japanese languages. There is a Japanese translation of the English word *identity*—"to be aware of one-self as oneself"—but its significance lies in the suggestion that this awareness of self is constituted on the basis of connections with others. The *katakana* (the Japanese language system that uses foreign words) word for *identity* is used. But using the word does not necessarily imply conceptual equivalence.

Even among individualistic cultures, a brand personality that can be recognized by, or is attractive to, the average public of one culture will not necessarily be recognized or found attractive by the average public of another culture. As a result, advertising campaigns that are effective in one culture because they are based on a strong brand personality are not necessarily as effective in another culture. Brands acquire their personalities over time, and these are largely derived from the market context in which they develop. This context consists of a series of peculiarities that might not repeat itself in the same ways in other intended markets.[17] If the human personality trait construct is culture-bound, so also the brand personality construct will be culture-bound.

Jennifer Aaker[18] has conducted several studies to define brand personality dimensions across cultures. She found five brand personality factors in the United States that she labeled "Sincerity," "Excitement," "Competence," "Sophistication," and "Ruggedness." The first three resemble the human personality factors agreeableness, extraversion, and conscientiousness. Similar studies in Japan and Spain led to additional, but country-specific, factors: "Peacefulness" in Japan and Spain and a specific Spanish dimension, which she labeled "Passion."

A general aspect of the brand personality concept is that it is less relevant for members of collectivistic cultures than for members of individualistic cultures. If, as in collectivistic cultures, people are not used to describing themselves in abstract terms, they are likely not able to do so for brands either. For members of collectivistic cultures, the brand concept is too abstract to be discussed the way members of individualistic cultures do. The Reader's Digest Trusted Brands survey in 2002 asked people in 18 different countries[19] in Europe about the probability of buying unknown brands. The responses "extremely/quite likely to consider buying a brand which I've heard of but haven't tried before" correlated significantly with individualism ($r = .82***$). A brand out of context is less relevant to members of collectivistic cultures than to members of individualistic cultures.

Whereas American companies have developed product brands with unique characteristics, Japanese companies have generally emphasized the corporate brand. In essence, this means inspiring trust among consumers in a company and so persuading them to buy its products.

The consequences for the brand concept are that in individualistic cultures, brands have to be unique and distinct with consistent characteristics, whereas in collectivistic cultures the brand should be viewed as being part of a larger whole, a product of a trusted company.

Attitude

Western consumer behaviorists view an *attitude* as a lasting, general evaluation of people (including oneself), objects, advertisements, or issues.[20] Attitudes have affective and cognitive components. The affective component includes feelings and emotions one experiences in response to an attitude object. The cognitive component includes attributes and functions of the object.[21]

In the Western definitions, attitudes help to organize and structure one's environment and to provide consistency in one's frame of reference. Individualists want consistency between their attitudes, feelings, and behaviors.[22] This need for consistency between attitude and behavior implies that under certain conditions (in individualistic cultures), the behavior of consumers can be predicted from their attitudes toward products, services, and brands. In collectivistic cultures, however, people form attitudes that fulfill their social identity functions, and there is not a consistent relationship between attitude and future behavior. Also in individualistic cultures, there will be some discrepancy between attitude and behavior, but in collectivistic cultures the discrepancy is likely larger than in individualistic cultures because of the greater sensitivity to situational demands, for example, others' expectations.

For assessing advertising effectiveness, the attitude toward the advertisement (A_{ad}) tends to be measured, which in turn is used as an indication of buying intention. This is a logical practice in individualistic cultures where individuals want consistency between their attitudes and behaviors. In collectivistic cultures where situational factors can influence the various elements of attitude and behavior, the practice will not work the same way.

The most widely known model that measures the relationship between attitude and behavior is the Fishbein behavioral intentions model, also referred to as the theory of *reasoned action*. Fishbein hypothesizes that a person's behavioral intentions are determined by an attitudinal or personal component and a normative or social component. The personal component or attitude toward the act refers to personal judgment of behavior, whereas the normative or social component refers to social pressures on behavior such as expectations of others.[23] What in Western terms is called "social pressure" has relatively weak influence on individualists, who will refer to their own personal attitudes as having influenced their buying decisions.[24] The individualistic social norm has a different loading in collectivistic cultures, as it does not capture "face." Face motivates collectivists to act in accordance with their social position. If one acts contrary to expectations of one's social position, "a shadow is cast over one's moral integrity."[25] Thus in collectivistic cultures, the norm is to live up to the standards of one's position, whereas the social norm component of the Fishbein model measures perceptions of opinions of other persons.

Lifestyle

Lifestyle is described in terms of shared values or tastes as reflected in consumption patterns. Personal characteristics are viewed as the "raw" ingredients to develop a unique lifestyle. In an economic sense, one's lifestyle represents the way one allocates income, but lifestyle is more viewed as a mental construct that explains, but is not identical with, actual behavior.[26]

Lifestyle is viewed as a useful within-country criterion, but it is less useful for defining segments across cultures because lifestyles are country-specific. No one has ever produced an empirical base to support the argument that across countries, lifestyle similarities are stronger than cultural differences. In contrast, increasingly evidence is found that culture overrides lifestyle. To understand consumer behavior across cultures, it is necessary to go beyond lifestyle and distinguish value variations by product category. Even if across cultures certain groups of people can be identified with respect to ownership of specific products, the motives for buying these products vary so strongly that for developing international advertising, these lifestyle groups are not useful (see also Chapter 5 under the heading Value and Lifestyle Research).

Social Processes

Social processes deal with the *how*'s of consumer behavior and include motivation, needs, drives, emotion, and group processes. All are processes that steer behavior. Although some emotions are internal, many result from interaction with the social environment.

Needs

Consumption can be driven by functional or social needs. Clothes satisfy a functional need; fashion satisfies a social need. A car may satisfy a functional need, but the type of car can satisfy a social need. Buying motives cannot be viewed as purely internal drives; they are strongly related to the social environment. Many global brands that seem universal are bought for different reasons across cultures. What in one culture may be a functional need can be a social need in others. The bicycle is a functional need to many Chinese, who need it for transportation, whereas it is a social need to most Americans, who use it for socializing or fitness.

Differences in sensitivity to certain product attributes and varying buying motives can be explained by the underlying cultural values that vary by product category. For example, in high uncertainty avoidance cultures, the generic motive for mineral water is purity, whereas this motive is irrelevant in low uncertainty avoidance cultures. Soft drinks and alcoholic beverages have status value in masculine cultures, not in feminine cultures, and whisky consumption is related to social status in high power distance cultures. For cars, needs vary between safety, status, design, and environmental friendliness, all related to different cultural values.

Maslow[27] categorized human needs in a hierarchy of importance: physiological needs, safety needs, social needs, esteem needs, and self-actualization. His hierarchy of needs concept is based on the assumption that a person's behavior is directed at satisfying needs and that some needs will take precedence over others when the individual is faced with choices as to which needs to satisfy. Physiological needs will take precedence over security or safety, group membership, or esteem needs. The supreme category then is self-actualization. Figure 6.4 depicts Maslow's hierarchy.

Maslow's hierarchy of needs is generally presented as a universal model, but the cross-cultural relevance is increasingly questioned. There is little evidence to support Maslow's hypothesis that there is a universal order among the nonphysiological goals. A universal human pattern may be that physiological needs take precedence

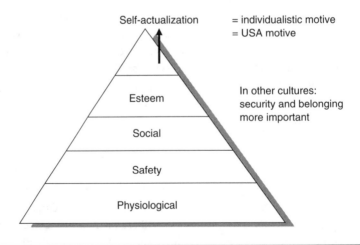

Figure 6.4   Maslow's Hierarchy of Needs

over higher-order needs, but the ranking of the nonphysiological needs varies across cultures.

Self-actualization is a highly individualistic U.S. motive. In collectivistic cultures, what will be actualized is not the self but the interest and honor of the in-group (not its individual members). In collectivistic cultures, belonging and safety will converge: It is very risky to distinguish oneself from the group. Security or safety is likely to prevail over other needs where uncertainty avoidance is strong. Belonging will prevail over esteem in feminine cultures, but esteem over belonging in masculine cultures.[28]

Motivation

Motivation can be defined as the internal state of an organism that drives it to behave in a certain way. *Drives* are the motivational forces that cause individuals to be active and to strive for certain goals. The study of motivation, the mixture of wants, needs, and drives within the individual, is seen as of prime importance to understanding behavior. Motivation research seeks to find the underlying "why" of our behavior; it seeks to identify the attitudes, beliefs, motives, and other pressures that influence our purchase decisions. In the 1950s, researchers such as Ernest Dichter used Freudian psychoanalytical ideas to explain behavior on the basis of unconscious motivation. Motivation theories are particularly based on Freud's idea of anxiety.

Freud's concepts related to the self, quoted in many textbooks on consumer behavior, are culturally determined. In developing his concepts of the id, ego, and superego, Freud was a true product of Austrian-Hungarian culture. Austria and Hungary score extremely low on power distance and high on uncertainty avoidance. Strong uncertainty avoidance implies that parents raise their children with the message that life is threatening, dangerous, so the children have to create structures to cope with threat. If combined with large power distance, this attitude does not pose a problem for children, as parents will create the structures for them. Small power distance, however, implies that children become independent at early age and have to structure reality for themselves. This leads to frustration. Freud's superego is meant to control the id, thus taking the role of the parent. It serves as an inner uncertainty-absorbing device.[29] One conclusion is that if Freud's theory is true or useful, it will be most useful for the Austrians and Hungarians and other cultures of a similar configuration of dimensions. It will be less useful for cultures of weak uncertainty avoidance, such as the United Kingdom and Scandinavia, or for cultures of large power distance such as France and Asian cultures.

Buying Motives

Understanding the variations in what motivates people is important for positioning brands in different markets. Motives underlie brand loyalty, brand preference, brand image, and the importance of luxury brands. The diagram in Figure 6.5 maps the different roles of luxury brands in the cultures of the configuration of individualism and masculinity.

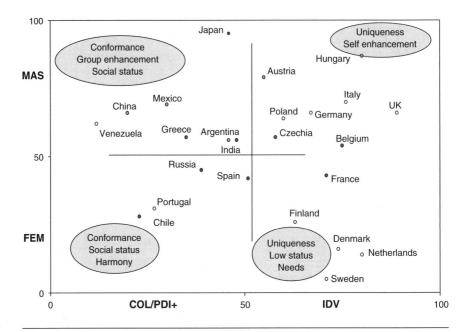

Figure 6.5 Motives for Luxury Brands

SOURCE: Data from Hofstede (2001) (see Appendix A)

In collectivistic cultures in the two left-hand quadrants that are also of large power distance, people have the need to conform, and luxury brands provide social status. Russians, being both collectivistic and very high on power distance, are very status sensitive. When combined with low masculinity, harmony and a relationship orientation prevail, and luxury brands mainly serve a social function. When combined with high masculinity, status needs are reinforced to enhance group identity, to show that you belong to an important social class. The cultures in the right quadrants are individualistic. When combined with high masculinity, luxury brands help to enhance the unique self. In the individualistic and low masculine cultures, people have low status needs. They want to be unique but will not use luxury brands to demonstrate their uniqueness.

Buying motives can be recognized in the appeals used in advertising. Several scholars have developed lists of consumption motives by analyzing advertising. Pollay's[30] list of values in advertising is an early inventory of North American buying motives. Some motives may exist across cultures, but the degree of importance will vary. Some motives are category-bound (e.g., purity for mineral water). For other categories, motives can strongly vary across cultures. An example is how motives for buying automobiles vary by culture.

Figure 6.6 shows motives for buying automobiles by cultural clusters according to two of Hofstede's dimensions, masculinity and uncertainty avoidance. These motives are recognized in the design of cars and in the appeals used by advertisers of successful car brands.

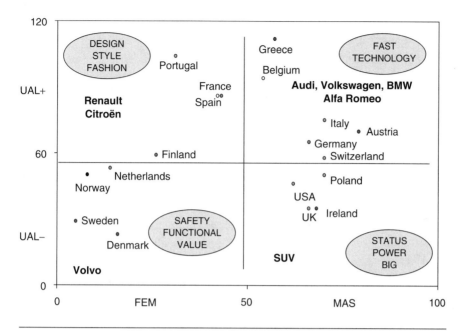

Figure 6.6   *Car-Buying Motives*

SOURCE: Data from Hofstede (2001) (see Appendix A)

The lower left quadrant shows the configuration of low masculinity and weak uncertainty avoidance. In this culture cluster, people have a preference for safety to protect their family and value for money. Safety (to protect the weak) and the functional aspects of a car are more important than technology or design. The Swedish Volvo car brand is well known for the safety claim. In feminine cultures, people have little interest in the motor of their car. Data from several surveys show that they don't even know the power of their car engines, as compared with masculine cultures. The lower right quadrant shows a cluster of cultures with the configuration masculinity and weak uncertainty avoidance. People in these cultures have status needs and prefer cars with big, powerful motors. This is the culture cluster where people will be most attracted to the sturdy SUV. The upper right quadrant shows the cluster of cultures with the configuration of masculinity and strong uncertainty avoidance. People in these cultures are aggressive drivers, and they prefer cars with rapid acceleration. This seems paradoxical, as one would expect to see risk aversion translated into a safety motive. Not so: The explanation is that people of strong uncertainty avoidance cultures build up stress, which they also want to release. Fast and aggressive driving serves as an emotional safety valve. But cars must also be technologically advanced, well designed, and well tested. These are the cultures where people prefer the German brands like Audi and BMW and the Italian Alfa Romeo. Volkswagen's claim, "Vorsprung durch Technik" ("head start" through technology), reflects the technology motive. In the upper left quadrant, in the combination of low masculine and strong uncertainty avoidance, one sees the need for "sporty" driving, fast acceleration but not so aggressive. This is combined with a preference for design (but more in the art/fashion sphere), pleasure, and enjoyment. This is the area where the stylish brands like Renault and Citroën originate and are preferred.

Emotion

Emotion tends to be described as a process that involves an interaction between cognition and physiology. Emotions consist of various components like experience, facial expression, and physiological response that are closely linked together. Emotions are affective responses that are learned. This aspect of emotion makes it culture-bound. It is unlikely that people in all cultures have learned to express their feelings and to recognize feelings of others in the same way. Concept, definition, understanding, and meaning of emotion vary across cultures. Yet emotion psychologists have argued that many emotions are universal.

One argument in favor of universal basic emotions is that most languages possess limited sets of central emotion-labeling words, referring to a small number of commonly occurring emotions. Examples of such words in the English language are anger, fear, sadness, and joy. Another argument is based on research of recognition of facial expressions. The question is whether it is justified to take facial expression as an index of the presence of emotions, because it is possible that in some societies emotions occur without facial expressions and in others facial expressions occur without emotions.[31] Seeing a facial expression allows an observer to draw a conclusion about a situation, but one specific facial expression is not necessarily connected to one specific emotion. For example, a smile is generally viewed as an expression of happiness. However, seeing a friend can make a person smile, but this does not imply that the person is happy. He or she can, in fact, be sad or lonely.

The psychologists Mesquita and Frijda[32] reviewed various elements of emotions across cultures and concluded that several elements of emotion, but not all, are related to culture. For example, among individualistic independent selves, "ego focused" emotions like anger, frustration, and pride are more marked than among collectivistic interdependent selves where "other focused" emotions such as sympathy, shame, and feelings of interpersonal communion are more marked.

Meaning and intensity of emotions vary. Emotions are, for example, more subdued in hierarchical, high power distance, and collectivistic cultures.[33] The degree to which and how people display their emotions are culturally defined. East Asian collectivists try to display only positive emotions and tend to control negative emotions.[34] Within Europe, members of cultures of weak uncertainty avoidance are less inclined to show emotions than cultures of strong uncertainty avoidance. The British "stiff upper lip" can serve as an example.

The same expressions may have different meanings in different cultures. Children in Western societies protrude their tongue show contempt; among Chinese it means surprise. A smile may be an expression of pleasure or embarrassment. Instead of suppressing expression of displeasure, Asians may display an expression of polite intercourse, what Westerners may perceive as a smile. In personal encounters, the author of this book has often seen Chinese or Indonesians smile or even laugh to hide their embarrassment. This sort of smile is certainly not a reflection of happiness.

Emotions in Advertising

The use of emotions in advertising originated in the United States and is a reaction to the strong historical focus on argumentation, persuasion, and information. In the early 1980s, the American advertising industry realized that using advertising mainly at the attribute and benefit levels had resulted in parity advertising. Any manufacturer claiming superiority on the basis of attributes finds competitors responding with identical or even better claims in a short span of time. In the 1980s, the use of emotions in advertising was a response to that problem and the need to stand out from an increasingly cluttered advertising environment.[35] Yet in the United States, use of rational appeals is usually preferred to the use of emotions. When emotions are used, they tend to be part of the argumentation. Disgust goes with dirty, and happiness goes with clean.

The concept of global (standardized) advertising as first introduced by the advertising agency Saatchi & Saatchi in the early 1980s was based on the assumed universality of basic emotions such as happiness or love. This has led to parity advertising showing happy people connected to the brand. Because the ways people show their emotions are so different across cultures, the use of emotions in global advertising is not advisable. Those who rely on so-called mood boards to visualize different brand positions have found they cannot use the same visuals to express moods across cultures. Experience at international advertising agency BBDO has taught that for their "photo sort" method, which they used to position brands, photographs of facial expressions produced in the United States to represent and be recognized as "mood" could not be transplanted to Europe. The way American actors expressed specific moods could not be recognized by European respondents. The same is true within Europe: No single "photo deck" could be developed for the whole of Europe.

Group Processes

The behavior of individuals is based partly on their personal characteristics and partly on their group memberships. The different groups to which a person belongs, however, are not all equally important. The role of the group, its reference function, and the individual's place and role in the group vary by culture.

Western consumer behavior theory distinguishes between formal (associations) and informal groups (family and friends) that may influence behavior and decision-making. Another group that is distinguished as influencing consumer behavior is the reference group.

Group Influence

The Western individualistic assumption is that people can choose group membership. Individuals select other people, groups, or associations that match or reinforce their identity. In collectivistic cultures, members of the inner circle are part of one's identity. They are not selected; they are part of your being. Whereas in individualistic cultures few other people will influence the buying process, which is an individual activity, Japanese housewives refer to a group of on average eight other housewives who influence their decision making.[36] This explains the success of network marketing in collectivistic cultures.

In consumer decision making, the degree to which group members depend on others, in particular family members, varies with collectivism and power distance. Comparative content analysis of Chinese and American advertising demonstrates that group consensus and conformity to family preference rather than individual choice is found more in Chinese than in American advertising.[37] When in individualistic cultures people refer to friends and family as influencing their decisions, this process is not the same as in-group influence in collectivistic cultures. The latter is an automatic process of in-group interpersonal communication, and people are not inclined to view this process as an active information-gathering process.

In feminine cultures, the marriage partner plays a stronger role in the buying process than in masculine cultures. An example of how strongly this difference can affect advertising is a 1996 television commercial for the Renault Mégane (automobile). It depicted a man who wanted to surprise his wife with the new Renault Mégane, at the same time demonstrating the short stopping distance. He stops in front of what he thinks is his house, shouting "Darling, I have bought the Renault Mégane," and it appears he has entered his neighbor's (similar) house because he is not used to the short stopping distance. The text of this Belgian commercial was changed radically for the Netherlands, although it was in the same language (as part of Belgium and the Netherlands share the same language). In Belgium, apparently, the husband can buy a car without consulting his wife, but this is not done in the Netherlands.

Reference group generally is defined as an actual or imaginary individual or group that is relevant for an individual's evaluations, aspirations, or behavior.[38] The terms "reference group" and "aspirational group" tend to be used more loosely to describe any external influence that provides social clues. The importance of reference groups will vary, not only with culture but also with the type of product. If a product is consumed privately (e.g., necessities), the opinions of others are viewed to be less important than if a product is used publicly (e.g., luxury goods). In individualistic cultures, the degree to which peers influence an individual in nuclear families is stronger for public than for private products and brands whereas this is not the case for individual members of extended families. This occurs because in nuclear families the number of immediate family members and their importance to the individual is limited, whereas in extended families there are numerous family members available to influence the individual's decision making.

Opinion Leaders

In Western decision-making theory, specific individuals are assumed to influence the decision-making process through word-of-mouth communication, generally within a certain product category. Opinion leaders are strong, informal sources of product information. They achieve their status through technical competence and social accessibility. They serve as role models and play an important role in the process of diffusion of innovations. The concept of opinion leadership is basically an American concept, derived from the diffusion of innovation theory by Rogers,[39] which resulted from investigation of the speed and pattern of the spread of new farming techniques across the United States.

The roles of opinion leaders vary across cultures. People with technical competence, or competent people in general, are likely to be favored in strong uncertainty avoidance cultures. Masculine cultures have high regard for the successful. In large power distance cultures, the power holders may have an important role as opinion leaders.

An important difference is in the way opinion leaders get their information. Whereas the theory says they get their information from the mass media in individualistic cultures, in collectivistic cultures they obtain their information from the social network. This is an informal and implicit process as compared with the explicit process of individualistic cultures.

Mental Processes

How people see, what they see and do not see, how they think, how language structures their thinking, how they learn, and how people communicate are mental processes. These processes—called cognitive processes in psychology—deal with understanding of several *how*'s of behavior.

The term *cognition* covers the main internal psychological processes that are involved in making sense of the environment and deciding what action might be appropriate. These processes include thinking and reasoning, understanding and interpreting stimuli and events, attention, perception, learning, memory, language, and decision making. A few of these topics are reviewed in the following sections.

Language, Perception, and Memory

The structure of a language (e.g., its grammar and type of writing system) has consequences for basic consumer processes such as perception and memory. Structural differences, such as in scripts of Indo-European and Asian languages, seem to affect mental representations, which in turn influence memory. Chinese native speakers rely more on visual representations whereas English speakers rely primarily on phonological representations (verbal sounds). In the English language, verbal sounds are most used to encode the brand name and facilitate memory. Explicit repetition of words enables consumers to encode and recall the brand name. An example is, "If anyone can, Canon can," used as payoff in ads for Canon in the United Kingdom, or the more recent, "You can, Canon" payoff that is used all over Europe, as in Illustration 6.2.

Illustration 6.2   Canon, International

Because of their own focus on sound and pronunciation, Western companies are inclined to adapt their brand names to other cultures more vocally than visually. Chinese consumers, however, are more likely to recall information when the visual memory is accessed and are more likely to recall brands when they can write them down.[40] Visually distinct brand name writings or calligraphy and logo designs that enforce the writing will be more effective in China, whereas for English native speakers the sound qualities of brand names should be exploited by the use of jingles and onomatopoeic names (names resembling the sound made by the object).

Locus of Control

An important mental phenomenon that explains the influence of others on behavior is *locus of control,* introduced by Julian Rotter.[41] Internal or external locus of control refers to the degree to which persons expect that an outcome of their behavior depends on their own behavior or personal characteristics versus the degree to which persons expect that the outcome is a function of chance, luck, or fate; is under the control of powerful others; or is simply unpredictable.[42] At the culture level, the difference suggests that in some cultures people are more inclined to take social action to better life's conditions (also called "civic competence") whereas in other cultures people are more dependent on institutions such as authorities and governments. The belief in the West that the locus of control resides in the individual and that behavior is a function of the individual's own action is deeply implanted in decision theory. In collectivistic cultures, however, where people are used to the fact that other people may make decisions about them and for them, external locus of control operates; and this is reinforced by large power distance, where the power holders will ultimately make the decisions. Particularly, the combination of large power distance, collectivism, and strong uncertainty avoidance appears to be linked with external locus of control. An example is how, across 12 countries in Europe, people answer the question when asked how globalization should be controlled.[43] The higher countries score on power distance, the higher the percentage of people who say there should be more regulation by their governments to control globalization. In Figure 6.7, countries are mapped according to internal-external locus of control.

Understanding the difference is important because internal locus of control is part of the fundamental assumptions in consumer behavior—for example, in behavior intention models and in decision-making theories.

Information Processing

Information processing theory is a psychological approach to analyze how people acquire, organize, and use information to assist choice behavior. The underlying assumption is that people want to solve problems and choose rationally. This assumption is increasingly disputed in the Western world and can be even less generalized for consumers of non-Western cultures. How people acquire information varies with individualism. In collectivistic cultures, people will acquire information

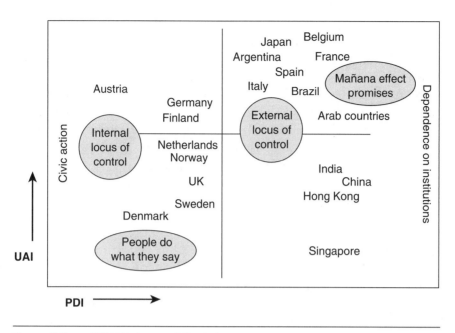

Figure 6.7   PDI-UAI: Locus of Control

SOURCE: Data from Hofstede (2001) (see Appendix A)

more via implicit, interpersonal communication and base their buying decisions more on feelings and trust in the company, whereas in individualistic cultures people will actively acquire information via the media and friends to prepare for purchases.

Eurobarometer[44] asks people to what degree they view themselves as well-informed consumers. Across 14 west European countries, the answers "well-informed" correlate with individualism, which explains 53% of variance. Next to this, what people consider to be information will vary.

Information processing theory further says that the information a person has acquired must be organized in order for it to be placed in one's memory. The human memory is arranged according to *schemata,* structures of knowledge a person possesses about objects, events, people, or phenomena. To place the acquired information in memory, it must be encoded according to the existing schemata. One's generic schema for a product would include what to do with the product, the consequences of using it, and the environment in which it is used.[45] The independent self of individualistic cultures forms context-independent schemata and a context-independent processing style whereas the interdependent self of collectivistic cultures forms context-dependent schemata and thus forms a context-dependent processing style, paying attention to specific social contexts.[46] Thus, East Asians are more likely to process information in terms of the context within which it is presented, whereas Westerners will process the various components separately.

When processing advertising, either the information presented in an advertisement will fit an existing schema or a new schema is established. Most acquired information is organized in schemata that already exist in the memory. Often only the information relevant and important to the activated schema is selected; the rest is lost. Next, the meaning (semantic content) is interpreted so as to be consistent with the schema, to make it fit. Finally, schematically stored information can be used to make judgments, evaluations, and choices. However, the information must be retrievable before it can be used; it must be remembered.

Western information-processing theory generally states that distinctive (unusual) information is easier to remember than ordinary information. Salient information is easier to remember than unimportant information.[47] Many things can go wrong in this process. First, one's own cultural roots may inhibit the perception of stimuli coming from another cultural perspective. Second, interpretation of the meaning may not be as intended. Third, the evaluation and decision-making process may vary.

Decision Making

The fundamental assumption in decision-making theory is that decisions do not "happen," someone "makes them." This is a Western view. The Japanese are more likely to prefer events to shape whatever actions are required, to stand back from an event rather than attempt to control it by decision making.[48] A fundamental difference between individualistic and collectivistic cultures is in decision making: In collectivistic cultures, if an individual makes the decision, that decision will be made in consensus with the group, so it is not an individual decision. Consensus seeking will also pay a role in feminine cultures, which are also intuitive.

The need for information and the type of information desired will vary for low-context and high-context cultures. Buyers in high-context, collectivistic cultures will seek more social information than those in low-context, individualistic cultures. Strong uncertainty avoidance will lead to the need for more, structured, and detailed information. Club Mediterranée "learned that Japanese tourists crave infinite detail in their travel plans. So, along with brochures and activity schedules for the villages they'll visit, Club Med sends them maps of airports at both ends of the trip, showing toilets, customs booths, and other facilities."[49]

A sharp difference between Americans and Japanese is the difference in control of time (management of deadlines) and control of human relationships. To a lesser degree, this is similar to the differences among countries in Europe, for example between the Germans and the Spanish. What colloquially is called the "mañana syndrome" (postponing decisions, related to external locus of control) may affect decision making. Another difference related to time orientation is the thought that a decision or expressed buying intent will lead to action. People with an action attitude actively seek progress. People with a reaction attitude will wait with action until confronted with a new situation. This behavior is not necessarily related to expressed intentions.

Another difference is between people who make definite, concrete plans with well-described actions and people who leave their plans more abstract, more philosophical, without a specific sequence of actions. Differences can lead to wrong expectations with respect to buying intentions. If 55% of the people who try a new product in Italy say they will definitely buy it, the product will probably fail. But in

Japan, if 5% say they will definitely buy it, the product is likely to succeed.[50] This phenomenon is related to external or internal locus of control. If one is used to fate or power holders interfering at any time in the realization of an expressed intention, and if cancelled appointments are acceptable, this is part of daily life, thus part of people's values. This is reflected in the way buying intention is expressed. Extreme response style (ERS), the tendency to score in the extremes of a bipolar scale, has the same origin. In collectivistic cultures, people do not like to say no, and in large power distance cultures, there is a need to please, resulting in "yesmanship."

Consumer Decision-Making Styles

Consumer decision-making style can be defined "as a mental orientation characterizing a consumer's approach to making choices."[51] The underlying thought of most Western consumer decision-making models is that all consumers engage in shopping with certain fundamental decision-making modes or styles, including rational shopping and consciousness regarding brand, price, and quality. The search for a universal instrument that can describe consumers' decision-making styles across cultures seems to be problematic.

An approach that focuses on consumers' orientations in making decisions is the consumer characteristics approach by Sproles and Kendall,[52] who developed an instrument to measure consumer decision-making styles analogous to the personality traits concept, called the consumer style inventory (CSI). The CSI identifies eight mental characteristics of consumer decision making: (a) perfectionism or high quality consciousness; (b) brand consciousness; (c) novelty-fashion consciousness; (d) recreational, hedonistic shopping consciousness; (e) price and "value-for-money" shopping consciousness; (f) impulsiveness; (g) confusion over choice of brands, stores, and consumer information; and (h) habitual, brand-loyal orientation toward consumption.

This approach has been applied to different cultures with varying results. For example, among Koreans[53] the brand-conscious, perfectionist style was found most, and price-consciousness and value for money were not found in Greece and India.[54]

Business Decision Making

In the business or industrial decision-making process, the number of members in the decision-making unit (DMU) varies; so does the importance of the individual members. The average size of the decision-making team within the EU varies from 10 in France, to 8 in Germany, 6 in Italy, 10 in Sweden, and 9 in Britain.[55] Also, the members of the DMU behave differently, related to the country's management style and culture. In Britain, specialist expertise is not highly regarded. Decisions tend to come about by informal consensus developed in meetings, discussions, and out-of-office contacts among middle managers. Top management normally refuses any routine contacts with suppliers. This is due to the high level of delegation, a characteristic of small power distance cultures. In France, although middle or specialist managers may be consulted, in the end the president directeur général must give permission. In the Netherlands, business relationships are more relaxed and informal. In Italy, businesses have to take relatively large amounts of time and resources to deal with industrial relations problems. Successful managers have to be flexible improvisers. Authority may be delegated to trusted individuals rather than to holders of particular job titles so that finding the right decision maker is an art. Interpersonal contact is of great importance. Business relationships are based on mutual dependence and a sense of mutual obligation. A distinctively Spanish company is likely to have a strong leader, an entrepreneurial autocrat with boldness and personal charisma. Good personal relations are necessary to prevent middle management blocking approaches, and anything important may have to be sent "up the line" for final approval.

In large power distance cultures, the boss will make the decision, and the roles of influentials below his or her level will be less pronounced than in small power distance cultures. In the latter cultures, secretaries have an important influence on decisions related to their work, such as for office equipment. The decision-making process will also vary according to the degree of masculinity. In feminine cultures, where reaching consensus is important, all people concerned must be allowed to give their opinion, whereas in masculine cultures decisiveness is seen as a virtue that will make the decision-making process more expedient.

Finding the influence of others in decision making is not easy, as culture influences the degree to which people think they are involved in decision making, which may be different from actual decision-making power. Because of egalitarian values in low power distance cultures, more people think they are involved in decision making on corporate buying aspects than in high power distance cultures. Whereas in Denmark a secretary who assists her or his boss in gathering information on products to buy may view this as involvement in decision making, a secretary in France giving the same assistance probably will not view this as being involved in making the decision, as the boss implicitly makes all decisions.[56]

Consumer Behavior Domains

Behavior refers to the physical actions of consumers that can be directly observed and measured by others. It is also called overt behavior to distinguish it from mental activities. A trip to a shop and usage and ownership of products involve behavior. All processes such as motivation, emotion, cognition, and affect are involved in behavior, but they operate differently across the various consumer behavior domains, such as product acquisition, ownership and usage, shopping and buying behavior, complaining behavior, brand loyalty, and adoption of innovations.

Product Acquisition, Ownership, and Usage

There are substantial differences between countries with respect to product ownership and usage, and many of these can be explained by culture. People's values have a direct and an indirect effect on product ownership. A product has physical characteristics (attributes) that have functional or psychosocial consequences or benefits. Product ownership or usage can also express the (desired) values of the consumer. A car is not only a means of transportation; it also says something about its owner. Each product category has its own cultural relationship. In this section, we give a few examples.[57]

Food consumption varies with climate and historical, economic, and cultural factors. Food carries cultural meaning. In collectivistic cultures, the symbolic function of food is much stronger than in individualistic cultures, and variety of food is important. Food should be available in the house for any unexpected guest.

In high uncertainty avoidance cultures, purity is an important attribute of many food and drink products. In Chapter 4, the example of bottled water consumption was used. The relationship between uncertainty avoidance and mineral water has been consistent over time. Although in the past 30 years the quality of tap water has improved everywhere in Europe, the differences between countries have remained similar since 1970 or have become even larger. Since 1970, high uncertainty avoidance has explained between 44% and 53% of variance of various data on mineral water consumption in Europe. A different cultural relationship is found for soft drinks, which are more consumed in masculine cultures than in feminine cultures. For decades, the soft drinks category has been dominated by Anglo-Saxon brands and related masculine values, which has been a likely cause of lower consumption in feminine cultures.

Expenditures on clothing and footwear as a percentage of household expenditures are higher in collectivistic and high uncertainty avoidance cultures. In collectivistic cultures, for reasons of face, people want to be well groomed when going out into the streets. In high uncertainty avoidance cultures, it is one way of facing a threatening world. Spending money on clothing and footwear also serves needs for self-esteem and self-enhancement. In large power distance cultures, people dress according to occasion.

Many consumer electronics serve the individualistic need for variety and stimulation. Worldwide, television ownership (numbers per 1,000 people) is linked with individualism. The frequency of watching and the programs are culture-bound (see Chapter 7 on media usage). The role of television in social life varies. In modern China, the television has emerged as perhaps the most symbolic purchase people make. For most Chinese, owning an automobile is not yet possible, and consumer electronics, particularly the television, play an important role in establishing one's financial image as well as projecting an aura of success. The television one owns must project the right image to others.[58] In countries like China, a television set also serves another social need, as an important application is karaoke.

PC ownership is a matter of wealth, but an important explanation of differences in ownership is uncertainty avoidance, which explains variance of adoption of innovations; so also penetration and usage of the Internet. Variation in how people use the Internet is discussed in Chapter 7.

National income and individualism explain variance of the numbers of cars per 1,000 population, as well as car usage. High mobility in the individualistic cultures makes people use their car more. In 1998, individualism explained 50% of variance of the number of passenger kilometers per person per car.[59] Masculinity explains the differences in numbers of cars owned per family. In Italy, Germany, and the United Kingdom, there are more families with two cars than there are in the feminine cultures such as the Netherlands and the Scandinavian countries. In these cultures, people think one car is enough (although they may be able to afford two), and larger percentages of people than in the masculine cultures say they do not want a car.[60]

Although worldwide, national wealth explains variance of leisure expenditures, in the developed world it is culture. In Europe, leisure expenditures are highest in individualistic cultures of low power distance and low uncertainty avoidance. The heavy spenders are Sweden and the United Kingdom; the low spenders are Spain and Portugal. An explanation is that in the latter cultures free time is spent with family and relatives whereas in the former people spend more time on paid organized leisure activities. Elements of low uncertainty avoidance that explain expenditures on leisure products and services are low anxiety, innovativeness, and a culture of fitness. Relevant individualistic values are pleasure, stimulation, variety, and adventure, so the sale of "pleasure" products and services like travel, theme parks, and sports activities tends to be higher in individualistic than in collectivistic cultures.

Complaining Behavior

Consumer complaining behavior can be classified into three categories: (a) voice response to the party directly involved in the complaint; (b) negative word of mouth or brand switching; and (c) legal action.[61] With varying concepts of self, consumers across cultures vary with respect to these three types of responses. Because of harmony needs, collectivistic consumers are relatively loyal and are less likely to voice complaints when they experience postpurchase problems, but they do engage in negative word of mouth to in-group members.

Data from Eurobarometer[62] consumer surveys show that individualists are more active in searching for information on consumer issues than collectivists and think that their rights are well protected. Collectivists will exit and engage in negative word of mouth. There is evidence that compared with Australians, the Chinese are less likely to lodge a formal complaint for a faulty product.[63] When collectivists do exit, it is particularly difficult for the offending supplier to regain them as customers.[64]

An aspect of American culture is the frequent use of legal action. It is related to the configuration individualism and masculinity, which makes people want to get the most out of life. This explains the high use of litigation in the United States. Also, consumers will take more legal action. For years, the cigarette industry has been sued for damaging smokers' health. In 2002 in the United States, obese people even started suing fast food chains, holding them responsible for their gaining weight.

Brand Loyalty

Conformance and harmony needs make collectivists more brand loyal. Purchasing products that are well known to the in-group may help to decrease uncertainty about in-group approval of the purchase.[65] Choosing another brand than the group members or changing brands distinguishes a person from the group. It is preferable to choose the popular or perceived popular brands. This will be reinforced by uncertainty avoidance. Trying a new product or brand involves some amount of risk taking, and it may also satisfy a variety-seeking motive.[66] Variety seeking and stimulation are aspects of individualistic cultures.

Large power distance implies respect for the status quo, the "proper place" of the power brand, the brand with the highest market share. In Asia, big market share brands are the kings of their "brand world," and consumers in Asia believe in them implicitly.[67] This is the reason brands like Coca-Cola, Nescafé, and San Miguel have such high and sustained market shares in a number of Asian countries. Being big automatically provides trust. This trust, combined with harmony and conformance needs of collectivistic cultures, leads to high brand loyalty. Consequently, it will be difficult for new entrants in these markets to gain market share.

Diffusion of Innovations

Consumers' degree of innovativeness influences their propensity to try new products. As innovativeness is related to tolerance for ambiguity and deviant ideas, members of weak uncertainty avoidance cultures are more innovative than members of strong uncertainty avoidance cultures. How innovativeness operates in cultures depends on its configuration with other dimensions. Power distance and individualism influence innovativeness in cultures in another way. Whereas it is internalized in the person in small power distance and individualistic cultures, in large power distance and collectivistic cultures, it is externalized. In the latter, the degree of innovation depends on the power holders and group process. Although the Chinese are a weak uncertainty avoidance culture and in the far past have proved to be extremely innovative, for some time their power holders have not stimulated innovativeness. The Chinese invented a number of processes or instruments that were not discovered or acknowledged in the West until more than 1,000 years later. Examples of inventions are the process of making steel from crude iron (2,000 years), deep drilling for natural gas (1,900 years), and the wheelbarrow (1,300 years).[68] In China, the incentive for inventions was service to the overlord or emperor, not personal ambition.

Rogers[69] identified five categories of (American) consumers according to their degree of acceptance of new products. These five categories of adopters are often illustrated in a normal distribution curve, as illustrated in Figure 6.8. They are called "Innovators," "Early Adopters," "Early Majority," "Late Majority," and "Laggards." Innovators represent 2.5% of (American) society; they are described as venturesome individuals who are willing to take risks. Early adopters (13.5%) are those who take up new ideas that have already been taken up by the innovators, who serve as role models. The early majority (34%) are risk avoiders, but they are relatively deliberate in their purchasing behavior. The late majority (34%) are skeptical and cautious of new ideas. Laggards (16%) are very traditional.

The percentages as well as the time span of the adoption process vary by culture. More innovative cultures have a larger percentage of early adopters than less innovative cultures. Collectivism plays another role. Particularly in Japan, after acceptance, the spreading of new products is rapid. On the one hand, change is not

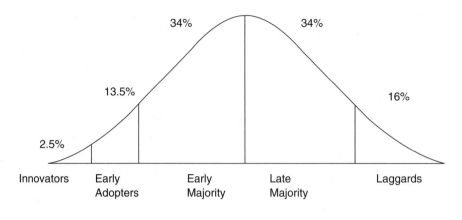

Figure 6.8 Adoption of Innovations, USA

appreciated, so adoption of new ideas and products takes longer. Yet the need for conformance leads to faster adoption as soon as a group member has taken the lead. In individualistic and strong uncertainty avoidance cultures, the adoption process takes longer because what is new is dangerous, and that relates to each person individually.

Dutch marketing professor Jan-Benedict Steenkamp[70] calculated percentages of adoption categories for packaged goods in five countries in Europe (Table 6.1). These were based on household panel data on the occurrence and timing of first purchases for 239 new consumer packaged goods over a 52-week period after introduction. Correlations with the cultural variables confirm the relationships with uncertainty avoidance and individualism.

The category innovators in the five European countries plus the United States correlates with low uncertainty avoidance and individualism, whereas the category late majority correlates with high uncertainty avoidance and collectivism. Also, in Latin America, where all countries are high on uncertainty avoidance, the percentages

Table 6.1 Diffusion of Innovations and Culture

	Innovators (%)	Early Majority (%)	Late Majority (%)	Laggards (%)
USA	16.0	34.0	34.0	16.0
UK	23.8	43.4	26.4	6.4
France	15.1	25.5	35.6	23.8
Germany	16.8	26.1	34.2	22.9
Spain	8.9	34.1	43.9	13.1
Italy	13.4	30.8	41.0	14.8
Correlation coefficients				
IDV	.75*		−.74*	
UAI	−.83*		.83*	

SOURCE: Steenkamp (2002)

of early adopters tend to be lower than in the United States. A Target Group Index (TGI) study in Chile found 7.5% of the average population that could be viewed as early adopters of technological innovations.[71]

Conclusion

Most concepts and theories of consumer behavior are Western-centric. The concepts of self, identity, and personality are integral parts of consumer psychology. They also are Western-centric concepts. They are used in theory, in practice, in research, and in strategy. To use them properly, they must be adapted. What people buy and why they buy certain products is influenced by their cultural values. A number of theories of consumer behavior commonly found in textbooks were reviewed in this chapter. Both mental and social processes vary by culture, and this influences decision making and choice behavior. Motives for buying products vary among and within geographic areas. Countries may share a border but be far apart with respect to buying motives. Finding relationships between actual buying behavior and cultural dimensions is exciting and assuring. Most value research relies on what people say about their values. Finding the relationship between actual consumption behavior and measured value differences provides strong proof of the influence of culture that cannot be ignored and that also brings understanding that can be used for developing effective cross-cultural strategies.

Notes

1. Solomon, M., Bamossy, G., & Askegaard, S. (1999). *Consumer behaviour: A European perspective.* London: Pearson Education, p. 8.

2. This model is based on Manrai, L. A., & Manrai, A. K. (1996). Current issues in cross-cultural and cross-national consumer research. In L. A. Manrai & A. K. Manrai (Eds.), *Global perspectives in cross-cultural and cross-national consumer research.* New York: International Business Press/Haworth Press, p. 13.

3. Markus, H. R., & Kitayama, S. (1991). Culture and the self: Implications for cognition, emotion and motivation. *Psychological Review, 98*(6), 224–253.

4. Roland, A. (1988). *In search of self in India and Japan.* Princeton, NJ: Princeton University Press; Triandis, H. C. (1995). *Individualism and collectivism.* Boulder, CO: Westview Press.

5. Roland, 1988, 242.

6. Watkins, D., Akande, A., Fleming, J., Ismail, M., Lefner, K., Regmi, M., et al. (1998). Cultural dimensions, gender, and the nature of self-concept: A fourteen-country study. *International Journal of Psychology, 33*, 17–31.

7. Jowell, R., et al. (2003). *European social survey 2002/2003* (technical report). London: Centre for Comparative Social Surveys, City University.

8. Roland, 1988, 3–13.

9. Markus, H. R., & Kitayama, S. (1998). The cultural psychology of personality. *Journal of Cross-Cultural Psychology, 29*, 63–87 (see p. 68).

10.   Norenzayan, A., Choi, I., & Nisbett, R. E. (2002). Cultural similarities and differences in social influence: Evidence from behavioral predictions and lay theories of behavior. *Personality and Social Psychology Bulletin, 28,* 109–120.

11.   Benedict, R. (1974). *The chrysanthemum and the sword.* Rutland, VT: Charles E. Tuttle, p. 195.

12.   Hofstede, G., & McCrae, R. R. (2004). Personality and culture revisited: Linking traits and dimensions of culture. *Cross-Cultural Research, 38*(1), 52–88.

13.   Antonides, G., & Van Raaij, W. F. (1998). *Consumer behaviour. A European perspective.* Chichester, UK: Wiley, pp. 162–163.

14.   Camilleri, C., & Malewska-Peyre, H. (1997). Socialization and identity strategies. In J. W. Berry, P. R. Dasen, & T. S. Saraswathi (Eds.), *Handbook of cross-cultural psychology.* Boston: Allyn & Bacon, p. 48.

15.   European Commission Directorate. (2000, September). *How Europeans see themselves* (Eurobarometer report). Brussells: Author (see Appendix B).

16.   Belk, R. W. (1984). Cultural and historical differences in concepts of self and their effects on attitudes toward having and giving. In T. C. Kinnear (Ed.), *Advances in consumer research.* Provo, UT: Association for Consumer Research, pp. 753–760.

17.   Campana, C., & Paulo, R. (1999, November). Evaluating the value of global brands in Latin America. *Marketing and Research Today,* 159–167.

18.   Aaker, J. L., Benet-Martínez, V., & Garolera, J. (2001). Consumption symbols as carriers of culture: A study of Japanese and Spanish brand personality constructs. *Journal of Personality and Social Psychology, 81,* 492–508.

19.   Belgium, Czech Republic, Denmark, Finland, France, Germany, Hungary, Italy, the Netherlands, Norway, Poland, Portugal, Russia, Slovakia, Spain, Sweden, Switzerland, and the United Kingdom.

20.   Solomon, Bamossy, & Askegaard, 1999, 121.

21.   Cervellon, M.-C., & Dubé, L. (2002). Assessing the cross-cultural applicability of affective and cognitive components of attitude. *Journal of Cross-Cultural Psychology, 33,* 346–357.

22.   Gudykunst, W. B., Matsumoto, Y., Ting-Toomey, S., Nishida, T., Kim, K., & Heyman, S. (1996). The influence of cultural individualism-collectivism, self construals, and individual values in communication styles across cultures. *Human Communication Research, 22,* 510–543.

23.   Antonides & Van Raaij, 1998, 202–205.

24.   Lee, C., & Green, R. L. (1991). Cross-cultural examination of the Fishbein behavioral intentions model. *Journal of International Business Studies, 22,* 289–305.

25.   Malhotra, N. K., & McCort, J. D. (2001). A cross-cultural comparison of behavioral intention models. *International Marketing Review, 18,* 235–269.

26.   Grunert, K. G., Brunsø, K., & Bisp, S. (1997). Food-related lifestyle: Development of a cross-culturally valid instrument for market surveillance. In L. R. Kahle & L. Chiagouris (Eds.), *Values, lifestyles and psychographics.* Mahwah, NJ: Lawrence Erlbaum, p. 343.

27.   Maslow, A. H. (1954). *Motivation and personality.* New York: Harper & Row.

28.   Hofstede, G. (1991). *Cultures and organizations: Software of the mind.* London: McGraw-Hill, p. 126.

29.   Hofstede, G. (2001). *Culture's consequences* (2nd ed.). Thousand Oaks, CA: Sage.

30.   Pollay, R. W. (1984). The identification and distribution of values manifest in print advertising 1900–1980. In R. E. Pitts Jr. & A. G. Woodside (Eds.), *Personal values and consumer psychology.* Lexington, MA: Lexington Books, D. C. Heath, pp. 111–135.

31.   Russell, J. A. (1995). Facial expressions of emotion: What lies beyond minimal universality? *Psychological Bulletin, 118,* 379–391.

32.   Mesquita, B., & Frijda, N. H. (1992). Cultural variations in emotions: A review. *Psychological Bulletin, 112,* 179–204.

33. Kagitçibasi, C. (1997). Individualism and collectivism. In J. W. Berry, M. H. Segall, & C. Kagitçibasi (Eds.), *Handbook of cross-cultural psychology* (Vol. 3). Boston: Allyn & Bacon, p. 23.

34. Triandis, 1995.

35. Holman, R. H. (1986). Advertising and emotionality. In R. A. Peterson, W. D. Hoyer, & W. R. Wilson (Eds.), *The role of affect in consumer behavior: Emerging theories and applications.* Lexington, MA: Lexington Books, D. C. Heath.

36. Interview with K. Ushikubo, November 1995.

37. Lin, C. (2001). Cultural values reflected in Chinese and American television advertising. *Journal of Advertising, 30,* 83–94.

38. Solomon, Bamossy, & Askegaard, 1999, 296.

39. Rogers, E. M. (1962). *Diffusion of innovations.* New York: Free Press.

40. Schmitt, B. H., Pan, Y., & Tavassoli, N. T. (1994). Language and consumer memory: The impact of linguistic differences between Chinese and English. *Journal of Consumer Research, 21,* 419–431.

41. Rotter, J. B. (1966). Generalized expectancies for internal versus external control of reinforcement. *Psychological Monographs, 80,* No. 609.

42. Rotter, J. B. (1990). Internal versus external control of reinforcement. *American Psychologist, 45,* 489–493.

43. *Globalisation.* (2003, October). Flash Eurobarometer No. 151b.

44. *Consumers Survey.* (2002, January). Flash Eurobarometer No. 117.

45. Domzal, T. J., Hunt, J. M., & Kernan, J. B. (1995). Achtung! The information processing of foreign words in advertising. *International Journal of Advertising, 14,* 95–114.

46. Kühnen, U. (2001). The semantic-procedural interface model of the self: The role of self-knowledge for context-dependent versus context-independent modes of thinking. *Journal of Personality and Social Psychology, 80,* 397–409.

47. Domzal, Hunt, & Kernan, 1995.

48. Stewart, E. C. (1985). Culture and decision making. In W. B. Gudykunst, L. P. Stewart, & S. T. Ting-Toomey (Eds.), *Communication, culture, and organizational processes.* Beverly Hills, CA: Sage, pp. 177–211.

49. Toy, S. (1995, October 16). Storm, terrorists, nuke tests: Why is Club Med smiling? *BusinessWeek,* 20.

50. *Nielsen SRG News Asia Pacific.* (1996, February). No. 80.

51. Lysonski, S., Durvasula, S., & Zotos, Y. (1996). Consumer decision-making styles: A multi-country investigation. *European Journal of Marketing, 30,* 10–21 (see p. 11).

52. Sproles, G. B., & Kendall, E. L. (1986). A methodology for profiling consumer decision making styles. *Journal of Consumer Affairs, 20,* 267–279; Lysonski, Durvasula, & Zotos, 1996.

53. Hafstrom, J. L., Jung, S. C., & Young, S. C. (1992). Consumer decision-making styles: Comparison between United States and Korean young consumers. *Journal of Consumer Affairs, 26,* 146–158.

54. Lysonski, Durvasula, & Zotos, 1996.

55. Wolfe, A. (1991, May). Stalking Euro-buyers in their lairs. *Business Marketing Digest,* 87–94.

56. De Mooij, M. (2003). *Consumer behavior and culture.* Thousand Oaks, CA: Sage, p. 224.

57. For a more in-depth description and evidence of relationships between culture and various product categories, see de Mooij, 2003.

58. Brewer, D. K. (1997). Symbolic consumption in China: The color television as a life statement. *Advances in Consumer Research, 24,* 128–131.

59. Office for Official Publications of the European Communities. (2001). *Consumers in Europe.* Luxembourg: Author, p. 23.

60. Office for Official Publications of the European Communities, 2001, 143.

61. Chelminski, P. (2001, December). The effects of individualism and collectivism on consumer complaining behavior. *Proceedings of the Eighth Cross-Cultural Research Conference,* Association for Consumer Research and American psychological Association. Kahuku, Oahu, Hawaii.

62. *Consumer Survey.* (2002, January). Flash Eurobarometer 117.

63. Lowe, A., Chun-Tung, A., & Corkindale, D. R. (1998). Differences in "cultural values" and their effects on responses to marketing stimuli: A cross-cultural study between Australians and Chinese from the People's Republic of China. *European Journal of Marketing, 32,* 843–867.

64. Watkins, H. S., & Liu, R. (1996). Collectivism, individualism and in-group membership: Implications for consumer complaining behaviors in multicultural contexts. In L. A. Manrai & A. K. Manrai (Eds.), *Global perspectives in cross-cultural and cross-national consumer research.* New York/London: International Business Press/Haworth Press.

65. Lee, J. A. (2000). Adapting Triandis' model of subjective culture and social behavior relations to consumer behavior. *Journal of Consumer Psychology, 2,* 117–126. Countries studied were Australia, the United States, Hong Kong, Singapore, and Malaysia.

66. Baumgartner, H., & Steenkamp, J.-B. E. M. (1996). Exploratory consumer buying behavior: Conceptualization and measurement. *International Journal of Research in Marketing, 13,* 121–137.

67. Robinson, C. (1996). Asian culture: The marketing consequences. *Journal of the Market Research Society, 38,* 55–66.

68. Temple, R. (1986). *China.* London: Multimedia Publications.

69. Rogers, 1962.

70. Steenkamp, J.-B. E. M. (2002, November 17). *Global consumers.* Presentation at Tilburg University. Based on *Consumer and market drivers of the trial probability of new consumer packaged goods* (Working paper). Tilburg University, Tilburg, The Netherlands.

71. TGI Chile. (2003). Early adopters of technological innovations. Retrieved November 5, 2004, from www.zonalatina.com/Zldata99.htm

SEVEN

Advertising and the Media

Because the United States is the birthplace of marketing and advertising techniques, American cultural assumptions are at the root of philosophies of how advertising works, not only in the United States but also in other parts of the world. If we want to understand how advertising works across cultures, we'll first have to learn how communication works. Styles of communication vary by culture. One of the clearest distinctions is between high-context and low-context communication. Related to this distinction is the way people process information and their expectations of the role, purpose, and effect of communication. Is advertising persuasive by nature, or can it have another role in the sales process? Understanding how advertising works across cultures is of great importance for international advertisers. The practice and philosophy of public relations, which involves managing relationships between organizations and publics, is also related to culture. Related to communication style are varying media preferences that are also related to culture.

Communication and Culture

In classic communication theory, communication in a broad sense includes all the procedures by which one mind may affect another. All communication is viewed as persuasive. The traditional model of communication, as depicted in Figure 7.1, includes the source or sender of a message (person, organization, company, brand), the message itself (story, picture, advertisement), the medium (any carrier of the message: a storyteller, newspaper, television), and the receiver of the message (person, consumer).

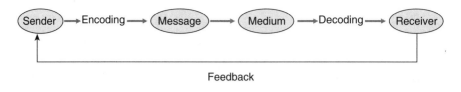

Figure 7.1   Classic Model of Communication

In this communication process, a message is selected and encoded in order to transfer meaning. The receiver of the message must be able to receive the message via the medium and decode it. Generally, the sender of the message wants to get feedback to find out if the message has been received and understood. It is easy to understand that in this process many things can go wrong. Even more in mass communications than in interpersonal communication, the process is difficult to control. In the coding and decoding process, anything may go wrong.

The sender (company, marketer) who formulates and shapes the message uses her cultural framework that will be reflected in the content and in the form of the message. Similarly, the media are shaped by the culture of the people who produce them, both in content and in form. Finally, the receiver of the message uses his cultural framework when decoding the message. In the decoding process, selective perception will operate in the sense that people will best understand messages that fit existing schemata. This concerns content, form, and style of the message. In order to understand the influence of culture on styles and forms of mass communication, we first have to understand variation in interpersonal communication across cultures.

Several cultural dimensions explain variance in communication across cultures, of which individualism-collectivism explains most. Interpersonal communication styles vary along with the self-concept. The independent self, when thinking about others, will consider the other's individual characteristics and attributes rather than relational or contextual factors. The interdependent self emphasizes status, roles, relationships, belonging and fitting in, and occupying one's proper place.[1] The distinction *high-* and *low-context communication* (as described in Chapter 4) fits the differences in communication behavior of interdependent selves of collectivistic cultures and independent selves of individualistic cultures. In low-context communication, information is in the words; in high-context communication, information is in the visuals, the symbols, and the associations attached to them. Because in high-context communication the meaning of the message is difficult to assess by outsiders, such communication is also considered to be inaccessible. In individualistic, low-context cultures, people are more oriented toward the written word, whereas in collectivistic, high-context cultures people are more visually oriented.

The verbal orientation of members of individualistic and low uncertainty avoidance cultures is reflected in the degree to which people read books. Over time, several European surveys have asked people for the degree to which they read books. Since 1970 in Europe, heavy book reading has been related to individualism, low power distance, and low uncertainty avoidance.

Various other factors explain differences in communication style. Rapid speech rate, for example, suggests to Americans that the speaker makes true and uncensored statements, whereas for Koreans, slow speech implies careful consideration of others and context.[2]

Interpersonal Communication Styles

Interpersonal communication style is made up of verbal and nonverbal styles. Gudykunst and Ting-Toomey have best described the influence of the various dimensions of culture on verbal and nonverbal communication style.[3] Verbal styles can be *verbal personal* or *verbal contextual*. The two styles focus on personhood versus situation or status. Verbal personal style is individual-centered language; it enhances the "I" identity and is person oriented (e.g., English). Verbal contextual style is role-centered language; it emphasizes a context-related role identity (e.g., Japanese, Chinese), which includes different ways of addressing different persons, related to their status. For example, the Japanese language adapts to situations where higher- or lower-placed people are addressed.

Verbal personal style is linked with low power distance (equal status) and individualism (low context), whereas verbal contextual style is linked with high power distance (hierarchical human relationships) and collectivism (high-context).

Another distinction is between elaborate, exacting, and succinct verbal style. *Elaborate* verbal style refers to the use of rich, expressive language. *Exacting* or *precise* style is a style where no more or no less information than required is given. *Succinct* or *understated* style includes the use of understatements, pauses, and silences. Silences between words carry meaning. High-context cultures of moderate to strong uncertainty avoidance tend to use the elaborate style. Arab cultures, for example, show this elaborate style of verbal communication, using metaphors, long arrays of adjectives, flowery expressions, and proverbs. Low-context cultures of weak uncertainty avoidance (e.g., United States, United Kingdom) tend to use the exacting style. The succinct style is found in high-context cultures (e.g., Japan). Silence is particularly appropriate in the contexts of uncertain and unpredictable social relations.

Nonverbal style possibilities are *unique-explicit* and *unique-implicit* style and *group-explicit* and *group-implicit* style, which echo the self-orientation of individualism versus the group orientation of collectivism, and *accessibility-inaccessibility,* which refers to the degree to which the home environment emphasizes the openness or closedness of occupants to outsiders. Strong uncertainty avoidance cultures perceive outsiders as more threatening than do weak uncertainty avoidance cultures, and power distance reinforces that.

Together, verbal and nonverbal styles can explain how we communicate. Figure 7.2 clusters countries according to these styles and summarizes the different interpersonal communication styles.

Communication in the cultures in the two left quadrants is direct, explicit, verbal, and personal. People like written communication. In business, they prefer using e-mail to using the phone. They use the exacting style and like data. The sender is

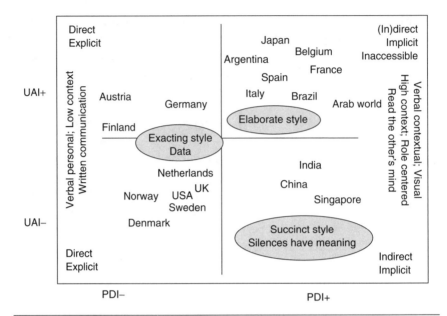

Figure 7.2 Interpersonal Communication Styles

SOURCE: Gudykunst and Ting-Toomey (1988) adapted by De Mooij 2004; Data from Hofstede (2001) (see Appendix A)

responsible for effective communication. Communication in the mostly collectivistic cultures in the two right quadrants is more implicit. France and Belgium, which are individualistic, are exceptions, and communication can be both explicit and implicit. Communication is role centered. Particularly in Asia, children learn to "read the other's mind." They learn to read subtle cues in the communication from others. The receiver is responsible for effective communication. In the cultures in the top right quadrant, the elaborate style is used and communication often is inaccessible. In the lower right quadrant, the succinct style is found.

The most pronounced difference is between the direct versus the indirect style, or the extent to which speakers reveal their intentions through explicit verbal communication. In the direct style, wants, needs, and desires are expressed explicitly. The indirect verbal style refers to verbal messages that conceal the speaker's true intentions. Wordings such as "absolutely" and "definitely" to express buying intentions are an example of the direct style, whereas "probably" or "somewhat" are examples of the indirect style.

Mass Communication Styles

Three aspects determine mass communication styles: content, form, and style. Differences in form and style of mass communications reflect interpersonal communication styles.

The influence of culture on these three elements can be recognized in literature, mass media programs, advertising, and public relations. American television, for example, is more action oriented than Finnish television. Domestically produced Finnish video dramas are much more static. They sacrifice action and setting for dialogue and extreme close-ups.[4] Both the Russians and the Japanese depict boredom in their novels, whereas American novels do not do much with the theme. "Fun is not a Russian concept," says Moscow sociologist Maria Zolotukhina on the difficulties faced by the creators of a Russian version of the popular American children's television program *Sesame Street*.[5] The "happy ending" is rare in Japanese novels and plays whereas American popular audiences crave solutions. This is reflected in American TV dramas and commercials. The essence of much drama in Western, individualistic literature is an eternal struggle of the hero ("to be or not to be"). Chinese essayist Bin Xin has noted that real tragedy has never existed in Chinese literature because the Chinese have hardly any struggles in their minds.[6] Also, how people behave in literature and what motivates them reflects cultural values. An example from literature is the Italian *Pinocchio,* by Carlo Collodi, who is an obedient and dependent child, as compared with the nephews of Disney's Donald Duck, who are much more independent and less obedient. Strong uncertainty avoidance is reflected in the novel *Das Schloss (The Castle),* by Franz Kafka, in how the main character K. is affected by bureaucracy. *Alice in Wonderland,* where the most unreal things happen, is a typical work to originate in a culture of weak uncertainty avoidance, England. It is no surprise that the Harry Potter books originated in the same culture. Press releases from American PR agencies reflect U.S. culture. They are short and to the point.

Advertising Styles

Advertising is a symbolic artifact constructed from the conventions of a particular culture. The sender crafts the message in anticipation of the audience's probable response, using shared knowledge of various conventions. Receivers of the message use the same body of cultural knowledge to read the message, infer the sender's intention, evaluate the content, and formulate a response. Cultural knowledge provides the basis for interaction. If advertising crosses cultures, it lacks the shared conventions. Content, form, and style are a reflection of interpersonal communication styles, but they also reflect different roles of advertising across cultures.

Four elements of advertising style can be distinguished. Each will vary by culture:

1. Appeal (including motives and values)

2. Communication style (e.g., explicit, implicit, direct, indirect)

3. Basic advertising form (e.g., testimonial, drama, entertainment)

4. Execution (e.g., how people are dressed)

Illustration 7.1
Gerolsteiner, Germany

Illustration 7.2 Vodafone
International

Illustration 7.3 Airtel,
Spain

An example of a typical appeal of high uncertainty avoidance cultures is purity, as in the German advertisement for Gerolsteiner, a German mineral water brand (Illustration 7.1). An example of an individualistic appeal is the international advertisement for Vodafone (Illustration 7.2), which focuses on the individual. The Spanish Airtel (acquired by Vodafone) used a collectivistic appeal, an example of group identity (Illustration 7.3). Chapter 8 describes more examples of relationships between culture and advertising appeals. How the basic forms used in advertising reflect culture will be discussed in Chapter 9. The term *execution* refers to the casting and activities of people, as well as the setting. A British kitchen, for example, looks different from a German kitchen. In this chapter, we focus on the cultural aspects of communication styles used in advertising.

A major distinction is between the direct style of individualistic cultures and the indirect style of collectivistic cultures. In advertising, the direct style uses the personal pronoun (you, we), whereas the indirect style doesn't address people directly but uses indirect methods such as drama or metaphors. There are variations in indirectness among collectivistic cultures. Singapore Chinese are, for example, more direct than are the people from Taiwan.[7] Cutler et al.[8] examined advertisements from eight different countries (U.S., U.K., France, India, Japan, Turkey, Taiwan/Hong Kong, and Korea) and measured the use of a direct, personalized headline, which appeared to be related to individualism.

Examples of the direct style are ads from the United Kingdom for Centrum (Illustration 7.4), ProViva (Illustration 7.5), and the German ZDF (Illustration 7.6). Examples of the indirect approach are the international advertisement for Thai Airlines (Illustration 7.7) that uses the eye of the needle to symbolize a small world, and a Spanish ad for Heineken (Illustration 7.8) that reflects the collectivist Friday feeling in an indirect way.

An example of the indirect style from Latin America is a Brazilian TV commercial for Sara Lee Piláo coffee. The message is that it is strong coffee. This message is

Illustration 7.4 Centrum,
United Kingdom

Illustration 7.5 ProViva,
United Kingdom

Illustration 7.6 ZDF,
Germany

Illustration 7.7 Thai
Airlines, International

Illustration 7.8 Heineken,
Spain

conveyed by showing just a cup of coffee and a continuous squirt of milk that doesn't make the coffee look lighter. This is a purely visual demonstration.

Direct style communication also tends to be more verbal, whereas indirect style tends to be more visual. Whereas U.S. advertising utilizes more copy, Japanese advertising uses more visual elements. The differences between cultures with respect to verbal and visual orientation are reflected in all aspects of marketing communications such as corporate identity, brand name, package design, and advertising styles. Chinese-speaking consumers tend to judge a brand name based on its visual appeal, whereas English speakers judge a brand name based on whether the name sounds appealing. In Asia, visual symbolism is a key aspect of a firm's corporate identity.[9] A comparative study of package design across seven countries

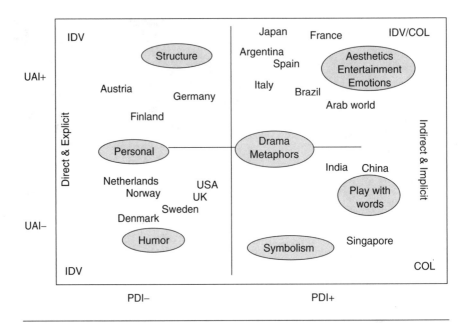

Figure 7.3   Advertising Styles

SOURCE: Data from Hofstede (2001) (see Appendix A)

found that packages differ both in three-dimensional design and in the way they communicate through graphic design. They vary in the use of textual information, use of color, shape and symbolism, and degree of structure and detail in the package design. Culture appears to be of great influence on the noted differences.[10]

Cultures can be mapped according to their advertising styles, similar to communication styles, as in Figure 7.3. The advertising style in the two left quadrants is direct and explicit. Within the direct-indirect distinction, there are also differences. In cultures of strong uncertainty avoidance positioned in the upper left quadrant, advertising is more serious and structured. The execution of the visuals will be detailed, often including demonstration of how the product works. An endorser must be an expert. That is the style of the Germanic cultures, where visuals are more exact than in weak uncertainty avoidance cultures. In the masculine cultures (U.S., U.K.), presenters are personalities or celebrities, whereas in the feminine cultures (Scandinavia, the Netherlands), the personality of the presenter will be downplayed. In the weak uncertainty avoidance cultures of the lower left quadrant, where ambiguity is tolerated, more humor is used in advertising. Many centrally developed television commercials for Anglo-American brands in the household cleaning products category and personal products have used the personalized testimonial format. They are carefully directed to focus on the personality of the endorser and not to include any implicit nonverbal behavior. For the U.S. market, the typical personal endorser and spokesperson have a positive impact on recall.[11]

The two quadrants at the right include styles that are implicit and indirect. The upper right quadrant covers several styles. It includes cultures that combine high to medium individualism with high power distance and high uncertainty avoidance (e.g., France), showing a communication style that expresses both uniqueness and inaccessibility. Inaccessibility is recognized in the frequent references in advertising to other forms of communication such as films, art, or even advertising by others. This quadrant also includes cultures that combine collectivism with high power distance and high uncertainty avoidance. Meaning is in the context. Communication is subdued and works on likeability or on bonding, building an emotional relationship between brand and consumer without too much focus on the product attributes. The use of aesthetics and entertainment as an advertising form is characteristic of this communication style. If celebrities are involved, they are not likely to address the audience directly. They play a more symbolic role and associate more with the product than endorse it in a direct way. Visual metaphors and symbols are used to create context and to position the product or brand in its "proper place." Drama (see Chapter 9) is an indirect style that fits countries like Spain and Italy, as well as Latin American cultures. Variations are found between masculine and feminine cultures. In Italy, high on masculinity, show is favored, and the drama form tends to be theatrical and often not based on real life. In Spain, drama style is softer, and metaphorical stories are used to place the product in a context that provides meaning. Although in the United States the drama style is also used, it is more popular in the countries in the upper right quadrant. Drama in the United States is more "slice-of-life," a form that demonstrates how a product is used in everyday life, whereas drama in the right quadrants is entertainment, meant to build a relationship between the consumer and the brand.

The advertising style of collectivistic cultures of medium to large power distance and weak to moderate uncertainty avoidance in the lower right quadrant must ensure group norms and help maintain face. Next to the use of drama and metaphors, visuals, play with words (visually), songs, and symbolism are important in advertising in these cultures, but the audience can be directly addressed. Advertising in Hong Kong, Singapore, and India fits this style. These cultures are more direct in their communication, which can be explained by low uncertainty avoidance. Chinese consumers like visual and straightforward, vivid ads with images. For India, the direct communication style is confirmed by Roland,[12] who states, "Indian modes of communication operate more overtly on more levels simultaneously than do the Japanese."

Illustrations 7.9, 7.10, and 7.11 show how in different countries different styles are applied in advertising for one international brand. All use the drama form, but the U.S. and the U.K. approach (Illustrations 7.9 and 7.10) is competitive. Both compare Bounty with another (not named) brand. Yet the U.S. approach is straightforward, comparing Bounty with the next leading brand, whereas the British one is humoristic, showing two males dressed as females, demonstrating that Bounty works faster. The Bounty user is drinking tea while his partner is still scrubbing. The Swiss commercial, which like the U.K. commercial is also focusing on wet usage of Bounty, shows a mother at leisure, phoning her partner to say that he has to clean up. He discovers Bounty and its effects and decides to use it to clean his motorbike. This is the more serious approach and also a reflection of strong role differentiation of a masculine culture.

Illustration 7.9 Bounty, United States

Illustration 7.10 Bounty, United Kingdom

Illustration 7.11 Bounty, Switzerland

The Purpose of Marketing Communication

How professionals think advertising works is based on theories that are derived from Western psychology. For example, the theory of information processing is based on cognitive psychology with a bias toward the use of verbal material and linguistic performance, disregarding pictorial and other nonlanguage stimuli.[13]

Americans view communication as a process of transmitting messages for the purpose of control. They see it as a means to persuade others, to change attitudes, and to influence or condition behavior. This view is reflected in the theories of how advertising works. The role and purpose of marketing communications vary across cultures, in particular between individualistic and collectivistic cultures. In individualistic culture, advertising must persuade, whereas in collectivistic cultures the purpose is to build relationships and trust between seller and buyer. The desire of Japanese consumers to establish trusting, in-group-like relationships with suppliers and their products is reflected in the tendency of Japanese advertising to focus on inducing positive feelings rather than to provide information.[14] The different purposes are reflected in the difference in timing and frequency of verbal or visual mention of the brand name in commercials.[15] In a typical Japanese television commercial, the first identification of a brand, company name, or product occurs later than in a typical U.S. television commercial. Japanese advertisers tend to take more of a commercial's time to develop trust, understanding, and dependency. In Japan, the brand name is shown for a longer time than in the United States, where it is more frequently mentioned verbally.

For Americans, persuasiveness, repetition, and hard sell arise from a model positing that "advertising and consumer are on two sides of a counter, and that some kind of confrontation is taking place with one side trying to persuade the other to change attitude or behavior."[16] The frequently used persuasion test to measure advertising effectiveness is based on this pattern of thinking. The basic procedure is measurement of purchasing intentions before and after exposure, which reflects a "digital," cause-effect way of thinking.

The persuasive communication function of advertising appears to be viewed with a bias toward rational claims and direct address of the public. All elements of advertising—words and pictures—tend to be evaluated on their persuasive role in the sales process. Although in other cultures sales will also be the ultimate goal of advertising, advertising's role in the sales process is obviously different. In collectivistic cultures, the use of a hard sell or directly addressing consumers turns them off instead of persuading them.

The U.S. persuasive communication model is based on U.S. information processing theory of how people acquire information (see also Chapter 6). How people acquire, organize, and utilize information is related to how they have learned to process information. It is related to the type of information they are used to. People of high-context cultures, used to symbols, signs, and indirect communication, will process information in a different way than people of low-context cultures, who are used to explanations, persuasive copy, and rhetoric.

There are significant cross-cultural differences in pictorial perception. Imagery is an important element of advertising, yet it is undervalued in research because of the historical focus on verbal communication. The phrases "copy research" and "copy testing" used for testing effectiveness of advertising, including visuals, demonstrate the bias toward thinking in verbal stimuli.

The eternal dilemma of advertising is whether to follow the conventions of advertising for a particular product category in a particular culture or to be distinctive in order to raise awareness and find a place in people's memories. Within countries, the danger of using distinctive, unusual information in advertising to attract attention is that it will not fit in consumers' schemata and will be discarded. This risk is even greater across cultures than within cultures because people's schemata vary.

Informational Versus Emotional

The American assumption that advertising's main role is to provide information as part of the persuasive process has undervalued other elements of advertising. It is not so long ago that advertisers started to realize that the consumption experience also includes emotional components. Consumers' emotions were recognized as having a significant influence on purchase and consumption decisions. As a result, "emotional," "transformational," "evaluative," or "feeling" messages are often contrasted with "rational," "informational," "factual," or "thinking" appeals. This suggests that emotions do not carry information. "Logical, objectively verifiable descriptions of tangible product features" and "emotional, subjective impressions of intangible aspects of the product" are viewed as contrasting.

Discussions of emotion have often been hampered by a lack of agreement on how emotion differs from rational concepts and from other, nonrational concepts like drives, needs, and affect. When discussing the role of emotions in advertising, one must distinguish between emotional stimuli (advertising content) and emotional response. Percy, Rossiter, and Elliott[17] view emotion as one of four main processing responses to advertising: attention, learning, accepting or believing what the ad says, and emotion that is stimulated by the ad. An emotional response will mediate what is learned and whether or how a particular point is accepted. Typical emotional responses may be connected to specific motivations. Examples are problem removal, portrayed by annoyance with the problem followed by relief, or social approval, ending with brand usage that flatters the user.

This description of the role of emotions fits the way emotions are exploited in Anglo-American advertising content, which is different in European advertising. Whereas in the United States emotions in advertising tend to be used as part of the argument (dirty goes with disgust and clean with relief or pleasure), in other cultures, in particular in the south of Europe, advertising reflects the pure emotional relationship between consumer and brand without the argumentation. In some cultures, the word *emotion*, in itself, is popular in advertising. An example is the Spanish payoff *Auto Emoción* for the Seat make of cars. A U.S. example is a TV commercial for Dixie disposable plates (Illustration 7.12). A French example is for Kelloggs (Illustration 7.13) and an Italian for Alfa Romeo (Illustration 7.14). U.S. Dixies uses disgust to debase the competitive brand that is not strong enough for the microwave oven. It becomes soft; the spaghetti falls and damages the shoes. In the French Kelloggs TV commercial, the actor drops the milk jug and spills the milk. He starts crying because he cannot enjoy the cereal. In the Italian ad for Alfa Romeo, a young man sees the car and gets so excited that he grabs a bottle of champagne and wets everybody.

As described in Chapter 6, emotions such as happiness and sadness are only universal when described abstractly. Rules for emotional displays are culture-specific. Expressive behavior varies by culture, which makes the emotional behavior of people of one culture often not understood by members of another culture. Also, what Americans call "emotional" can be perceived as "sentimental" by members of other cultures. Several researchers have tried to classify the emotional content and responses to advertising. A classic example is a study by Holbrook and Batra,[18] who identified dimensions of emotional content in U.S. advertising and linked these to emotional responses. To understand the role of emotions across cultures, this study should be replicated in other cultures. Typologies of emotional content can be useful to measure the effectiveness of emotional appeals for one culture but not for others.

Illustration 7.12   Dixie, United States

Illustration 7.13   Kelloggs, France

Illustration 7.14   Alfa Romeo, Italy

Because of the strong focus on verbal communication, problem solving, and assumed need for information in low-context cultures, Western advertising people tend to think of the rational elements as the "content" and the emotional element as "execution" and see them as separate entities. But execution is content. One cannot separate what is said from how it is said.

Theories of how advertising works are based on the assumption of an active information-gathering and rational consumer who wants to solve problems. To operationalize the distinction between informative and noninformative, the Resnik and Stern[19] typology is usually applied, in which the criterion for considering an advertisement informative is whether the informational cues are relevant enough to assist a typical buyer in making an intelligent choice among alternatives. Next to the fact that in some cultures people do not search for information, what is informational for members of one culture may not be informational for members of another culture.

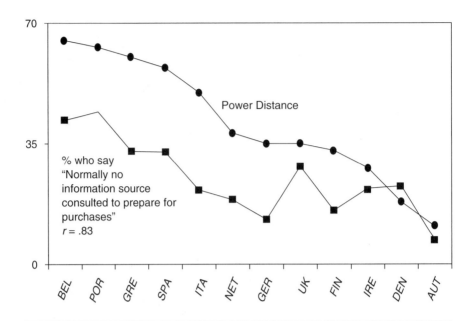

Figure 7.4   Information Behavior

SOURCE: Data from Hofstede (2001) (see Appendix A); *Consumer Survey,* Flash Eurobarometer 117 (2002) (see Appendix B)

Information-gathering behavior varies across cultures. Eurobarometer[20] asks European consumers which information sources (e.g., newspapers, TV, Internet, magazines, friends and relatives, consumer publications) they consult to prepare for purchases. The degree to which people inform themselves is related to individualism and power distance. In the Chapter 6 section "Information Processing," we mentioned that the degree to which people view themselves as well-informed consumers correlates with individualism. The percentages of answers, "Normally I don't consult any information source" correlate with high power distance, which explains 56% of variance. The problem-solving and argumentation approach to advertising will be less effective in cultures where people don't consciously search for information in the buying process and consumers' decision making is emotion based instead of information based. Figure 7.4 illustrates the relationship for 12 countries.

Measuring Advertising: Persuasion or Likeability

In view of the above, it seems inappropriate to use persuasion tests based on rational, linear processing to test advertising meant for people who process information in a different way. Yet often the effectiveness of advertising across cultures is measured by testing persuasiveness.

In advertising effectiveness research in the Western world, it has been recognized that persuasion measures do not capture a key element in the link between communication and the thoughts and behavior of consumers. That missing link is the degree to which an advertisement has personal significance for the consumer. When people experience advertising, they do not behave as passive, objective receivers of messages about brands. They interpret the advertisement for themselves, using their own "worldview" as an interpretative filter. They associate it with other information.[21] Next to persuasion, therefore, likeability has become a measure to predict sales. The following are aspects that contribute to the likeability of advertising:[22]

- Meaningful (worth remembering, effective, believable, true-to-life, not pointless)
- Does not rub the wrong way (not irritating, worn out, phony)
- Warm (gentle, warm, sensitive)
- Pleases the mind (entertaining, aesthetic)

This view of how consumers relate to advertising may be a better approach to apply to advertising across borders than the persuasion model. It certainly will be a better effectiveness measurement for Japanese advertising where pleasing the consumer is one of the objectives of advertising. In most cultures where the purpose of communication is to raise trust between the company and the consumer or to build an emotional relationship between consumer and brand, likeability will be a better purpose and measurement criterion than persuasion.

How Advertising Works

Most models of how advertising works are based on an assumed hierarchy of effects and on sequential thinking. Although academics worldwide have modified this hierarchy-of-effects model, the sequential way of thinking remains the basis of much of the thinking about how advertising works.

The Hierarchy of Effects

The underlying assumption of how advertising works is that advertising takes people from one stage to another. These "linear or sequential" or "transportation" models are based on a logical and rational process.[23] This hierarchy-of-effects model has strongly influenced American advertising style and the style used by U.S. advertisers elsewhere. Also, later models such as the FCB matrix[24] that categorizes products according to the degree of involvement and cognitive-affective attitude components are derived from the concept of multiple hierarchies.

High and Low Involvement

One of the early sequences in the theory of how advertising works was that people would first learn something about a product or brand, then form an attitude or feeling, and consequently take action, which meant purchasing the product or at least going to the shop with the intention of buying. This sequence is summarized as "learn-feel-do." It was later seen as mainly applicable to products of "high involvement," such as cars, for which the decision-making process was assumed to be highly rational. This so-called high-involvement model assumes that consumers are active participants in the process of gathering information and making a decision.

In contrast, there are low-involvement products, such as detergents or other fast-moving consumer goods, with related low-involvement behavior when there is little interest in the product. The concept of low involvement is based on Herbert Krugman's[25] theory that television is a low-involvement medium that can generate brand awareness but has little impact on people's attitudes. The low-involvement sequence was assumed to be "learn-do-feel." Again, knowledge comes first, after that purchase, and only after having used the product would one form an attitude.

The FCB planning model suggests four sequences in the process by which advertising influences consumers: (a) learn-feel-do, (b) feel-learn-do, (c) do-learn-feel, and (d) do-feel-learn. The first two sequences are related to high involvement; the third and fourth sequences are low involvement. International advertising scholar Gordon E. Miracle[26] argued that for the Japanese consumer another sequence is valid: "feel-do-learn." Japanese advertising is based on building trust, a relationship between the company and the consumer. The purpose of Japanese advertising is to please the consumer and to build *amae* (dependency),[27] and this is done by the indirect approach. As a result, "feel" is the initial response of the Japanese consumer, after which action is taken: a visit to the shop to purchase the product. Only after this comes knowledge. Miracle suggests that this sequence also applies to Korean and Chinese consumer responses. It may well apply to all collectivistic cultures.

Miracle summarized the logic of advertising in two distinct ways. The logic of advertising in Western societies is basically to tell the audience the following:

1. How you or your product is different.

2. Why your product is best, using clearly stated information and benefits.

3. Consumers then will want to buy, because they have a clear reason or justification for the purchase.

4. If they are satisfied, consumers will like and trust the company and the product and make repeat purchases.

The logic of advertising in Japan, which is probably valid for most Asian collectivistic cultures, is essentially the reverse:

1. Make friends with the target audience.

2. Prove that you understand their feelings.

3. Show that you are nice.

4. Consumers will then want to buy, because they trust you and feel familiar with you (i.e., the brand and the company).

5. After the purchase, consumers find out if the product is good or what the benefits are.

Later models continue to follow the assumption that the advertising concept is what classical rhetoricians call an "argument from consequence," following the cause-effect way of thinking. Petty and Cacioppo's[28] elaboration likelihood model (ELM) is one of the most advanced U.S. models of how advertising works. Taking into account the role of involvement, it states that persuasion follows a central route, peripheral route, or both. Within the central route, a person engages in thoughtful consideration (elaboration) of the issue-relevant information (arguments) within a message, so actively thinking about the arguments in the message is the central route. When the person is not motivated to think about the arguments, the peripheral route is followed. In the theory, the peripheral route generally includes visual cues like the package, pictures, or the context of the message.

The theory is embedded in Western advertising practice that uses pictures as illustration of words. Various studies have been conducted to find the influence of pictures, in both the central route and the peripheral route, reviewing affective responses as determinants of persuasion. In collectivistic cultures, where people process advertising holistically and pictures provide the context, the theory may not apply.

Little is known about how consumers from different cultures process visual images in print advertisements. Visuals have been used for standardizing print advertisements worldwide with the underlying assumption that consumers from all around the world can "read" a picture whereas the copy of the advertisement often needs to be translated. These highly standardized visual campaigns, however, do not always convey a uniform meaning among audiences. For example, Benetton's ad of a black woman nursing a white baby won awards for its message of unity and equality in Europe. At the same time, the ad stirred up controversy in the United States because many believed it depicted a black nanny in the subordinate role as a slave.[29] It is a misconception that visuals are universally understood across cultures. Pictures fit into schemata people have, and schemata vary by culture. A picture, meant in one culture to be associated with freedom (e.g., a lion), may be known in another culture to represent strength.[30] People can derive different meanings from the same message because contextual people will "see" more in the message than is intended by the producer of the message. Because in high-context cultures people are used to contextual messages, they will read more in pictures and derive "hidden" meaning from a visual image. Even for simple visual images with highly explicit information, the high-context audience may try to construct metaphorical meaning that is not intended by the sender of the message.

Differences in perception and visual processing result in a range of differences in the use of pictures in advertising. A multicountry comparison in the United States, the United Kingdom, France, Korea, and India[31] of visual components of print advertising found variations with respect to the size of the visual, frequency of usage of photographs and product portrayals, the size of the product, usage of metaphors, and frequency of persons in general, and specifically women and children, depicted in advertising.

Appreciation of Advertising in General

In the discussion of how advertising works, another aspect of advertising plays a role: variation in appreciation of advertising in general. Several factors influence perceptions of advertising in general: the political climate, culture, and the advertising landscape of a country. In small markets, where international advertisers dominate with messages that do not fit the culture of the consumer, people tend to dislike advertising more than in large markets with much homegrown advertising. U.S. students, for example, have been found to have a significantly greater number of affective responses to advertising than Danish and Greek students.[32]

A universal finding is that advertising in general is praised for its economic effects, whereas it is criticized for its social effects.[33] In developing economies, because of lesser knowledge of how advertising works, expectations of the economic effects may be higher than in developed economies. A study in 1994 found that Russians at that time viewed advertising very positively. They saw it as an "engine of trade."[34]

The degree to which people like or dislike, approve or disapprove of advertising in general is also related to their culture. Notoriously, the Dutch and the Scandinavians have a critical attitude toward advertising, whereas the Americans, British, and Japanese have made it a part of their daily lives. This is related to masculinity. A characteristic of feminine cultures is a critical attitude, so people will not readily say they like something. In masculine cultures, advertising is part of show business.

Appreciation of advertising is also related to media usage. Across countries, reading the news in newspapers every day goes together with viewing advertising in newspapers as a source of new product information.[35] For television, we see similar relationships. Heavy TV viewing is related to a positive attitude toward advertising on TV. The percentages of heavy viewers correlate positively with the percentages of respondents saying that advertising on TV is a useful source of product information ($r = .66^{***}$).[36]

Thus, certain value patterns make some people generally more receptive to advertising as a phenomenon than others, which must be taken into account when comparing advertising effectiveness across borders.

Models of How Advertising Works

Giep Franzen[37] described seven different models of how advertising works: the sales-response model, the persuasion model, the involvement model, the awareness model, the emotions model, the likeability model, and the symbolism model. These can be linked to different ways of thinking about how advertising works and can be used to explain how advertising works for different cultures. I have added hypotheses about which model might fit which culture best.

1. The *sales-response model* is based on the simple stimulus-response model. The message is very direct, with the only objective being direct sales—the "buy now" strategy. This is the ultimate Anglo-Saxon model, based on short-term effect. It will fit cultures of the configuration of small power distance, high individualism, high masculinity, weak uncertainty avoidance, and short-term thinking.

2. The *persuasion model* can be compared with the "injection needle" theory of how communication works. The objective is short-term shift of attitude, buying intention, and brand preference through providing arguments. The "lecture" advertising form, which uses presenters, demonstrations, and testimonials, fits this

model. The model is based on the assumption that advertising should be persuasive and direct. It fits cultures with the configuration low power distance, individualism, and masculinity—the United States, England, Germany, Switzerland, and Austria.

3. The *involvement model* has as its objective the building of relationships between consumers and brands by creating emotional closeness. The philosophy behind this model is that the brand must become a "personality" to which human characteristics are attributed. Advertising must transfer associations from the brand to the consumer. This model is based on a more indirect advertising process. It will fit relatively well in feminine and individualistic cultures—the Netherlands, Scandinavia, and France.

4. The *awareness model* is primarily based on creating awareness in order to differentiate brands from similar brands. Association, metaphors, humor, and other forms of indirect advertising are based on this model. This is a model that, depending on the execution, may well cross borders. It may fit well in those cultures that need awareness as part of building trust, namely collectivistic cultures (e.g., Spain, Asia, Latin America). Because of its lack of persuasiveness, it may not work in cultures that are masculine and individualistic (e.g., U.S., England, Germany).

5. The objective of the *emotions model* is to create a positive attitude and brand loyalty. It builds an emotional bond between consumers and brands. This is the model for collectivistic and feminine cultures, for building relationships and trust. The emotions as such and the intensity will vary across cultures according to the level of uncertainty avoidance.

6. The *likeability model* is based on the assumption that liking the advertisement will lead to liking the brand. In countries used to the direct approach, conditioned to expect arguments and persuasion, this is not a good model. This is the model of how advertising works in collectivistic cultures. Likeability is the most important criterion for Japanese advertising, where the objective of advertising is to make friends with consumers and get them to trust and depend on the seller. This goal is achieved by telling a story or by entertaining the audience to put the consumer in a good mood, to induce him or her to go to the shop where real information about the product is available.

7. The objective of the *symbolism model* is to turn the brand into a symbol, a code, to help distinguish the consumer from other consumers. It gives cohesion to a group. This model is very culture-specific. Symbols reflect culture: They can be symbols of status, success, self-expression, stability, or any other reflection of culture. Symbols are the communication mode of cultures of large power distance combined with strong uncertainty avoidance, but also of collectivistic cultures—all of Asia, France, and the south of Europe.

Public Relations

Public relations involves managing relationships between organizations and publics. It helps an organization and its publics adapt mutually to each other.

It implies among others a communications dialogue.[38] The PR profession is most advanced in the Anglo-Saxon world, where companies want to convey explicit information, based on the assumption that their target groups want to be informed.

PR communicates with publics via the media in all sorts of ways, for example by issuing press releases or by organizing events that are covered by the media. The Western, individualistic origin of PR is recognized by the importance of the press release. International PR has to take into account differences in media usage across cultures. Across cultures, different channels have to be selected. Because communication management is essential for PR, sensitivity to different communication styles is essential. The same cultural rules operate for international PR as for international advertising. Whereas in individualistic cultures press releases can be short and to the point, a different style is likely more effective in collectivistic cultures. PR also assumes a need for information, which is not necessarily the same in all cultures, as we have seen in the previous sections. In high power distance cultures, where power holders disperse information as they see fit, PR is likely to have a different function, more to persuade than to inform, as in low power distance cultures with more openness. In individualistic cultures, when a problem occurs, a company tends to organize a great PR effort, providing information to contain the damage. In collectivistic cultures, companies have problems admitting mistakes and see it as a loss of face.

In international PR, whatever is communicated should be locally relevant, or the message will be thrown into the wastebasket. Also, for journalists, what doesn't fit their mental maps will not be used. If you don't have locally relevant messages, it is difficult to maintain an ongoing relationship with journalists of the relevant media. Messages will have to be translated, as not all journalists are fluent enough to understand the essentials of a message. Better do a translation yourself than depend on the journalists' capabilities.

Unlike international advertising, not much has been published about international public relations. Comparative studies tend to focus on the legal aspects.

The Media

Worldwide, several types of mass media exist. The major types are newspapers, magazines, television, and radio. These media vary considerably, not only with respect to content but also with respect to usage by consumers. This section describes these differences for television, newspapers, radio, and the important new electronic medium, the Internet.

Television

Although penetration of television sets has converged across countries, differences in viewing time between countries are considerable, and these differences are more or less stable over time. In 1998, heavy viewing across 19 countries worldwide[39] was related to high masculinity and large power distance. In 2001, similar relationships were found for 24 countries in west and east Europe.[40] High masculinity explained 37% of variance, and high power distance explained an additional 14%. Television has increasingly become show and violence to which people in masculine cultures are more attracted than people in feminine cultures. An advertisement by CNN illustrates this (see Illustration 7.15).

In the masculine cultures, television is also more integrated into daily life. Across Latin American countries, the percentages of people who say they like having the TV set on while doing other things in the house correlate with masculinity.[41]

Across Europe, people hardly watch the programs of other countries, mainly because they do not understand the language. Even within countries, different language groups will watch different programs. Analysis of Peoplemeter data from Germany and the three cultural regions of Switzerland showed substantial differences in television viewing.[42]

In every European country, the most popular television program is a local production. *Navarro,* a French action drama, never had less than 33% market share in France. In Germany, local performers account for 48% of the $3.5 billion in yearly sales. In Spain, 58% of the total $1 billion music sales are generated by Spanish and Latin American artists.[43] The Los Medios y Mercados de Latinoamérica study of 1998 shows that in most Latin American countries people are more interested in programs from their own country than from the United States.[44]

tv ● mobile ● com

Money, extortion, greed, passion. Makes for a good night's tv viewing.

Charles Hodson. World Business Today 20:30 CET. World Business Tonight 22:30 CET.

Hosted by Charles Hodson with guest appearances from key business leaders. The show reflects on the day's financial market changes, big stock movers, commodities and currencies. The ultimate in reality TV. Be the first to know.   **CNN**

Illustration 7.15   CNN, International

As a result, many international TV channels have localized language and content. In 2001, CNN International, originally a pan-European channel, offered programs in English, German, Turkish, and Spanish. It offers local advertising windows to the Scandinavian countries and Germany. Programs by Cartoon network are in English, French, Danish, Swedish, Dutch, Spanish, Italian, and Polish. Local ad windows are offered to the United Kingdom, France, Denmark, Sweden, Italy, Spain, and Poland. Programs of Eurosport are in 18 different languages, and local ad windows are offered to Germany and Scandinavia. MTV programs are in German, Dutch, French, Italian, Nordic languages, Polish, Spanish, and English and offer 16 different local ad windows.[45] In 2002, MTV had 35 channels worldwide, 15 of them in Europe. Much of the content is local. Some 80% of the content of MTV Italy, for example, is Italian-made.[46]

How people watch TV—alone, with friends or family—is also related to culture. Although in all countries children increasingly have television sets in their bedrooms, French children watch it there less often than young Swedish children do. Also, the degree to which parents give freedom to their children with respect to what they watch varies enormously.[47] What people prefer to watch across Latin American cultures also varies. Although the "soap opera" was invented in the United States, in Latin America people even more frequently watch their version of the soap or "telenovela." In 1998, 53% of Latin Americans between the ages of 12 and 64 said they watched telenovelas regularly; but across the Latin American cultures, distinct styles have evolved, so they cannot all be transplanted to the other countries.[48]

Newspapers

National wealth and power distance explain differences in newspaper readership worldwide, whereas in the economically more homogeneous Europe, the configuration of power distance and uncertainty avoidance explains variance. More important to advertisers than circulation is readership. In 1996, of the measurement "read a newspaper yesterday" for 31 countries worldwide published by the advertising agency McCann Erickson,[49] 26% of variance was explained by low power distance and an additional 15% by low uncertainty avoidance. In cultures of high power distance and high uncertainty avoidance, people read fewer newspapers than in cultures of low power distance and low uncertainty avoidance. The latter countries are more participative democracies, where people want to be informed. Several data confirm the relationship with power distance. Answers to the statement "read the news in the newspaper every day" (each year measured by Eurobarometer) consistently correlate with low power distance. In 2001, low power distance explained 68% of variance. In a group of 24 countries in Europe, including the candidate EU countries, 57% of variance was explained by low uncertainty avoidance and an additional 11% by low power distance. Figure 7.5 illustrates the correlation between newspaper readership and power distance and the stability of the relationship for 13 countries in Europe.

The data of 1991 are from Reader's Digest and are the percentages of answers "read a newspaper yesterday," a more general question than the 2001

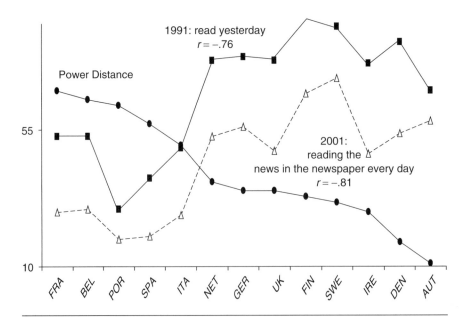

Figure 7.5   Newspaper Readership and Power Distance, Europe

SOURCE: Data from Hofstede (2001) (see Appendix A); Reader's Digest Survey (1991), Eurobarometer (2001) (see Appendix B)

Eurobarometer question that asks whether people read the *news* in the newspaper *every day*. So the percentages are lower. But the lines run parallel.

As the differences in newspaper readership between countries in Europe have existed for more than half a century, they are unlikely to disappear. Television will remain a more important medium in the collectivist cultures than newspapers. Usage differences with respect to the other printed media—magazines and books— are mainly related to individualism-collectivism.

The Internet

The new electronic media are concentrated in the developed world; and in the low uncertainty avoidance cultures, people have adopted the Internet fastest. In 2002, differences in the percentages of populations without access to the Internet, either at home or at work, was related to high uncertainty avoidance, which across 20 countries explained 46% of variance.[50] The relationship is illustrated in Figure 7.6 for 17 countries.

Next to uncertainty avoidance, masculinity explains variance of usage of all sorts of information technology. For example, in cultures of high masculinity people will use the Internet to be more competitive, whereas in the feminine cultures people have adopted it to enhance the quality of life.

Because of low penetration of personal computers in Japan, access to the Internet has lagged. The Internet has become more representative when new carriers were

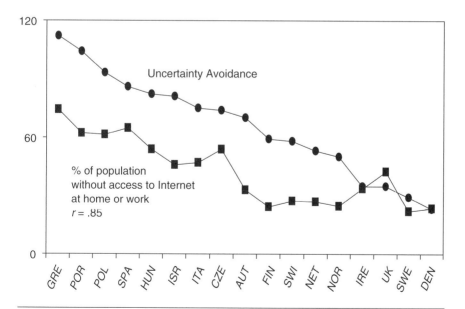

Figure 7.6   Internet Access and Uncertainty Avoidance

SOURCE: Data from Hofstede (2001) (see Appendix A); European Social Survey (2002/2003) (see Appendix B)

introduced such as Internet services by mobile phone. When in Japan Netphones (WAP phones) were introduced, the cell phone became the tool of access to the Internet.[51] A study by Roper Starch Worldwide[52] confirmed this difference in computer usage. Whereas Americans use their computers for lots of things related to children and education, in developed Asian countries people are less likely to use computers for teaching or entertaining children, or for school/college work. Also, Italians rarely use computers on children's behalf.

The Internet can be viewed as a new medium that takes time from the old media or other activities. In 2000, people across cultures had different views on what activities would be replaced by the Internet.[53] In the various countries, these were the activities on which people already spent relatively little time. An example is Internet usage replacing book reading in collectivistic cultures, where people anyway read fewer books than in individualistic cultures. In masculine and collectivistic cultures, where people generally participate less in active sports anyway, people expected that the Internet would reduce time spent on sport or physical activity. In the United States and in the United Kingdom, where people traditionally have read newspapers and magazines, there are indications that time spent on the Internet will come primarily from time spent watching television rather than from reading newspapers or magazines.[54] In Latin America (mostly collectivistic and polychronic cultures), where people are used to doing more things at the same time, Internet usage and TV viewing are not mutually exclusive activities. In the home, the TV is placed next to the computer monitor so that people can watch the two things at the same time. This is multitasking, or parallel processing.[55]

The Internet can be used for various applications: for e-mail and communication, for educational and scientific purposes, for business, for leisure, for banking, or for e-commerce. From various sources, we found that most differences in usage are explained by uncertainty avoidance and masculinity.[56] Low uncertainty avoidance is the main explaining variable of use of the Internet for e-mail. Variance of use for leisure and personal reasons is explained by low masculinity.

Web Site Design

When the Internet became operational for the world, it looked as if its users were part of a global community with similar interests. As we have seen in the previous section, however, people soon started to use it for different purposes. As a result, Web sites will have to be different to attract Internet users in different cultures. The first thing done by international companies who adopted it as a new global medium was allow for foreign names, zip codes, and countries, currency formats and units of measurement, and international telephone numbers. The next step was language. As described in Chapter 6, although many will say they speak English, the comprehension problems associated with reading a foreign language will affect the ease of use and appeal of a Web site.

Basically, Web site design for international usage has gone through steps similar to international advertising. Initially people thought the Web was a universal global means of communication, but soon they discovered that the same laws operate as in other communications. Across cultures, people vary in the ways they want to be addressed. Values and motives vary as well as communication styles. For example, university Web sites in feminine cultures have a softer approach and are more people oriented than Web sites of universities in masculine cultures that are more focused on achievement.[57]

Along with culture, there is variation in the way information is presented, the amount of data used, the use of extreme claims, rhetorical style, and the degree to which information is explicit, precise, and direct. Another culture-bound element is the option to contact people, which is, for example, limited in Spanish Web sites.[58] Offering the possibility to contact people in Web sites suggests equality in low power distance cultures, whereas it is limited in high power distance cultures.

Conclusion

How communication works and how advertising works is culture-bound. In one culture, advertising is persuasive by nature; in another, it is meant to build trust between companies and consumers. Thus, models of one culture cannot be projected to other cultures. The basic difference is between communication styles. Different verbal and nonverbal communication styles can be recognized in both interpersonal and mass communication, and culture clusters can be defined where one or the other style prevails. This is related to the way people process information. For some, pictures contain more information than words; for others, the only way to convey meaning is verbal. Academics and researchers across cultures have disputes about the different theories of how advertising works. Maybe no one is right, or maybe all are right. People look at how advertising works from the perspective of their own culture, which may indeed be very different from the perspective of their counterparts in other cultures. The consequence of the different roles of advertising across cultures is that international advertisers cannot use one standard for measuring effectiveness worldwide. Little is published about the effect of culture on international public relations. This chapter included a few assumptions. Finally, advertising uses the media to distribute its messages. As people across cultures use different media, it is also important to understand culture's influence on the media, both old and new, like the Internet.

Notes

1. Singelis, T. M., & Brown, W. J. (1995). Culture, self, and collectivist communication. *Human Communication Research, 21,* 354–389.

2. Oyserman, D., Coon, H., & Kemmelmeier, M. (2002). Rethinking individualism and collectivism: Evaluation of theoretical assumptions and meta-analyses. *Psychological Bulletin, 128,* 3–72.

3. Gudykunst, W., & Ting-Toomey, S. (1988). *Culture and interpersonal communication.* Newbury Park, CA: Sage, pp. 99–116.

4. Levo-Henriksson, R. (1994, January). *Eyes upon wings: Culture in Finnish and US television news.* Unpublished doctoral dissertation. Oy. Yleisradio Ab., Helsinki, p. 84.

5. Perspectives. (1996, September 9). *Newsweek,* 11.

6. Li, Z. (2001). *Cultural impact on international branding: A case of marketing Finnish mobile phones in China.* Academic dissertation, University of Jyväskylä, Finland.

7. Bresnahan, M. J., Ohashi, R., Liu, W. Y., Nebashi, R., & Liao, C.-C. (1999). A comparison of response styles in Singapore and Taiwan. *Journal of Cross-Cultural Psychology, 30,* 342–358.

8. Cutler, B. D., Erdem, S. A., & Javalgi, R. G. (1997). Advertiser's relative reliance on collectivism-individualism appeals: A cross-cultural study. *Journal of International Consumer Marketing, 9,* 43–55.

9. Schmitt, B. H. (1995). Language and visual imagery: Issues of corporate identity in East Asia. *Columbia Journal of World Business, 3,* 28–37.

10. Van den Berg-Weitzel, L., & Van de Laar, G. (2001). Relation between culture and communication in packaging design. *Brand Management, 8,* 171–184.

11. Laskey, H. A., Fox, R. J., & Crask, M. R. (1994, November/December). Investigating the impact of executional style on television commercial effectiveness. *Journal of Advertising Research,* 9–16.

12. Roland, A. (1988). *In search of self in India and Japan.* Princeton, NJ: Princeton University Press.

13. Scott, L. M. (1994). Images in advertising: The need for a theory of visual rhetoric. *Journal of Consumer Research, 21,* 269.

14. Watkins, H. S., & Liu, R. (1996). Collectivism, individualism and in-group membership: Implications for consumer complaining behaviors in multicultural contexts. In L. A. Manrai & A. K. Manrai (Eds.), *Global perspectives in cross-cultural and cross-national consumer research.* New York: International Business Press/Haworth Press.

15. Miracle, G. E., Taylor, C. R., & Chang, K. Y. (1992). Culture and advertising executions: A comparison of selected characteristics of Japanese and U.S. television commercials. *Journal of International Consumer Marketing, 4,* 89–113.

16. Lannon, J. (1994). Mosaics of meaning: Anthropology and marketing. *Journal of Brand Management, 2,* 160.

17. Percy, L., Rossiter, J. R., & Elliott, R. (2001). *Strategic advertising management.* Oxford, UK: Oxford University Press, pp. 167–180.

18. Holbrook, M., & Batra, R. (1987). Assessing the role of emotions as mediators of consumer responses to advertising. *Journal of Consumer Research, 14,* 404–420.

19. Resnik, A., & Stern, B. L. (1977). An analysis of information content in television advertising. *Journal of Marketing, 41,* 50–53; Stern, B. L., & Resnik, A. J. (1991, June/July). Information content in television advertising: A replication and extension. *Journal of Advertising Research,* 36–46.

20. *Consumer Survey.* (2002, January). Flash Eurobarometer 117.

21. Blackston, M. (1996). Can advertising pre-tests predict the longevity of advertising effects? *Marketing and Research Today, 24,* 11–17.

22. Biel, A. L. (1990, September). Love the ad. Buy the product? *Admap.*

23. Lannon, J. (1992, March). Asking the right questions: What do people do with advertising? *Admap,* 11–16.

24. Vaughn, R. (1980, June 9). The consumer mind: How to tailor ad strategies. *Advertising Age.*

25. Krugman, H. E. (1965). The impact of television advertising: Learning without involvement. *Public Opinion Quarterly, 29,* 349–356.

26. Miracle, G. E. (1987). Feel-do-learn: An alternative sequence underlying Japanese consumer response to television commercials. In F. Feasley (Ed.), *The Proceedings of the 1987 Conference of the American Academy of Advertising, USA,* R73–R78.

27.   Doi, T., (1973). *Amae No Kouzou* [The Anatomy of Dependence]. Tokyo: Kodansha. *Amae* can be explained as follows: The Japanese divide their lives into inner and outer sectors, each with its own different standards of behavior. In the inner circle, the individual is automatically accepted. There is interdependence and automatic warmth, love, or *amae,* the best translation of which is "passive love" or dependency. Members of the inner circle experience *amae* between each other, but it does not exist in the outer circle. You lose *amae* when you enter the outer circle. You don't expect *amae* in the outer circle.

28.   Petty, R. E., & Cacioppo, J. T. (1986). The elaboration likelihood model of persuasion. In L. Berkowitz (Ed.), *Advances in experimental social psychology.* New York: Academic Press. Also in Petty, R. E., & Cacioppo, J. T. (1986). *Communication and persuasion: Central and peripheral routes to attitude change.* New York: Springer.

29.   Callow, M., & Schiffman, L. (2002). Implicit meaning in visual print advertisements: A cross-cultural examination of the contextual communication effect. *International Journal of Advertising, 21,* 259–277.

30.   Müller, W. (1998). Verlust von Werbewirkung durch Standardisierung [Loss of advertising effectiveness through standardization]. *Absatzwirtschaft, 9,* 80–88.

31.   Cutler, B. D., Javalgi, R. G., & Erramilli, M. K. (1992). The visual components of print advertising: A five-country cross-cultural analysis. *European Journal of Marketing, 26,* 7–20.

32.   Andrews, J. C., Lysonski, S., & Durvasula, S. (1991). Understanding cross-cultural student perceptions of advertising in general: Implications for advertising educators and practitioners. *Journal of Advertising, 20,* 15–28.

33.   Ramaprasad, J. (2001). South Asian students' beliefs about and attitude toward advertising. *Journal of Current Issues and Research in Advertising, 23,* 55–70.

34.   Andrews, J. C., Durvasula, S., & Netemeyer, R. G. (1994). Testing the cross-national applicability of U.S. and Russian advertising belief and attitude measures. *Journal of Advertising, 23,* 71–82.

35.   Data from Eurobarometer, 1997–1999 (see Appendix B).

36.   European Media and Marketing Survey, 1999 (see Appendix B).

37.   Franzen, G. (1994, September 16). Reclame: Geloofshandeling of verkoopinstrument? [Advertising, an act of belief or sales instrument?] Unpublished inaugural lecture as Professor of Advertising, University of Amsterdam, the Netherlands.

38.   Elements of the definition by the Public Relations Society of America, 1988.

39.   Austria, Belgium, Denmark, Finland, France, Germany, Greece, Ireland, Italy, Japan, the Netherlands, Norway, Portugal, Spain, Sweden, Switzerland, Turkey, the United Kingdom, the United States. Source: Initiative Media, 1998 (www.initiativemedia.com).

40.   Eurostat. Cinema, TV, and Radio in the EU. Statistics on audiovisual services. Data 1980–2002 (see Appendix B).

41.   Soong, R. (1998, December 31). Television as companion. Message posted to TGI Latina (http://www.zonalatina.com/Zldata47.htm).

42.   Krotz, F., & Hasebrink, U. (1998). The analysis of people-meter data: Individual patterns of viewing behavior and viewers' cultural backgrounds. *The European Journal of Communication Research, 23,* 151–174.

43.   Culture wars. (1998, September 12). *Economist,* 99–103.

44.   Soong, R. (2000, May 11). Television program preferences by national origin. Message posted to TGI Latina (http://www.zonalatina.com/Zldata113.htm).

45.   M&M pocket guide on pan-European television (5th ed.). (2001, October). London: *Media and Marketing Europe.*

46.   Think local. Cultural imperialism doesn't sell. (2002, April 13). *Economist,* 13.

47. Pasquier, D., Buzzi, C., d'Haenens, L., & Sjöberg, U. (1998). Family lifestyles and media use patterns: An analysis of domestic media among Flemish, French, Italian and Swedish children and teenagers. *European Journal of Communication, 13,* 503–519.

48. Soong, R. (1999, November 8). Telenovelas in Latin America. Message posted to TGI Latina (http://www.zonalatina.com/Zldata70.htm).

49. Coen, R. J. (1997). *The insider's report.* New York: McCann-Erickson.

50. European Social Survey, 2003 (see Appendix B).

51. Kunii, I. (1999, July 12). The company that got Japan to log on. *BusinessWeek,* 40–41.

52. *The public pulse.* (1997). *12*(10/11), p. 5.

53. *Measuring information society.* (2000). Eurobarometer report (see Appendix B).

54. Mareck, M. (1999, December). Research watch. *M&M Europe,* 47.

55. Soong, R. (1999, September 4). The impact of the internet on television viewing. Message posted to TGI Latina (http://www.zonalatina.com/Zldata57.htm).

56. *Measuring information society.* (2000). Eurobarometer report (see Appendix B).

57. Dormann, C., & Chisalita, C. (2002, September 8–11). *Cultural values in Web site design.* Paper presented at the 11th European Conference on Cognitive Ergonomics, ECCEII Catania, Italy.

58. Husmann, Y. (2001). Localization of website interfaces. Cross-cultural differences in home page design. Wissenschaftliche Arbeit zur Erlangung des Diplomgrades im Studiengang Sprachen-, Wirtschafts- und Kulturraumstudien (Diplom-Kulturwirt). Universität Passau, Germany.

EIGHT

Value Paradoxes in Advertising Appeals

Three aspects of advertising style were pointed out that are each prone to influence by culture: (a) the values and motives included in the appeal, the central message; (b) the basic advertising form; and (c) the execution: the casting and activities of people, the setting, and the interrelationship. This chapter will focus on the appeals in advertising.

Appeals in Advertising

The appeal in advertising is a comprehensive concept. The appeal includes values and motives that define the central message. Wells, Burnett, and Moriarty[1] define an appeal as "something that makes the product particularly attractive or interesting to the consumer." Examples of appeals provided by Wells and colleagues are security, esteem, fear, sex, and sensory pleasure. The appeal is also used to describe a general creative strategy. Emphasis on the price is an economy appeal. A status appeal is used for presenting quality, expensive products.

The combination of the appeal (including motives), basic advertising form, and execution makes up advertising style. In this chapter, we will focus on how appeals reflect the core values of culture and use them as illustrations of how the Hofstede dimensions can explain what makes advertising culture-bound. Advertising appeals do not necessarily follow the norms of a culture. They may even go against them. To understand this, we first have to return to the value paradox.

The Value Paradox:
The Desirable and the Desired

Some values can easily be recognized as a reflection of culture. Self-actualization, self-interest, and self-esteem are examples of such values. They fit individualistic cultures. Also, doing it your own way and going it alone are expressions of an individualistic culture. But belonging is also a strong value of individualistic cultures. This seems paradoxical. That is because there are often opposing elements in one value. Thus, advertising appeals or claims may represent two opposing statements about values. This is related to the desirable and the desired, the distinction between what people think ought to be desired and what people actually desire, or how people think the world ought to be versus what people want for themselves.[2] The desired and the desirable do not always overlap. The desirable refers to the general norms of a society and is worded in terms of right or wrong, in absolute terms. The desired is what we want, what we consider important for ourselves. It is what the majority in a country actually do.

There is another paradox: the reflection of the gap between "words" and "deeds," between what people say they do or will do and what they actually do. Values as the desired are closer to deeds than values as the desirable. Because of the gaps between the desirable, the desired, and actual behavior, behavior may not correspond with the desirable, and norms for the desirable can be completely detached from behavior.

We speak of norms as soon as we deal with a collectivity. In the case of the desired, the norm is statistical: It indicates the values actually held by the majority. In the case of the desirable, the norm is absolute, pertaining to what is ethically right. The desired relates more to pragmatic issues, the desirable to ideology. The desired relates to choice, to what is important and preferred; it relates to the "me" and the "you." The desirable relates to what is approved or disapproved, to what is good, right, what one ought to do, and what one should agree with; it refers to people in general (see Table 8.1).[3]

The distinction between the desirable and the desired leads to seemingly paradoxical values within one culture. This paradox may even make cultures appear to be similar or to be moving in a similar direction. It may confuse people in the sense that they think cultures are becoming alike. An example is the conclusion that the Japanese are becoming individualistic because of an increased focus on

Table 8.1   The Desirable Versus the Desired

The Desirable	The Desired
The norm, what ought	What people want for themselves
Words	Deeds
Approval, disapproval	Choice
What is good, right	Attractive, preferred
For people in general	For me and for you
Ideology	Pragmatism

individuality in behavior and communication. In reality, individuality in Japan reflects the need for performance and competitiveness.

Individualism means "doing things your way, going it alone." This is the norm of an individualistic society. Yet companies cannot perform well if all individuals do things their own way. As a result, there is a great deal of focus on teamwork in individualistic societies. Because too much individualism also creates loneliness, the desired or actual behavior is opposed to the desirable: belonging. Belonging is an important American value. In Japan, the opposite is of importance: individuality, or any other value, need, or want that carries the desire to be different. In a collectivistic society, belonging to the in-group is an implicit part of culture, the desirable. Yet to be an entrepreneur, one has to distinguish oneself from the group. The value related to entrepreneurship is called individuality. It is the desired of Japanese culture: In order to be competitive, the Japanese must be more individualistic. This explains the Japanese focus on individuality. It reflects the decline of extreme subordination of the individual to the group.

The Value Paradox as an Effective Advertising Instrument

In advertising, the opposing values of a culture, although often paradoxical, appear to be effective because they relate to the important aspects of people's lives. Belonging is a ubiquitous value in American advertising, particularly in the sentimental, emotional form. It is included in the concept of "homecoming." It is not a value to use in an appeal in Japanese advertising.

The desired and the desirable are reflected in people's behavior and in how they relate to each other. Both the desired and the desirable are recognized in advertising appeals or claims, but they may be expressed in opposing ways. This makes it even more difficult to understand words and concepts that are labels of values of a culture other than one's own. An example is the concept of sharing in the English language. Superficially, this may imply a nonindividualistic and/or feminine, caring concept, meaning "not keeping things for oneself." Yet in masculine and individualistic culture, it reflects more. It reflects winning, communicating one's success and achievement to others. "One shares only the positive things of oneself—success. One does not share failure." One has to be very cautious with such concepts as they are ambiguous and when translated into other languages half of the meaning may be lost. If translated, a positive meaning may also change into a negative one.

Paradoxical value statements can be recognized in three ways:

1. Statements contrary to common belief, for example that the Japanese are individualizing whereas they actually are collectivistic. As in all increasingly wealthy societies, the Japanese are focusing more on individuality, but their behavior is collectivistic compared with Western societies. What is perceived as individualizing is changing competitive behavior.

2. Statements that seem contradictory but that may in fact be true. Seemingly opposing values of one dimension, such as "belonging" and "going it alone" in an individualistic culture.

3. As paradox type 2: Values that seem to be paradoxical within one dimension but can be explained by the configuration with other dimensions. An example is simultaneous "equality" and "large wage differences," a paradox of the configuration low power distance and masculinity.

"Trends," or temporary movements in society, often first adopted by the young, may reflect a reaction to a too strong focus on the desirable. Cocooning (withdrawing from the outside world into the inner world of home and friends) was an example of such a trend in the United States: a counterreaction to too strong individualism and competitiveness in an individualistic and masculine society. Cocooning has not been of great significance in feminine cultures and is absent in collectivistic cultures. There are more examples of paradoxes.

Equality Paradox

Equality is a strong desirable value of U.S. culture, but the actual behavior of Americans does not show so much equality. American behavior is related to fairness or that people should get what they deserve if they have the capabilities and work hard. This value results in inequality: If you have worked hard, you have earned the right to be different, to earn more—sometimes excessively more—money than others. CEOs of U.S. companies can earn 40 times as much as an ordinary production worker. The biggest increases in income inequalities have occurred in America, Britain, and New Zealand. Wage differences in most of continental Europe changed by much less.[4] Since then, wage differences in the Anglo-Saxon countries have not diminished. In continental Europe, increased wages of top managers of large companies have caused protests, and CEOs have even been asked to lower their salaries.

Equality in the United States means the poor have equal rights to become rich.

Equality in a large part of Europe means the rich should be equally "poor."

Dependence and Freedom Paradoxes

Another paradox can be found in dependence versus independence, the opposing values related to power distance and individualism. In large power distance and collectivistic cultures, children remain dependent on their parents much longer than in small power distance and individualistic cultures where children are supposed to go their own way, be self-reliant, and make their own decisions at an early age. This is extreme in the United States. An example is an event in 1996, when a 7-year-old girl, who wanted to set the record as the youngest pilot in the world, crashed and died. Her mother was quoted as saying: "It was her own decision."

Independence is a widely used concept or cue in Western advertising, but also in Japan. There, an appeal in advertising is independence as opposed to dependency, which is such a strong part of Japanese culture.

Related to dependency are the opposing values and paradoxes of freedom. In small power distance cultures, freedom means independence. In a collectivistic culture, the opposing values are freedom and harmony. Freedom can mean disharmony, as one ought to conform to the group. Freedom versus belonging can be opposing values for feminine cultures. Because of the affiliation needs in feminine cultures, belonging is an implicit value and is related to conformance, consensus. Yet in order to succeed, one wants to express oneself, be different. This goes against the norm, the desirable. Freedom reflects the desired. The freedom-belonging paradox is typical of the Scandinavian cultures and the Netherlands. The Dutch, for example, are notorious for searching for freedom in their holidays by traveling to France or Spain, but they take their own mobile home (caravan or trailer) with them and go to a camping area where they are sure they will find their compatriots.

In a strong uncertainty avoidance culture, too much freedom may lead toward undesired chaos, which cannot be tolerated, so the opposing value is order. In strong uncertainty avoidance cultures, freedom breeds uncertainty, whereas in weak uncertainty avoidance cultures freedom breeds success. People in strong uncertainty avoidance cultures take calculated risks to avoid failure; in weak uncertainty avoidance cultures, people take risks to succeed. Freedom paradoxes vary by culture.

Freedom/Dependence (France)

Freedom/Harmony (Japan)

Freedom/Belonging (the Netherlands)

Freedom/Order (Germany)

Success Paradoxes

The norm, the desirable, in masculine societies is that one wants to shine, to show one's success. Success is communicated, shared, and displayed because it is natural to show off. This is not the norm, the desirable, in feminine societies. Although a universal desire is to be recognized when one achieves something, success cannot be demonstrated directly. Because showing off is against the norm, demonstrating success must be done indirectly. Whereas the British (masculine culture) can say straightforwardly that they are the best, as British Telecom does: "We have the best connections," the Dutch, Danes, and Swedes (feminine) are not likely to do so. The paradox is frequently found in appeals such as, "There is more to it than meets the eye" or "True refinement comes from within" (Volvo, Sweden). Advertising in a masculine culture says: "Show your neighbors," whereas in a feminine culture advertising will say: "Don't show your neighbors." The paradox is in an advertising claim like, "Brilliant in its simpleness" (Omega watches, the Netherlands): On the one hand, one should not show off (the desirable), yet if successful, one wants to be recognized (the desired). It can also be recognized in payoffs or tag lines that tend to summarize the company's mission statement, as in the statement by Philips Electronics below.

Mazda Miata, United States: "The best selling car in the world."

Carlsberg, Denmark: "Probably the best beer in the world."

Swissair, Switzerland: "Best in Business."

Philips Electronics, the Netherlands: "Let's make things better."

The Innovation Paradox

The paradox traditional-innovative is found in most of western Europe and the United States. Innovativeness, embracing the new, is something that is implicit in weak uncertainty avoidance cultures. Characteristic of strong uncertainty avoidance is resistance to change, a desire for stability. For strong uncertainty avoidance cultures, accepting the new is the desirable value, but resistance to change is the desired value. Thus, advertising appeals may be paradoxical: *nouveau* or *neu* is an appeal that is as important for the French and the Germans as it is for the British, although the French and Germans are cultures of strong uncertainty avoidance. In France and Germany, innovativeness may represent the desirable, the norm for a society, while the actual behavior of consumers may be conservative, preferring tradition over innovation.[5] Although the cue word *new* is much seen in advertising, actual buying behavior may not be so innovative. In particular in Spain, the innovation paradox is strong. The Spanish way of life as reflected in advertising is warm, caring about others, different and original, even if full of unpredictable factors. On the one hand, the Spanish feel the desire to be modern and innovative; on the other hand, the desirable is stability, because of the difficulty of coping with ambiguity.

It should be like it used to be.

New is better.

Examples of Appeals by Dimension

In this section, examples of appeals found in advertising will be described by dimension, as well as activities and interactions between people in television commercials that are often deemed to be "only executional," but that reflect basic cultural values.

Power Distance

Status symbols are more frequently used in large power distance cultures than in small power distance cultures. An example is the use of certain status sports such as golf and related symbols such as golf balls. Power claims can be verbal and direct: "Save your power for the workplace" (from an advertisement for the Lexus in

Singapore) or as a verbal or visual metaphor: blue blood or yachts, referring to royalty (found in advertising in Portugal; see Illustration 8.1). In the execution, power distance can be shown in the way people interrelate or by the type of people shown (older vs. younger). In large power distance cultures, the elder (grand-mother, mother, or aunt) advises the younger (daughter or niece). Procter & Gamble has carefully differentiated its advertising for this cultural difference, as found in commercials for the brand ACE and washing liquid brands Dreft and Yes. In small power distance cultures, the younger advises the elder (daughter advises mother), as in P&G commercials for Yes in Sweden and Dreft in the Netherlands. A typical Japanese example of large power distance behavior is in a commercial for Shinko Sangyo "Saideria Home" that reflects the custom that, when a group of people share a car, the boss or any higher-placed person must always be brought home first, even if others live closer to the road taken. In this commercial, this custom allows the whole group to admire the nice home of the boss.

Another example is a TV commercial for Boss canned coffee, which reflects the *senpai-kohai* (elder-younger in work) relationship. A famous Japanese rock singer (Eikichi Yazawa) plays the role of an elder (*senpai*) Japanese salaryman. It is raining when he leaves the office and a younger colleague (*kohai*) offers to get his older colleague's car, so he will not get wet. This is a situation not found in low power distance cultures where equality values are strong.

In high power distance cultures, where elders are respected, ads also tend to refer to generations and refer, for example, to fathers and grandfathers who also used the product or brand. This reference to generations is reflected in the advertisement for Azzaro, showing three generations (Illustration 8.2). In high power distance cultures, elder people who dress up as young ones are viewed as "not grown up."

A global advertisement for Carrera sunglasses shows what is perceived as an older man (known to Americans as the professional wrestler Terry Bollea, nick-named "Hulk Hogan") dressed up as a young hippie. This is not a particularly attractive picture to people in high power distance cultures (Illustration 8.3). People will judge such a person as not grown up.

Illustration 8.1 Alfa 33, Portugal

Illustration 8.2 Azzaro, International

Illustration 8.3 Carrera, International

Illustration 8.4 Blue Band, Netherlands

Independence is an appeal reflecting the desirable in small power distance cultures. In large power distance cultures, it reflects the desired. A Japanese ad for Honda uses the words in the copy, "I'm independent" in English. In large power distance cultures, children are more protected and are independent at a later age than in small power distance cultures. Showing a young child alone, struggling to enter a building with his bicycle, as in a Dutch commercial for Blue Band margarine (Illustration 8.4), is not accepted in large power distance cultures. The Dutch will see the boy as an enterprising, independent child, whereas in other cultures he will be pitied because he is left on his own. In contrast, an Italian TV commercial for Granarolo milk shows a young (spoiled) boy in a high-status setting (country manor, servants). He doesn't want to drink milk, although the servants offer him all sorts of cookies, but when Granarolo is offered, he accepts and everybody applauds (Illustration 8.5).

Illustration 8.5 Granarolo, Italy

Children's behavior in school, when depicted in television commercials, will vary according to the degree of power distance. A scene showing a schoolteacher who is being driven crazy by her students would fit in a low power distance culture but not in a high power distance culture, where generally students show more respect for their teachers. This was reflected in an offer by the Belgian telecom company Mobistar, who offered special after-school rates for schoolchildren to motivate them to use their phones only in after-school hours.

The same is true for advertisements referring to the relationship between bosses and subordinates. A Danish advertisement for Lipton tea saying, "Drive your boss mad by making him drink your tea" (Illustration 8.6) should not be used in France, Spain, or Italy. Small power distance is reflected in the antiauthoritarian elements of parody and humorous advertising.

The concept of an "empowered consumer" included in a company's claim, "Judge for yourself"—or more implicitly when a company stresses its role as a facilitator instead of imposing ideas or creating a dependency relationship with the consumer—is part of small power distance cultures.

Illustration 8.6 Lipton, Denmark

Individualism/Collectivism

As described in Chapter 7, an important difference between individualistic and collectivistic cultures is between low-context and high-context communication. In individualistic cultures, the public tends to be addressed in a direct and personalized way. Words like *you, we,* and *I* are frequently used. So are imperatives. U.S. examples are "You flip a switch and . . ." (Detroit Edison), "Treat yourself right" (Crystal Light), "You have a dream, make a wish . . ." (Reebok). Whereas presenters in individualistic cultures address the public directly, the purpose of using well-known presenters or endorsers in collectivistic cultures is that the audience can associate with them. In individualistic cultures, the personal pronoun *I* is frequently used, as in the global advertisement for Nike (Illustration 8.7) and in the advertisement for Lucky Strike (Illustration 8.8). The latter was used in Spain, where this approach is not very attractive. A better approach is in the advertisement for the cigarette brand L&M (Illustration 8.9) that says, "Better in companionship."

The difference between the independent and interdependent self has an important impact on advertising appeals. Members of individualistic and collectivistic societies will respond differently to advertisements emphasizing individualistic or collectivistic appeals. In collectivistic cultures such as China and Korea appeals focusing on in-group benefits, harmony, and family are more effective, whereas in individualistic cultures like the United States, advertising is more effective that appeals to individual benefits and preferences, personal success, and independence.[6] A commercial where a man breaks out from a group and starts doing something on his own that the group hasn't thought of would be seen as positive in the individualistic cultures of the West, but negative in collectivistic Asian cultures.[7]

Whereas in collectivistic cultures people like to share things, in individualistic cultures people tend to keep the nice things for themselves. The ice cream brand

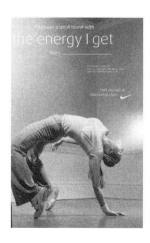

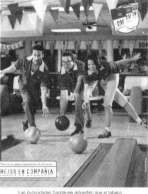

Illustration 8.7   Nike, Spain

Illustration 8.8   Lucky Strike, Spain

Illustration 8.9   L&M, Spain

Illustration 8.10 Magnum, Germany

Magnum has used this approach, as illustrated in the German advertisement that says, "I share many things, but not everything" (Illustration 8.10).

With respect to time, individualistic cultures are monochronic and collectivistic cultures are polychronic. The clock as a symbol of efficiency will not be understood in polychronic cultures.

In collectivistic societies, people do not like being alone or eating alone, whereas in individualistic societies people cherish their privacy. In collectivistic cultures, being alone means you have no friends, no identity. If alone, one is outside the group to which one belongs. In the United States, Levi's changed their advertising for the Hispanic market and downplayed individualism. Although in the United States the independent hipsters in Levi's TV ads had been drawing young customers, they didn't work for Levi's Hispanic customers. "Why is that guy walking down the street alone?" they asked. "Doesn't he have any friends?"[8] This difference between showing individuals, loners, or showing people as part of groups can be explicit and presented directly or implicit and presented indirectly, as shown in Chapter 7. Whereas in individualistic cultures people can enjoy a beer alone and being alone can even have a relaxing function, this is not the case in collectivistic cultures where people enjoy beer together. Images from a German TV commercial for Jever beer (Illustration 8.11) and for the Spanish Mahou (Illustration 8.12) illustrate the difference.

Illustration 8.11 Jever, Germany

Illustration 8.12 Mahou, Spain

Concepts reflecting collectivism may be more successful across borders than the highly individualistic approach. Marlboro was more successful in Asia than Camel. The Camel man represented the lonely, masculine individual whereas the (also very masculine) Marlboro cowboy was implicitly part of a group. Sometimes he was seen alone, but he always returned to the campfire, to his companions. Presenters in advertising in individualistic cultures can be—and often are—alone whereas in collectivistic cultures more than one presenter is seen. The value paradox belonging-independence can be recognized in Japanese advertising where on the one hand one sees groups of people in advertising, but celebrities frequently are depicted alone. This reflects the desired, dreaming of another world of individual success as a contrast to conformance to the group.

Appeals in individualistic cultures can refer explicitly to the independent self, for example the text of a Tampax commercial: "Free yourself, to be yourself. Do what you want, wear what you want any day you want." Examples of individualistic claims are "Designed for the individual" (Mitsubishi), "Privat concert" for Privat cigarettes (Denmark), "In a world of conformity some things are still made for the individual" (Herblein watch), "Go your own way" (Ford Probe), and "It's my crazy life. Be yourself, king of your craziness" (Chrysler PT Cruiser, U.K.). Examples of collectivistic claims are "Prospering together" (International ad for Japanese Chiyoda Bank, Illustration 8.13), "Be part of the group" (J&B whisky, Portugal), or showing a group of happy people with the tag line, "the best moments" (Ballentines, Spain).

Illustration 8.13   Chiyoda, International

Strong examples of the different appeals in collectivistic and individualistic societies are the two following appeals: "It is so good, you want to share it with others" (Hermesetas, Portugal) versus "It is so good, you want to keep it for yourself" (Evers, confectionery, Denmark). Philips Electronics in Spain presented the slogan, *"Juntos hacemos tu vida mejor"* (Together we make your life better). They said "together" and show more than one person. This is in contrast with the Dutch and German advertisements using the overall claim, "Let's make things better," and in which the "working together" aspect is missing. The name "Tchibo Privat Kaffee" reflects individualism, as do such universalistic claims as *"Überall auf der Welt"* (everywhere in the world), supposing that the feeling will be the same for all people in the world who drink coffee. *Worldwide* and *world* are power words for individualistic societies.

Members of collectivistic cultures have a different perception of hospitality than members of individualistic cultures. In collectivistic cultures, an unexpected guest will always be served food, so there is always enough food available. A claim like the Dutch one for party snacks, saying "Duyvis, for when there is a party," is not effective for collectivistic cultures, where this sort of product should always be available, not just for a party.

Popular appeals in collectivistic cultures are "modern" and "international," because they appeal to the need to conform, belonging to a new and greater world. Reader's Digest[9] publishes data on personal traits found in readership surveys. One of the traits is measured by the scale modern-traditional. The percentages of answers by people who considered themselves modern correlate with collectivism.

The importance of both context and the relationship orientation of the self in collectivistic cultures can explain the frequent use of celebrities in Japanese advertising. The use of celebrities in advertising varies across cultures. There are indications that in the Western world these variations are related to the degree of masculinity (need for success), which is likely to explain why in the United States the cult of personality and obsession with celebrity and stardom is most pronounced. In collectivistic cultures, the acceptance of celebrities would be expected to be lower because being individually distinctive in the context of daily life is not advised. In the collectivistic Japan, however, celebrities are even more frequently used in advertising than in the United States. In his description of the celebrity phenomenon in Japan, Carolus Praet,[10] a Dutch professor who teaches international marketing in Japan, provides explanations that refer to two collectivistic aspects: the relational self and context. In Japan, celebrity appearances are not limited to famous actors, singers, sports stars, or comedians. Advertising is a stage for established celebrities to capitalize on their fame, but it also is the stepping-stone for models and aspiring actors toward fame. In Japan, the word *talent* (*tarento*) is used to describe most celebrities in the entertainment world, and *star* is reserved for those who are seen to have long-lasting popularity. Many of the talents are selected on the basis of their cute looks. In the context of entertainment and advertising, this phenomenon seems not to pose problems of distinctiveness, which it might give in the context of the family or a work-related environment. The function of such *tarento* is also to give the brand "face" in the world of brands with similar product attributes. Instead of adding abstract personal characteristics to the product, it is linked to concrete persons. This is also explained as part of the creative process in which a creative team in the advertising agency prefers to explain a proposed campaign by showing the client a popular talent around whom the campaign is to be built rather than talking about an abstract creative concept.

Considering the fact that approximately 70% of the world population is more or less collectivistic and many global advertising campaigns (usually made in the international advertising centers London or New York) reflect individualistic values, it is fair to assume that much global advertising is only effective for a small part of the target. Most global ads address people in a direct way, show people alone, and refer to all sorts of individualistic claims such as "the power for self-expression" (e.g., in an international ad for Lexus).

Masculinity/Femininity

More winners per second

Razor-sharp in every shot, even the most difficult

Illustration 8.14 Nikon, International

Winning, a characteristic of masculine cultures, is frequently reflected in U.S. advertising. In particular, the combination of individualism and masculinity (the configuration of Anglo-German cultures) leads to the strong need to win, to be successful and show it, combined with the wish to dominate. Examples of wordings are "Being first," "The one and only in the world," and "Be the best." Hyperbole, persuasiveness, and comparative advertising are reflections of masculinity. A claim like "We'd like to set the record straight on who finished first in Client/Server Applications" (SAP integrated software) is typical for a masculine culture and reflects competitiveness. Another example is "Compete with the document company" (Xerox). An advertisement for Nikon cameras says, "More winners per second" (Illustration 8.14), and a German ad for Skiny underwear says, "Simply the Best" (Illustration 8.15).

Aggressive typology and layout are another reflection of competitiveness. Dreams and great expectations are expressions of masculine cultures. Statements like "A dream come true," "A world without limits," reflect the value "mastery," the idea that anyone can do anything as long as they try hard. This is opposed to feminine cultures, where dreams are said to be delusions. In masculine cultures, status is important for demonstrating one's success. To become Man (Woman) of the Year is the ideal for people in masculine cultures because mediocrity is the proof of failure. In Chapter 4, we showed how this was used in a commercial for Tylenol in the United States. Another reflection of masculinity, typical of American culture, is "bigness." America is a land of big egos, big cars, the Big Mac, the Quarter Pounder (or even a half pounder), and the big idea.[11] Illustration 8.16 shows an image from a TV commercial for Taco Bell.

The configuration of individualism and masculinity explains the frequent hyperbole in American advertising with statements like "All the cosmetics in the world can't do what we can," "The only plastic wrap with Reynolds strength behind it," "The greatest of ease" (for a white plastic garden chair), "You'll never find a softer toilet paper than new Northern Ultra," "The pain reliever that hospitals use most," or "The world's number one contact lens" (Acuvue).

Although both the United States and the United Kingdom score high on the masculinity index, there is a difference. The United States scores much higher on uncertainty avoidance, which also influences the difference between overstatement and understatement. In the United Kingdom, one also wants to state that one has success, but this is often done "tongue in cheek."

Feminine cultures are characterized by favoring caring, softness, and the small. An international business advertisement for Russian Norilsk Nickel expresses love for the weak, showing a child in their advertising (Illustration 8.17). Instead of hyperbole, feminine cultures like understatement, as in the international advertising campaign for Carlsberg, with the tag line "Probably the best beer in the world" (Illustration 8.18). Much of Volvo advertising (Volvo is from Sweden, the most feminine culture in the world) tends to focus on safety, protecting the family. In feminine cultures, showing off is negative. The Volvo advertisement in Illustration 8.19 says, "True refinement comes from within," meaning to say you don't have to show off.

Another example of understatement was in an advertisement for the Audi 100 in the Netherlands: "You have a small house (the visual is a mansion), and a small car, but your neighbors live far enough away, they cannot see it. Moreover, the most important part cannot be seen, it is under the hood." An opposing claim was by Seat, Italy, showing the car in a garage with a glass door: "It can always be shown, it can always be seen."

Understatement is also recognized in a Spanish print advertisement for the Audi A4 Avant, an expensive top model of Audi, which reads as follows:

Illustration 8.15   Skiny, Germany

Illustration 8.16   Taco Bell, United States

Illustration 8.17   Norilsk, International

Illustration 8.18   Carlsberg, International

Illustration 8.19   Volvo, International

Deceive all of them, saying it's a family car. The new Audi A4 Avant. Never speak about power in public. If, one day, someone mentions something about the 5 valves per cylinder, change the topic, tell him it seems like it's going to rain. 150 hp?—You don't know anything.—Quattro-traction?—What's that? Use the interior space and the variability as a pretext. So that no one thinks that you actually love its design. While traveling with friends make them think that you are bored. Even yawn. Do it and everybody will think that the Audi A4 Avant is only a family car. After all, there are a lot who want to deceive you, saying that they drive a sports car.

This text reflects the configuration of collectivism, high power distance, femininity, and strong uncertainty avoidance. You are not allowed to talk about power in public. You just have it. To avoid confrontations, things should not be said directly. Indirectly, a number of important details are communicated about the technical aspects. It reflects modesty and harmony.

Celebrity endorsement, an advertising form frequently used in Anglo-Saxon cultures, is less used in feminine cultures. In the latter, well-known people and presenters tend to downplay the fact that they are well known or they are belittled or even ridiculed. In more extreme cases, the parody style will be utilized. In the Netherlands, a look-alike of Pamela Andersen was used for an optician retail chain called Hans Anders, belittling her body shape and suggesting that these are as much a prosthesis as eyeglasses are. In Spain, a retail chain in opticals used another "hero" of the soap *Baywatch* running fast and bumping into a shack, for the audience to conclude that he should have worn glasses.

Strong and weak role differentiation are both reflected in advertising. An example of strong role differentiation is the claim in a Mexican ad for Jethro jeans: "Be his pin-up girl" (Illustration 8.20). In Danish advertisements, men can be seen wearing aprons, as in the advertisement for Matas (Illustration 8.21).

Illustration 8.20   Jethro,
Mexico

Illustration 8.21   Matas,
Denmark

Strong role differentiation is also reflected in Japanese advertising, for example for the energy drink Guronsan in which a salaryman is seen working and entertaining with his colleagues and his wife is waiting at home. He needs the energy drink for his many activities.

Men wearing aprons and playing an active role in family life cooking or caring for children are also seen in Spanish advertising, as illustrated in an image from a TV commercial for Avecrem by Gallina Blanca (Illustration 8.22). Also, in France fathers are seen in ads with their children, as in an image from a TV commercial for Maggi (Illustration 8.23). An image from a TV commercial for Ajax in Sweden (Illustration 8.24) shows a man wiping the floor with pleasure. He swings the mop as if it is a golf club.

Illustration 8.22   Gallina
Blanca, Spain

Illustration 8.23   Maggi,
France

Illustration 8.24   Ajax,
Sweden

When in masculine cultures men play a role in the household in TV commercials, they often are depicted as the stupid guy, and the woman knows better. She will play the role of the expert and advises how to use the product. Women want to be the competent housewife and be in control of their men. In the advertisement for Triumph underwear, it is called the "control thing" (Illustration 8.25).

Illustration 8.25 Triumph, United Kingdom

The women serve the family, as in the image from an Italian TV commercial for Casa Modena (Illustration 8.26). If men do something with babies, it likely serves their own purposes. A U.S. TV commercial for Honda shows a man with a baby approaching his car. He sees a spot on it and uses the baby's nappy to clean the car (Illustration 8.27). In masculine cultures, women can be shown to be tough; in feminine cultures, men can be shown to be tender. Illustration 8.28 shows three images from a classic award-winning Japanese TV commercial for a Hitachi vacuum cleaner in which a woman fights the flies. Illustration 8.29 shows three images of a Thai award-winning TV commercial for Asia Telecom in which in an airport a father tells a bedtime story to his daughter by videophone.

Appeals of masculine cultures are more task or success oriented, whereas appeals of feminine cultures will be more affiliation and relationship oriented. German commercials for detergents tend to argue

Illustration 8.26 Casa Modena, Italy

Illustration 8.27 Honda, United States

Illustration 8.28 Hitachi, Japan

Illustration 8.29 Asia Telecom, Thailand

the effectiveness of the detergent by showing large piles of dirty clothes or many dirty children and the result: large piles of clean clothes or many clean children in brilliant white clothes. Women are cast in the role of effective housewives. In a feminine culture like the Netherlands, a more affiliation-oriented approach will be more successful, casting the woman in her role of affective mother who has a happy relationship with her children. Clean children are part of her relationship with them. The two are very different approaches.

In international business journals like *Newsweek* and *BusinessWeek,* much of international advertising is from U.S. companies, and masculine values can be recognized in the ubiquitous use of women who are only used as illustrations and have no role at all in the message. An example is an advertisement for CA, Computer Associates (Illustration 8.30).

Illustration 8.30
CA, International

Uncertainty Avoidance

Strong uncertainty avoidance translates into the need for explanations, structure, testing, test reports, scientific proof and advice, and testimonials by experts, but also into high regard for technology and design. An example is an advertisement for the Italian car brand Lancia (Illustration 8.31). Advertisements tend to be highly structured and detailed. An example of a detailed advertisement is a Russian one for a facial cream, the name of which means something like "Purity Line" (Illustration 8.32). It includes a lot of information plus a picture of a laboratory, thus illustrating scientific proof.

Illustration 8.31   Lancia, Italy

Illustration 8.32   Purity Line, Russia

In high uncertainty avoidance advertising, the competence of the manufacturer must be demonstrated. Showing how a product works, with all the technical details, is important. This is in contrast with weak uncertainty avoidance cultures where the result is more important. Two advertisements for toothpaste illustrate the difference. In the advertisement for elmex and aronal (Illustration 8.33), the brands are called experts for tooth health and the details of how the product works are illustrated. In contrast, an English advertisement for Crest focuses on the results of using the product: beauty (Illustration 8.34).

Illustration 8.33   elmex and aronal, Germany

Illustration 8.34   Crest, United Kingdom

Illustration 8.35   Ariel, Germany

Design is a strong element of German and Italian advertising, though German advertisements also tend to focus on the technological aspect, whereas the Italians focus more on the outer appearance. The French and the Spanish are more art and fashion oriented.

Testing and test reports are favored in all strong uncertainty avoidance cultures, although the execution tends to be different. Favorite German expressions are *"Die Besten im Testen"* (The best in the test) and *"Testsieger"* (Test winner). A German advertisement for Ariel (Illustration 8.35) says, "Test it" and "The best product in the test." Technical explanations about the product can be very detailed for all sorts of products, be they cars, toothpaste, or shampoo.

In strong uncertainty avoidance cultures, people tend to be better groomed than in weak uncertainty avoidance cultures. In advertisements from the southern European and Germanic countries, people are significantly better dressed than in advertising

Stella Artois. About as sophisticated as a beer can get.

Illustration 8.36   Honda, Spain

Illustration 8.37   Stella Artois, Australia

from the northern European cultures. Being well groomed means matching the right colors and picking the right accessories. A Spanish advertisement for Honda illustrates this (Illustration 8.36). It suggests that people match the color of their car with their shoes, bag, sunglasses, mobile phone, and so forth. The ultimate understatement of sophistication is an Australian advertisement for Stella Artois beer (Illustration 8.37). Other examples are two breakfast situations, an Italian one for Saccottino (Illustration 8.38) where mother and father are well groomed and, in contrast, a Dutch one for Blue Band Goede Start—Good Start (of the day)—showing a father in his underwear (Illustration 8.39).

Illustration 8.38   Saccottino, Italy

In strong uncertainty avoidance cultures, presenters tend to be experts, the competent professional, or the competent boss—the professor or physician type—

Illustration 8.39   Blue Band Goede Start, Netherlands

preferably wearing a white coat. In small power distance, weak uncertainty avoidance cultures, a parody of the expert is favored.

In high uncertainty avoidance cultures, emotions can be shown, and the word *emotion* as such is attractive. An example is the payoff used for the Spanish Seat brand, *"Auto emoción."*

An appeal recognized in advertising in strong uncertainty avoidance cultures is relaxation in the sense of relief from anxiety and tension. This is expressed explicitly, whereas relief from tension is more implicit in weak uncertainty avoidance cultures. Stability is an important value of strong uncertainty avoidance cultures; change is not perceived as favorable. Fear of change is found in expressions like "no compromises."

Long-Term Orientation

The opposing values of long-term orientation are "save for tomorrow" versus "buy now, pay later." Short-term orientation is reflected in the sense of urgency so frequently encountered in U.S. advertising. Examples are "Hurry," "Don't wait," or "Now 50% off, no money down, two full years' free credit, it's on now!" Another expression of short-term thinking is "instant pleasure," as in an advertisement for Häagen-Dazs ice cream (Illustration 8.40) or living in the now and not thinking about the future, as in the advertisement for CK: "Be good, be bad, just be" (Illustration 8.41).

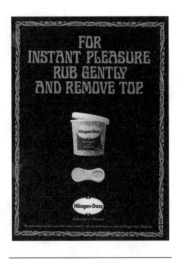

Illustration 8.40   Häagen-Dasz, UK

Illustration 8.41   CK, Spain

Symbols of long-term orientation are thick trees or explicit referral to future generations, as the Japanese telecom company NTT DoCoMo does in the international advertisement in Illustration 8.42. An international campaign by Korean LG also used long-term orientation symbolism, as in Illustration 8.43 that symbolizes continuity: What the old man cannot finish in his life, the baby will. The advertisement also symbolizes man in harmony with nature.

Illustration 8.42   NTT
DoCoMo, International

Illustration 8.43
LG, International

Harmony, with both nature and fellow humans, is a popular appeal in Asian advertising. It is part of an indirect approach that helps to build trust in the company. Much advertising is pure entertainment, and visuals and objects are used that please the eye, many of which relate to nature: bamboo trees, flowers, autumn leaves, or other representations of the seasons, which often have a symbolic meaning unknown to foreigners. Many Westerners do not understand the butterflies in ads for computers or other nature elements in Asian advertising. The combination of collectivism and long-term orientation demands harmony with nature and thus explains this advertising style, the objective of which is to please the customer, not to intrude.

Consequences for Advertising Concepts

Certain configurations of dimensions have significant consequences for the effectiveness of advertising appeals. Appeals or concepts can be presented in two-dimensional maps showing culture clusters where the appeal will be more or less effective. An example is the use of status, an appeal that varies with power distance and masculinity. Status is used to show power and social position in large power distance cultures and to show success in masculine cultures. In feminine cultures, particularly those of small power distance (Scandinavia and the Netherlands), status needs are low. Feminine cultures are characterized by modesty and jealousy, and so the use of status will be counterproductive. Cultures that score high on both masculinity and power distance will be particularly sensitive to the status motive.

Figure 8.1 shows a two-dimensional map of 30 countries, with culture clusters that will be more or less sensitive to status as an appeal in advertising. In the lower left quadrant are the Scandinavian countries and the Netherlands, cultures in which the status appeal will not work very well. In the upper left quadrant is the Anglo-German

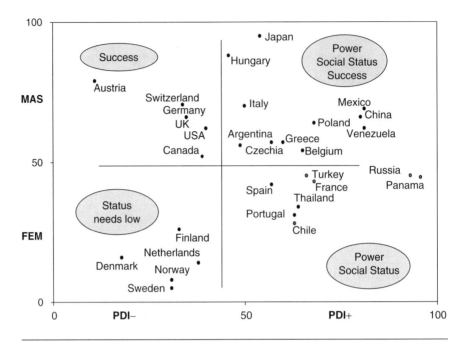

Figure 8.1   Status Needs

SOURCE: Data from Hofstede (2001) (see Appendix A)

cluster, where status will be most appealing if connected with success. The two right quadrants show a mixture of European, Latin American, and Asian cultures. In the lower right quadrant, status is mostly linked with power. The extremes are in the upper right quadrant, where both power and success are drivers for status brands and appeals in advertising: Mexico, Venezuela, Japan, and China are high-status cultures.

Do Great Ideas Travel?

Great ideas or concepts, if they are based on values, are ideas that touch the heart of the consumer. That type of concept tends to reflect the core values of the home country and can travel to only a limited number of other countries. The international advertising world is full of examples of concepts that cannot travel. A concept that is particularly attractive to the British is freedom of choice as used, for example, by British Telecom. The literal translation into Dutch (*Vrijheid om te kiezen*), as in Illustration 8.44, doesn't give the Dutch a similar warm feeling. Worse, it is irrelevant. Why wouldn't consumers in a free country have freedom of choice? Also Canon uses the "freedom of choice" concept (Illustration 8.45). The Dutch translation says, "Can I choose the best in all freedom?" which to the Dutch is utter nonsense.

A concept that is frequently used for wireless technology, "Work where you want," is typical of individualistic cultures, where people mix work and home life

Illustration 8.44
BT, Netherlands

Illustration 8.45   Canon,
Netherlands

more easily than in collectivistic cultures (Illustration 8.46). In Chapter 4 (under Individualism/Collectivism), we discussed the influence of individualism on penetration of home computers. Whereas in individualistic cultures people like to move their work from the office to the home, the park, or even the beach, in collectivistic cultures the workplace is part of one's "family," and people like to stay there with their colleagues to finish the job. So an advertisement like the one for Toshiba (Illustration 8.46) is culture-specific and cannot travel farther than northwest Europe and the Anglo-Saxon world. It shows a man with his laptop at the seaside and says, "It works outside the office."

Many international advertisements reflect the home values of the advertiser, not the values of a globally diverse audience. In this chapter, we presented several examples of culture-bound international advertising taken from international journals such as *Newsweek* or *BusinessWeek*. If these advertisers all keep targeting their home-culture audiences with their home culture's values, why are they using a cross-border medium? Their advertising would be more effective if adapted to different culture clusters. Modern printing techniques allow differentiating print runs for different regions or countries.

Illustration 8.46   Toshiba,
Netherlands

Why Humor Doesn't Travel

In some cultures, humor is a much used device in advertising and in others it is scarce. The statement that humor doesn't travel is frequently heard. Why? Because humor is a subversive play with conventions and established ideas; it is based on breaking taboos. Comedy plays with ways of breaking the rules of convention, going against what ought to be, the desired of a culture. Because it uses cultural conventions, it can only be understood by those who share the culture. An example is a fragment in Gogol's play *The Revisor,* where the Revisor's servant is seen lying on a bed. To the Russians of Gogol's time (1836), this was very funny because servants used to sleep on the floor and being on a bed meant being on one's master's bed, which was seen as an unheard-of liberty.[12] This fits Russian culture, which was and still is one of the largest power distance cultures in the world. The servant's act would have been impossible to understand by members of small power distance cultures and thus not be viewed as funny.

Culture also influences the type of humor used. Parody, for example, fits small power distance cultures because it disguises the voice of authority. Much of British humor is based on antiauthoritarianism. Weak uncertainty avoidance cultures, being able to cope with ambiguity, will use the more subtle types of humor, parody, and understatement. In strong uncertainty avoidance cultures, the more straightforward type of slapstick humor tends to be used. The admonishing humor of the Germans has to do with their need for perfectionism, which explains their infrequent use of irony.[13] Much of Belgian humor is straightforward. It is a likely effect of strong power distance. In Belgian humor, the oppressed entrench themselves.[14] A characteristic of humor is incongruity, or the contrast between the expected and the unexpected, the possible/plausible and the impossible/implausible. This element of surprise is an important part of humor: It is often the unexpected turn in a story or event that makes people laugh, and that helps them unwind.

Using humor in advertising is a management decision. The reason it is used more in some countries than in others has to do with the cultural values of management; it does not reflect the sense of humor of advertising audiences. Humor in advertising is found particularly in cultures of small power distance and weak to medium uncertainty avoidance such as the United Kingdom, Denmark, Sweden, Norway, and the Netherlands. Obviously, this configuration of dimensions makes managers willing to use humor in advertising, whereas in strong uncertainty avoidance cultures, management is not likely to do so.

In studies of the use of humor in advertising, a number of different humorous devices are usually distinguished: puns or word games, understatements, jokes, the ludicrous, the "comic" (as in comic strip), comedy, slapstick, satire, parody, irony, and black humor. In contrast to the stereotype of the German lack of humor, German studies (see Hillebrand[15] and Merz[16]) distinguished a similar number of types of humor with only one difference: in English/American studies, "understatement" is mentioned as a humorous device. This was not specified as a humorous device in the two German studies, which mentioned *Schadenfreude* (malicious pleasure) as a humorous device, one not mentioned in the Anglo-Saxon studies. The fact that in Germany less humor is used in advertising than in England doesn't mean that the Germans have a lesser sense of humor, but it reflects the risk aversion attitude of the German advertising industry as well as the purpose of advertising in Germany that follows the persuasion model.

Weinberger and Spotts[17] distinguished six categories of humor in the United States and the United Kingdom: pun, understatement, joke, the ludicrous, satire, and irony.[17] The U.S. advertising style included more of the ludicrous and the United Kingdom's more satire. This can be explained by the different scores on the uncertainty avoidance dimension. Alden, Hoyer, and Lee[18] examined the content of humorous television advertising from Korea, Germany, Thailand, and the United States and found one type of humor that worked across all compared countries: incongruous. Almost 60% of the humorous ads in all four nations contained incongruent contrasts, but there were some cultural differences. In the collectivistic cultures of Thailand and Korea, humorous appeals involved groups—three or more central characters were included—whereas in the United States and Germany, both individualistic cultures, substantially fewer ads with three or more characters were found. In the large power distance cultures (Thailand and Korea), more humorous ads featured unequal status between main characters than in the two small power distance cultures (Germany and the United States). Scheijgrond and Volker[19] conducted a study to compare differences in the liking of humorous television commercials between the Netherlands and Flanders (Flemish Belgium). Because in the Netherlands and Flanders, the Dutch-speaking part of Belgium, the same language is spoken, many advertisers assume that the people have similar cultural traits. But in fact it is Flanders and Wallonia (the French-speaking Belgian region) that share basically the same culture, one that resembles French culture more than Dutch. The culture gap between the Netherlands and Flanders is somewhat smaller than that between the Netherlands and Wallonia, the French-speaking part of Belgium, but it is still very wide. In fact, no two countries with a common border and a common language are so far apart culturally. Holland scores low on power distance, masculinity, and uncertainty avoidance. Belgium scores high on the same three dimensions. This difference became apparent when Dutch and Flemish television commercials were tested among Flemish and Dutch young men and women via in-depth interviews. The types of humor distinguished were (a) uncomplicated, explicit humor, including jokes, anecdotes, and slapstick; (b) linguistic humor, including puns and word games; and (c) complicated humor, including satire, irony, parody, understatements, and absurdism. Findings were that explicit jokes were liked better in Belgium than in the Netherlands, which can be explained by high uncertainty avoidance. Linguistic humor appeared to be liked less by the Flemish than by the Dutch. In particular, the anecdote type seemed to be culturally sensitive, because it relies on context. A typical slapstick commercial appeared to be liked better by the Belgians than by the Dutch. Slapstick usually is at the cost of one of the parties, which is more fitting in masculine cultures than in feminine cultures. In this particular case, one slapstick commercial involved throwing food, which is a no-go item in Dutch culture. Wasting food is "not done" in the thrifty Dutch culture. Absurdism, parody, and satire, particularly commercials that do not take experts seriously, were not appreciated by the Flemish but were appreciated by the Dutch.

Conclusion

Within each culture, there are opposing, seemingly paradoxical, values. The contrast is between the desirable and the desired values of each culture. Those who do not understand the cultural value paradoxes may be tempted to think that the world's values are converging, which is not the case. Each culture has its value paradoxes, and they are different from the value paradoxes of other cultures. They can be understood through the five dimensions.

A culture's opposing values appear to be important for advertising because they are recognized as the most meaningful elements of a culture. Both the desirable and the desired values are used for developing meaningful appeals in advertising. Particularly, the value paradoxes of culture appear to be able to trigger people's feelings.

Sometimes a desired value of one culture may seem to be similar to a desirable value of another culture. An example is independence, a desirable American value, a desired Japanese value. Yet there is a world of difference behind the same word. It is not a single concept.

Showing people alone in advertising in collectivistic cultures implies that they have no friends. It may go deeper than that: It may mean they have no identity because their identity would be in the group. As more than 70% of the world's population is more or less collectivistic, advertisers would be wise to show more people in their advertisements. It doesn't hurt the members of individualistic cultures to see more people in advertising, but it is negative to show solitary people in collectivistic cultures.

Because of the domination of American advertising, there is much more hype in international advertising than members of less masculine cultures appreciate. Taking into account that a large number of cultures of the European continent are more or less feminine, international advertisers focusing on Europe might consider using less hype or competitive advertising.

Finally, understanding the values of culture helps explain why humor doesn't travel: Humor uses the conventions of culture that cannot be understood by those who do not share the culture.

Notes

1. Wells, W., Burnett, J., & Moriarty, S. (1992). *Advertising: Principles and practice* (2nd ed.). Englewood Cliffs, NJ: Prentice Hall, p. 249.

2. Hofstede, G. (1991). *Cultures and organizations: Software of the mind.* New York: McGraw-Hill, p. 9.

3. Hofstede, G. (2001). *Culture's consequences* (2nd ed.). Thousand Oaks, CA: Sage, pp. 6–7.

4. Inequality: For richer, for poorer. (1994, November 5). *Economist,* 19.

5. Maleville, M. (1993). How boringly respectable can you get? A study of business slogans in three countries. *Toegepaste Taalwetenschap, 2.*

6. Han, S.-P., & Shavitt, S. (1994). Persuasion and culture: Advertising appeals in individualistic and collectivistic societies. *Journal of Experimental Social Psychology, 30,* 326–350; Zhang, Y., & Gelb, B. D. (1996). Matching advertising appeals to culture: The influence of products' use condition. *Journal of Advertising, 25,* 29–46.

7. Bowman, J. (2002). Commercials rise in the East. *M&M Europe: Pocket Guide on Asian TV.* London: Emap Media, p. 8.

8. Mitchell, R., & Oneal, M. (1994, September 12). Managing by values. *BusinessWeek,* 38–43.

9.   These surveys are conducted each year. Data are available for 2001, 2002, and 2003 (www.rdtrustedbrands.com) (see Appendix B).

10.   Praet, C. L. C. (2001). Japanese advertising, the world's number one celebrity showcase? A cross-cultural comparison of the frequency of celebrity appearances in TV advertising. In M. Roberts & R. L. King (Eds.), *Proceedings of the 2001 Special Asia-Pacific Conference of the American Academy of Advertising* (pp. 6–13). Kisarazu, Japan.

11.   Land of the big. (1996, December 21). *Economist*, 68.

12.   Van den Bergh, H. (1996, November 14). Lachen als bevrediging. *NRC Handelsblad*, 33.

13.   Bik, J. M. (1996, November 14). Variant op ernst. *NRC Handelsblad*, 35.

14.   Camps, H. (1996, November 14). Ondertoon van schuld. *NRC Handelsblad*, 35.

15.   Hillebrand, K. (1992). *Erfolgsvoraussetzungen und Erscheinungsformen des Humors in der Werbung—Dargestellt am Beispiel von Low-Involvement-Produkten* [Effect hypotheses and manifestations of humor in advertising: Described for low involvement products]. Prüfungsamt für wirtschaftswissenschaftliche Prüfungen der Westfälischen Wilhelms-Universität Münster. Unpublished.

16.   Merz, G. (1989). *Humor in der Werbung* [Humor in advertising]. Freie Wissentschaftliche Arbeit zur Erlangung des akademischen Grades Diplomkaufmann und der Wirtschaftsend Sozialwissenschaftlichen Fakultät der Friedrich-Alexander-Universität Erlangen-Nürnberg, Nürnberg. Unpublished.

17.   Weinberger, M. C., & Spotts, H. E. (1989). Humor in U.S. versus U.K. TV commercials: A comparison. *Journal of Advertising, 18,* 39–44.

18.   Alden, D. L., Hoyer, W. D., & Lee, C. (1993). Identifying global and culture-specific dimensions of humor in advertising: A multinational analysis. *Journal of Marketing, 57,* 64–75.

19.   Scheijgrond, L., & Volker, J. (1995). *Zo dichtbij, maar toch ver weg* [So close yet so far away]. Unpublished study for the Hogeschool Eindhoven, studierichting Communicatie.

NINE

Executional Style and Culture

Executional styles or basic forms used in advertising represent contexts for the advertising message.[1] A number of basic advertising forms that are used in different variations can be distinguished. Major international advertisers have used a single form indiscriminately across cultures. An example is the testimonial form used worldwide by Procter & Gamble. That does not mean that these formats are a first choice of all cultures. The "comparison" form, for example, is controversial. Certain forms have proved to be effective in one culture but not in others, like entertainment, which is effective in Japan but not in the United States. For international advertising, it is necessary to determine which basic forms are universal and which are not. There is little knowledge of the relative effectiveness of forms of one culture in others. The purpose of this chapter is to review basic advertising forms—how they reflect culture and serve different advertising purposes. Classifications of advertising forms are reviewed and one will be described comprehensively.

Classifications of Advertising Forms

For the purpose of comparing advertising across cultures, all sorts of classification systems have been developed. Some are very comprehensive, covering all aspects of advertising style; others cover only a few aspects. This section reviews the systems that tend to be used for classifying the various aspects of a print advertisement or a television commercial.

Classifications found in literature tend to mix two elements of advertising: strategy (level of communication) and form. The most used classification of advertising, *message strategy,* is based on the distinction *informational-transformational.*[2]

Moriarty[3] mentions it as two main message strategies. Informational advertising covers explicit messages; transformational advertising covers images. German professor Kroeber-Riel[4] uses the terms *functional* and *emotional*. Another term used for the same classification is *soft sell* versus *hard sell* as used by, for example, Mueller[5] to distinguish comparative advertising from mood or atmosphere. Yet another similar distinction is between *product information* and *product image,* which includes symbolic information.[6] This type of classification originates in the United States, where the dichotomy information-emotion is pronounced, as described in Chapter 7.

The most basic categorization of advertising forms is by Wells, Burnett, and Moriarty,[7] who distinguish between drama and lecture. According to Wells and colleagues, *drama* is a form of indirect address, like a movie or a play, because in a drama the characters speak to each other, not to the audience. A *lecture* is a form of direct address; the speaker addresses the audience from the television screen or the written page. In a lecture, the speaker presents evidence (data) and employs techniques such as arguments to persuade the audience.

Several other authors have distinguished basic forms such as slice of life; little story around the product; testimonial (from experts, stars, or "average" people); talking heads; characters associated with the product; demonstration; product in action; cartoon; lifestyle (connection between product, person, and usage); personalization (people talking about the product); product image (symbolic information on product and context); description (what the brand looks like); comparative (naming competitors); association (lifestyle or situation); and symbolic (metaphor, story telling and aesthetics).[8] These classifications cover most of American advertising forms.

French advertising professionals have provided a classification of descriptors:[9] *la Séduction* or temptation (French advertising tempts the consumer with its offering); *le Spectacle* (French advertising is theater, drama, show); *l'Amour* or romance (erotics, desire, display of affection); and *l'Humour* (amusing associations, playful use of words, humor). This classification reflects a totally different advertising style than the classifications developed by American researchers.

The most comprehensive classification of advertising forms is by Moriarty,[10] who lists 14 types of commonly used execution forms in the United States: (a) news announcement; (b) problem solution; (c) product as hero; (d) demonstration; (e) torture test; (f) song-and-dance spectacular; (g) special effect; (h) before-and-after and side-by-side comparison; (i) competitive comparison; (j) announcer; (k) dialogue/interview/conversation; (l) slice of life; (m) spokesperson; and (n) vignette. Six of these seem to cover most of U.S. advertising forms: comparative advertising, announcer, dialogue/conversation, slice-of-life, testimonials, and vignettes.

Seven Basic Advertising Forms Worldwide

The classification system for comparing advertising forms across cultures that is presented in this chapter is an adaptation of a classification model by Franzen,[11] who used this model to analyze the characteristics of advertising that influence effectiveness and found that a limited number of basic forms and executions accounted for differences in effectiveness. Franzen's categorization of eight forms was based on literature and a lifelong advertising experience in Europe. It was tested by content

Table 9.1   Seven Basic Advertising Forms

Basic Form	Subcategories	
1. Announcement	1.1	Pure display
	1.2	Product message
	1.3	Corporate presentation, documentary
2. Association transfer	2.1	Lifestyle
	2.2	Metaphor
	2.3	Metonymy
	2.4	Celebrity transfer
3. Lesson	3.1	Presenter
	3.2	Testimonial/endorsement
	3.3	Demonstration
	3.4	Comparison
	3.5	"How to"
4. Drama	4.1	Slice of life
	4.2	Problem-solution
	4.3	Vignettes
	4.4	Theatre
5. Entertainment	5.1	Humor
	5.2	Play or act around product
6. Imagination	6.1	Cartoons
	6.2	Film properties in action
	6.3	Other, unrealistic acts
7. Special effects	7.1	Product in action, animation
	7.2	Film, video techniques, artistic stimuli

analysis of Dutch advertising using a comprehensive code list of 112 variables and by statistical analysis. My adaptation is based on analysis of television commercials of more than 11 different cultures. The model consists of seven[12] groups and a number of subgroups. The seven main groups are announcement, association transfer, lesson, drama, pure entertainment, imagination, and special effects.

Analysis of advertising across cultures demonstrates that Franzen's basic forms exist in all cultures, although the distribution and the way they are executed vary. An adapted version of Franzen's model is presented in this section (see Table 9.1). Each basic form is described and related to culture. There are seven groups, and each group has subdivisions. The basic forms are not mutually exclusive, so a commercial or print advertisement may represent more than one main form or subcategory. The forms can be recognized in layers: There may be a dominant form, but the underlying tone of the advertisement may represent another form. Some combinations are found more often than others.

1. Announcement

Announcements are presentations of facts with no use of people. The facts or visuals are assumed to speak for themselves. This is the most basic type of advertisement: the product and information about the product.

Illustration 9.1 Clinique, International

1.1 Pure display. Pure displays include all forms that are based primarily on a product's appearance, rather like a product in a shop window or showroom. The product is the hero. This is a relatively culture-free form and may be useful for international advertising. It is found in advertising for fashion items, jewelry, and perfume. An example is an international advertisement for Clinique (Illustration 9.1)

1.2 Product message. This form is based on presentation of product attributes. It can include visual presentation or explanation of facts about the product or brand. It is found most often in low-context cultures because factual, logical explanation is a characteristic of individualistic, low-context cultures. This form is typical for new products or services, cameras, business-to-business products, printers, copiers, computers, and innovations. Messages can be about ingredients or availability of the product, news about products and services, discounts, sales, locations, films, and more. Examples of this form are also found in retail advertising. When used internationally, translations (voice-over and text) of instructional text are used.

An example is an international TV commercial for Dremel (the German version) illustrated by three TV images (Illustration 9.2).

1.3 Corporate presentation. This is the typical form used for corporate advertising. It can be compared with a documentary and concerns the presentation of the company and its products or services verbally and visually, sometimes including people in relation to the company or product to illustrate its activities. In an international commercial, people from all parts of the world may be shown. The visuals, products, or people should be of interest to the company's stakeholders. The company's message may be presented in a voice-over or a song. This is a form that can easily be internationalized by translating the voice-over, which can present facts. The amount of facts used is culture-bound: more in low-context cultures and less in high-context cultures. The style used for corporate presentation tends to be related to the culture of the company. Thus, American corporate advertising will be more direct and personalized and include facts, whereas Asian corporate advertising will be more indirect and include Asian values. This is recognized in corporate advertising by Asian companies, for example by Korean LG, of which we showed examples in

Illustration 9.2 Dremel, Germany

Illustration 9.3   Shell, International

Illustration 9.4   Vinci, France

Chapters 3 (Illustration 3.6) and 8 (Illustration 8.43), visuals that were also used in corporate TV advertising by LG. Different styles are illustrated by images of an international TV commercial for Shell (Illustration 9.3) and for the French construction company Vinci (Illustration 9.4). The Shell commercial shows a young female Shell employee who studies the environmental effects of oil drilling. The French commercial for Vinci demonstrates the Vinci products in an indirect way, reflecting the art orientation of the French. The viewer is led into the famous Mona Lisa painting. The camera zooms into details of the picture where the viewer sees bridges and roads. The commercial ends with a person using his mobile phone while watching a picture of the Mona Lisa.

2. Association Transfer

In association transfers, the product is combined with another object, a person or situation, or an environment. Associations with the objects or persons are meant to be transferred to the brand. Subforms include lifestyle, metaphor, metonymy, and celebrity transfer.

2.1 Lifestyle. The lifestyle concept is meant to transfer an association with people (young, successful, etc.). The type of lifestyle is culture-bound. Masculine cultures prefer to associate with the successful, the rich; feminine cultures will want to associate with nice, friendly people. High power distance culture will associate with people who have the right social status. As people are often depicted interacting with other people, the execution of the form is culture-bound. The type of lifestyle depicted will vary by product category. Illustration 9.5 shows images of a Spanish commercial for Tio Pepe, which reflects high society. Illustration 9.6 shows images of an international commercial for McDonald's, showing "young lifestyle." Illustration 9.7 shows images of a commercial for the German Beck's beer, the sporty lifestyle of young, 20+ people.

Illustration 9.5   Tio Pepe, Spain

Illustration 9.6   McDonald's, International

Illustration 9.7   Beck's, Germany

2.2 Metaphor. A metaphor can be used to transfer the characteristics of an object or an animal (concrete) or an idea (abstract) to the brand by drawing a parallel. Metaphors are used in advertising for all product categories. They can be verbal or visual, concrete or abstract. Visual mctaphors are used more in high-context cultures, verbal metaphors more in low-context cultures. Illustration 9.8 shows a Spanish advertisement for the Peugeot 206 using the horns of the bull to symbolize safety.

2.3 Metonymy. Metonymy transfers the meaning of the original object to the brand, for example a flower turning into a perfume, a piece of fruit turning into syrup, or a strawberry turning into jam. Because it is an indirect and visual way of explaining, it will be more appealing to high-context than low-context cultures. In a Spanish TV commercial for the railway Renfe, the zipper of the girl's dress turns into a railway track (Illustration 9.9)

Illustration 9.8   Peugeot, Spain

Illustration 9.9   Renfe, Spain

2.4 Celebrity transfer. This subform covers advertising in which a celebrity is shown or in which a celebrity acts with other persons without demonstrating, endorsing, or giving a testimonial. The only objective of showing the celebrity is for the target group to associate the product with the celebrity. Examples are showing Michael Jordan with Nike or Gatorade or showing an elegant actress who puts on a fashionable watch and engages happily in a party. The image of the sports star is transferred to the sports shoes or the sports drink; the image of the actress, or "elegance," is transferred to the watch. An actress playing the role of a housewife and referring to a refrigerator is viewed as an endorsement, not as pure association, because there is no transfer of "elegance" to a fridge. If in a commercial for Martini in Italy the model Naomi Campbell appears at the end and says no more than "Martini, it's a party," it is an association with a celebrity or celebrity transfer rather than an endorsement by a celebrity. In a collectivistic and masculine culture such as Japan, segments or age-groups have their own stars. The many famous people who appear in commercials usually support the brand indirectly so that people can associate with the stars. They may say only a few words, such as "tastes good." Many so-called *tarento* are professional models who became famous by first appearing in commercials

Illustration 9.10   Norit, Spain

Illustration 9.11   Epson, Japan

and then, on the basis of popularity attained through these commercials, started their own singing and/or acting careers.[13] Individualistic, low-context cultures need more facts and thus will use more endorsements than association transfers, which are a more indirect form fit for collectivistic cultures. Illustration 9.10 shows the Spanish actress Judit Mascó, who is pregnant and looks at the baby clothes of her first child that still look like new because she washed them with Norit. Illustration 9.11 shows images of a Japanese TV commercial for Epson color printers. People in the office discuss the need for color printing and the cost. At the end, a famous actor (Tamura) just says "Epson."

3. Lesson

Lessons are direct communications—presentations of facts and arguments—meant to lecture the audience. They state, explain, show, or try to convince or persuade. There may be presenters or voice-overs telling or explaining something to the audience, demonstrating, or comparing, often with the help of visuals. The audience is addressed in the "we-style" or the "you-style," and imperatives can be used. Examples from the United States are "Meet the all-new Ford 150," "Take control with Nicotrol," "The only good wrinkle is the wrinkle you never get" (Oil of Olay), "Any time you need us, anywhere you need us" (Wells Fargo), "You are over 50 and have not lost your edge . . ." (Centrum Silver nutritional supplements).

There is little or no interaction or dialogue. The lesson form is typical of low-context cultures, and it particularly fits the American preoccupation with facts. Wells, Burnett, and Moriarty[14] state that it is the dominant commercial message form (in the United States). Advantages of the lecture form are that it costs little to produce and is compact and efficient. A lecture can deliver a dozen selling points in seconds, if need be. There are several variations.

3.1 Presenter. Presenters are persons with a dominant presence speaking into the camera and conveying the main message. They can give a demonstration, make a comment only, interview or be interviewed with or without the interviewer being shown. The role of the presenter and the way he or she behaves will vary by culture. In high power distance cultures, presenters will be older or have certain status. A single dominant presenter is characteristic of individualistic cultures. More than one presenter will be used in collectivistic cultures. In cultures scoring high on masculinity, the presenter will be a "personality" or play a dominant role. In cultures of the configuration masculinity-individualism, presenters use a persuasive style that is perceived as "pushy" and irritating by members of feminine cultures. Feminine cultures do not like dominant people, so the presenter and the approach will be more soft-spoken. Presenters in cultures of strong uncertainty avoidance must convey competence related to the product or service. In low uncertainty avoidance cultures, presenter's expertise will be understated because people don't like experts.

Illustration 9.12 shows images from a TV commercial for Ariel in Ukraine. At the time, not all people were used to modern washing machines and detergent. The presenter shows the product and compares it with old-fashioned hand soap. A laboratory situation is added to add credibility. Illustration 9.13 shows images of a Spanish commercial for Leche Asturiana (milk). Two experts (a beekeeper and a cattle farmer) are discussing the quality of the ingredients. Illustration 9.14 shows images of a Dutch TV commercial for milk. The presenter treats the cow as a dog. In the final shot, the cow wants to bury the bone. The only message is that milk contains calcium, which is good for your bones.

3.2 Endorsement and testimonial. In this subform, a presenter or spokesperson suggests that he or she is a user of the product (testimonial) or has an opinion about it and therefore endorses the product (endorsement). Pure user testimonials are

Illustration 9.12   Ariel, Ukraine

Illustration 9.13 Leche Asturiana, Spain

Illustration 9.14 Melkunie, Netherlands

used in low-context cultures and particularly by American companies. Procter & Gamble has used this form worldwide for a number of brands in the category of disposable products (diapers, sanitary napkins/towels). Unilever has used the form successfully for the international introduction of Dove. In several countries, local users testified about the effectiveness of soap and deodorant. Illustration 9.15 shows images of such testimonials. People have tried the product for 7 days and testify about the effects. Dutch Linda Schelvis-Bijl testifies and so does Italian Dariella Camuniti. Other examples are for Dove deodorant. Polish Sylwia Broda tells how effective it is, raising her arms to demonstrate her shirt is clean, and so does Iratxe Martín from the Spanish Basque area.

Endorsements include celebrities or experts who, because of their role in society or expertise, are supposed to have an opinion, are credible, can convince. Credibility is an important element for cultures occupied with seeking the truth where testimonials must be credible. The celebrity must actually use the product. Football shoes, for example, should be endorsed by a football player. Models must use the shampoo they endorse. Credibility is less of a requirement for Asian cultures.

The French company L'Oréal uses celebrity endorsement for selling their shampoos and facial care products. All sorts of international film and TV celebrities endorse the various shampoo brands. The universal payoff used is "because I am worth it," which is subtitled or used in voice-over, depending on what various countries are used to. Illustration 9.16 shows examples from the United States, Germany, and the Netherlands.

Illustration 9.15 Dove soap, Netherlands and Italy; Dove deodorant, Poland and Spain

Illustration 9.16 L'Oréal, USA, Germany, Netherlands

For low-context cultures, another effective type of testimonial is the expert testimonial, for example, used in comarketing communications by Procter & Gamble. Two examples are in Illustration 9.17. Horst Kett of Bosch (washing machines) endorses Ariel Futur in Germany, and Stewart Nowell of Puma endorses Ariel Futur in the United Kingdom, demonstrating that the product doesn't damage the Puma sports shirts.

The testimonial form is used in various cultures, but the roles of the presenters in both endorsements and testimonials vary. In masculine cultures, presenters tend to be high profile—celebrities, stars, or known people. If ordinary people give testimonials, they are identified, their name is mentioned, and sometimes their signature is added. In feminine cultures, they like to be anonymous. In a high-context society like Japan, things are said indirectly and implicitly, for example, "They say it is good" (instead of saying, "It is good for you"), without the explicit argumentation and product merit found in U.S. testimonials. A typical Japanese testimonial, therefore, is an implicit recommendation by a familiar talent.

Western cultures combining masculinity and strong uncertainty avoidance use high-profile presenters who are also experts: competent experts who must provide

Illustration 9.17   Ariel Germany with Bosch and United Kingdom with Puma

credibility. This is the type found in countries like Germany and Italy. Feminine cultures don't take their heroes seriously or else downplay their importance. The presenter is preferably anonymous; person and message are low profile. Big egos are not appreciated. A testimonial by a celebrity, if given at all, should be credible. For example, may use well-known people, but these do not present themselves in a serious way, resulting in a parody on the testimonial. The roles of presenters can be summarized according to four culture clusters, as illustrated in Figure 9.1.

3.3 Demonstration. The advertisement shows how (well) the product works. Product attributes and benefits may be shown or the situation before and after use. A presenter may demonstrate how the product works. the amount of information, details, and instruction will vary with the degree of uncertainty avoidance. Strong

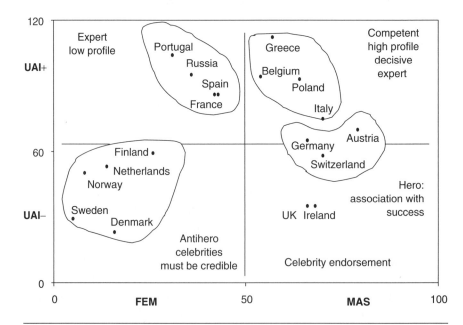

Figure 9.1   Roles of Presenters

SOURCE: Data from Hofstede (2001) (see Appendix A)

Illustration 9.18   Listerine, Spain

uncertainty avoidance cultures will need more detailed information than weak uncertaintly avoidance cultures. Focus can be on the attributes and benefits of the product—before and after using the product—and testing. An example is an international TV commercial for Listerine, shown in Spain. The presenter is walking on human teeth and tells how the product works. Pictures show how Listerine removes the bacteria in the mouth. It is the direct approach of a low-context culture but used in a high-context culture (Illustration 9.18).

3.4 Comparison. Four types of comparative advertising can be distinguished:

- Competitive comparison: the brand is compared with another, identified brand
- The brand is compared with an unidentified product, not named, called "Brand X," "the other brand leader," or a "conventional" product, often presented in the form of side-by-side comparison, or the brand is said to be better than "other products in the category"
- "The best" or "the best in the world"

Examples of competitive comparison are Electrasol (U.S.) and Halifax (U.K.) (Illustrations 9.19 and 9.20). The TV commercial for Electrasol Powerball shows how the product works, then a package of the competitive brand, Cascade, and a hand that covers the Cascade package with an Electrasol package. The Halifax commercial shows a singing bank employee who shows boards with the interest rates of Halifax and competing banks. An example of a brand compared with an unidentified competitive brand is Illustration 9.21, which shows images of a TV commercial for

Illustration 9.19   Electrasol, US

Illustration 9.20   Halifax, UK

Illustration 9.21   Persil, Germany

the German detergent brand Persil. Two sisters meet, and one gets a dress of one of the children of her sister, who has washed the dress in Persil. The good quality is compared with clothes that are washed with another, not named detergent. Examples of "the best" were given in Chapter 8, under masculinity.

The appreciation of comparative advertising is culture-bound. It is a typical form of the United States. It fits best in cultures of the configuration individualism-masculinity and weak to medium uncertainty avoidance. It is not appreciated in most other cultures. Acceptance and nonacceptance can best be explained by the varying configurations of individualism-collectivism and masculinity. Figure 9.2 shows four culture clusters. In three of them, the form is not acceptable.

The lower left quadrant shows the combination collectivism-femininity, with Portugal and Spain. Feminine Asian and Latin American cultures would also fit in this quadrant. This is no-go area for competitive comparative advertising. In collectivistic cultures, comparison with the competition is not acceptable because it makes the other party lose face. It will backfire: You are the one who loses face, as it is not proper. More than two thirds of the world population is more or less collectivistic, which may explain the relatively low use of comparative advertising. It is not perceived as an attractive form in feminine cultures either because it is considered too aggressive. Also, modesty makes people feel that it is not proper to demonstrate how good you are.

The upper left quadrant shows the combination collectivism-masculinity. Masculine cultures, characterized by their interest in winning and fighting, are basically in favor of competitive comparative advertising. Although these cultures may want to express the fact that they are good, the combination with collectivism makes avoiding loss of face for others overriding. If comparison is used, the comparison is with another product of the same company to show, for example, that an innovative new product is better than

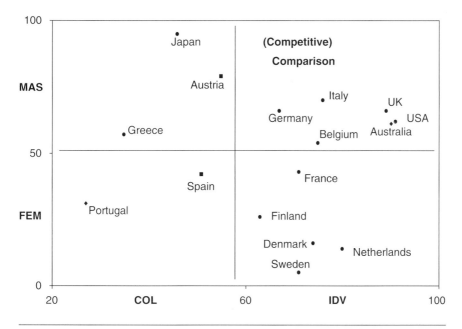

Figure 9.2   Comparative Advertising

SOURCE: Data from Hofstede (2001) (see Appendix A)

an old product from that company. Japan is the typical example of such a culture, but a number of Latin American cultures are also in this cluster.

The lower right quadrant shows cultures of the configuration individualistic-feminine. This is the Scandinavian-Dutch cluster. Feminine cultures, because of affiliation needs, are more in favor of the soft approach. They do not like the confrontation included in direct comparison. Being the best is OK, but saying so is not: "Probably the best beer in the world" (Carlsberg, Denmark).

The upper right quadrant shows the combination masculinity-individualism. In cultures of this combination, people tend to focus on their rights. As a result, Anglo-Saxon cultures, and in particular U.S. culture, tend to see comparative advertising as informational, offering the consumer "the right to choose." Only the Anglo-Saxon cultures like the hard confrontation as represented by the "cola wars." Germany, Austria, and Switzerland may also like it but are inhibited by their strong uncertainty avoidance, which makes it difficult to cope with the related ambiguities—such as having to prove the correctness of the claim. Various types of competitive comparison are used in the United States. Examples include side-by-side comparisons, demonstrations with competitor's name mentioned, or pictures of packages of competitors' brands with a cross through them.

3.5 "How to" Use of the product and the result achieved are explained or demonstrated. All recipe advertising is covered by this form. Another example is demonstrating how to use technical products. This basic form can be used internationally, but differences in design (kitchens, living rooms), how people look, and the like, must be taken into account. Illustration 9.22 gives an example of how to use the Moulinex mixer in a Spanish commercial.

Illustration 9.22   Moulinex, Spain

4. Drama

Drama entails the interplay between two or more people. There is a continuity of action, a beginning, middle, and "happy ending." The performers deliver the message. Although drama is intended to convey a product message, it is a more indirect form than lesson. It originated in the United States and was blown across the ocean with the soap operas. Small stories and plots are included; people experience things, interact and react to situations, and relate to each other. Unlike in the lesson forms, viewers are not addressed directly; they are observers. They are assumed to watch how other people interact and to draw their own conclusions. Subforms are slice of life, problem-solution, and vignettes. The indirectness of the form makes it useful for high-context cultures, yet we should keep in mind that the form is based on the typical "solution" or "happy ending" orientation of the United States.

4.1 Slice of life. Slice-of-life advertisements have dramatized dialogue dealing with everyday events and "true-to-life" situations. The product is pivotal to the story. There is usually an emotional reward for using the product. A slice of life from one culture cannot be implanted in another culture without adaptation. The adaptation will concern not only how people look but also how they relate to each other. For example, in Italy, France, and Spain the elder will advise the younger whereas in the Netherlands, Germany, the United Kingdom, and Scandinavia the younger person will advise the elder. Related to this is the choice of depicting people alone or in groups—a family consisting only of parents and two children or an extended family showing older and younger people including grandparents. Another important choice is whether to show people inside or outside the home. In southern Europe, the social context of many products is outside the home, whereas in northern Europe the social context is inside the home.

There also are differences in how products deliver emotional rewards to consumers. A first distinction is between two types of emotional reward: task orientation or relationship orientation. Individualistic cultures are task oriented; collectivistic cultures are relationship oriented. A second distinction is between ego needs and affiliation needs. Masculine societies are characterized by ego needs, whereas feminine societies are characterized by affiliation needs. These characteristics can be recognized in commercials. The role of the housewife in German commercials is task and ego oriented. The results shown can be lots of dirty clothes

Illustration 9.23   Bounty, Germany

and then lots of clean, white clothes. In feminine cultures, the emotional reward will be the relationship between mother and children.

An example of slice of life is a German TV commercial for the disposable kitchen towel Bounty. At a barbecue party, all sorts of people are shown who need to wipe something (Illustration 9.23).

4.2 Problem-solution. This is an easily recognized advertising form in Western society. It is related to cause-effect thinking. The problem is dirt—the detergent cleans. The problem is dandruff—the solution is Head & Shoulders. Not all problems are viewed as such. Dandruff, for example, is not viewed as equally problematic in all countries.

The form is most used for detergents. An example is a TV commercial for Clorox (Illustration 9.24). A boy catches a frog in a brook, wipes his hands on his shirt. The best detergent is Clorox (in comparison with a regular one). The shirt is clean—mother and son look happily at the frog. Another example is a Polish TV commercial for the antidandruff shampoo Denorex (Illustration 9.25). A boy points at dandruff on his father's shoulder. A scientist in a laboratory gives evidence of the effectiveness of Denorex, including a detailed picture of how it works on the hair. The happy ending is the boy who touches his father's hair and there is no dandruff. The variations in these examples are comparison in the U.S. Clorox commercial and scientific evidence in the Denorex commercial in Poland, a country that scores high on uncertainty avoidance.

4.3 Vignettes. Vignettes are a series of independent sketches or visual situations with no continuity in the action. The product plays a part in each vignette. Vignettes are characterized by interaction between people. There may not always be a dialogue but instead a voice-over or song suggesting the relationship between the product and visualized activities. An example is a German TV commercial for Merci chocolates,

Illustration 9.24   Clorox, USA

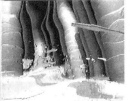

Illustration 9.25   Denorex, Poland

Illustration 9.26   Merci, Germany

which shows vignettes of a girl preparing a present for Mother's Day and all sorts of happy people (Illustration 9.26).

4.4 Theater. This subform is a story that is *not* "true-to-life" acted as in a theater. People might interact in an exaggerated way or there might be an unusual story around the product, as in the subform entertainment (5.2), as for example in illustration 9.27. Interaction takes place as part of a show, sketch, or play. This form is relatively frequently found in France and Italy.

5. Entertainment

A characteristic of entertainment is that it is an indirect form of communication. Entertainment can be in the form of theatrical drama, musicals, shows, comedies, slapstick, humor, horror, or satire. It is meant to please the audience rather than to sell. The form outshines the content of the advertising. Pure entertainment does not fit in the persuasive communication model. It is, however, a typical form for Japan and other collectivistic cultures where it is effective because it builds relationships and trust between consumers and companies. According to the Japanese advertising agency Dentsu, Japanese people don't want to be lectured, they want to be entertained.

What makes advertising entertaining can be judged only by the people of the culture in which it is meant to entertain. Entertainment is also relative: In countries where advertising generally uses much direct selling, even the slightest deviation from the direct address may be perceived as entertaining. Much of Japanese advertising may be perceived by the Japanese as a clear message to the consumer whereas to Western eyes it may seem to be purely entertaining. To low-context cultures, all high-context advertising may seem to be meant to entertain. Subforms are humor and plays or acts about the product, which includes a theatrical form of drama.

5.1 Humor. Humor is anything that makes an audience laugh. There are various types of humor, which were described in Chapter 8 under Why Humor Doesn't Travel. Humor doesn't travel because humor reflects culture: One often laughs about the most characteristic aspects of one's own culture. The type of humor that is said to travel is incongruity, the unexpected thing happening. Humor in advertising is most often encountered in cultures of weak uncertainty avoidance. England, Denmark, Norway, the Netherlands, South Africa, and Australia have produced award-winning humorous television commercials.

5.2 Play or act around the product. All nonhumorous entertaining commercials fit this subform. An example is an Italian TV commercial for Lavazza coffee (Illustration 9.27). In a surreal world in the clouds with flying horses (Pegasus), people are drinking coffee and discussing an accident with the Pegasus. In the end, two men have to apologize to the Pegasus. A Japanese award-winning TV commercial for Nissin Cup Noodle (Illustration 9.28) shows Stone Age people throwing rocks at a dinosaur. There is no relationship with the product. It only says: "Hungry? Cup Noodle."

Illustration 9.27   Lavazza, Italy

Illustration 9.28   Cup Noodle, Japan

Illustration 9.29   Bamseline, Denmark; Coccolino, Italy; Cajoline, Greece; Kuschelweich, Germany

6. Imagination

The imagination format covers cartoons or film and video techniques that depict events experienced as nonrealistic—presentations of a make-believe world. The form is often used for children's products or to avoid a too literal interpretation when conveying messages for sensitive products such as sanitary products. An international application is the promotion of film properties such as characters in Disney films. These can cross borders. Subforms include cartoons, film properties in action, or other unrealistic acts. Film properties are also used to convey associations with product attributes, like softness for fabric softeners. Examples of film properties are the monkeys used for OMO in France and the little men used for the household cleaning brand Cif. A fabric softener that carries different brand names in different countries uses a teddy bear to convey softness. The illustration shows images of TV commercials with the bear in four different countries in Europe: Bamseline in Denmark, Coccolino in Italy, Cajoline in Greece, and Kuschelweich in Germany (Illustration 9.29). The bear is the unifying international factor.

7. Special Effects

Illustration 9.30   M&Ms, Poland

The special effects format covers all sorts of artistic elements, animation, cartoons, camera effects, recording and video techniques, music, and tunes. Modern techniques offer a new range of artistic resources for developing creative advertising that can be adapted to the stimuli of particular target groups. This is a popular form for advertising on channels for the young, like MTV. The use of artistic stimuli is found more in some cultures than in others (e.g., more in art-oriented Spain than in Germany). Showing the "product in action" through animation is a visual that can cross borders, provided there is no value included. Illustration 9.30 shows an example of a product in action, two images of a TV commercial for M&Ms. Recent technology makes it possible to produce pieces of art, based mainly on video techniques that can be viewed as pure entertainment. This style appeals to the art-oriented cultures of southern Europe.

Relationships Among Basic Form, Culture, and Product Category

A few observations can be made with respect to the relationship, among basic forms, product category, and culture. Although the use of some basic forms seems to be related to specific product categories, an observation is that basic forms are more related to the market leader's culture than to the product category. The problem-solution form has been a basic form used for detergents in many countries. The likely cause is the fact that the leading company, American Procter & Gamble, has used this style for half a century. Henkel, the German detergent manufacturer, has followed the example and has used a similar form for much of its advertising for detergents and fabric softeners across European countries. Nestlé has its own style, as does Beiersdorf, the company selling the global brand Nivea. The French company L'Oréal has exploited the authority of film stars worldwide.

The basic form used in international advertising is decided by the culture of the advertiser but also by the international development phase of a company. New entrants into a market tend to present themselves by the product attributes. In 1996, a number of new Asian entrants into European markets (e.g., Daewoo and Hyundai) used a simple announcement style. More experience in foreign markets has led to a more sophisticated approach, although in many cases East Asian values are recognizable in their advertising. The styles of the country of origin of a company can be recognized in the approaches and basic forms used in their international advertising. P&G markets brands in a number of product categories from perfumes and cosmetics to detergents and sanitary napkins/towels. The basic forms used for their brands of different product categories have more in common with the culture of the company than with the culture of the audience or the product category. For several product categories, a few dominant multinationals like P&G, Unilever, and German Henkel have used the problem-solution form, testimonial, or side-by-side comparison. These are sanitary products (e.g., Always, Evax, Ausonia Seda, Carefree, Tampax), personal care and cosmetics (e.g., Max Factor, Oil of Ulay/Olay/Olaz, Dove), detergents and other cleaning products (e.g., Ariel, Dash, Vizir, Calgon, Dreft, Yes, Fairy, Fleuril, Sunil), diapers (e.g., Pampers, Liberos, Dototis), pet food (e.g., Whiskas, Pedigree Pal), and other brands such as Head & Shoulders, Clearasil, and American Express. Only slowly are advertising styles and forms being selected that fit the cultures of the target audiences of international companies.

Conclusion

Seven basic advertising forms can be distinguished that are used worldwide. Their distribution varies and appears to be related to culture. The lesson style is part of Anglo-German culture and exported to many other cultures where one might wonder if it is equally effective. Comparative advertising mainly fits individualistic-masculine, weak uncertainty avoidance cultures—only the Anglo-Saxon world. Pure entertainment will work better in collectivistic cultures than in individualistic cultures. Basic forms have become representative for product categories because companies from specific cultures have dominated the product category—they have become corporate forms. There are specific P&G, Unilever, and Henkel forms.

Although large multinationals like Procter & Gamble have been successful in using one basic form across cultures and adapting it to cultural differences in a meaningful way, they might be even more successful if they were to use the forms that fit the cultures where they want to sell their products or brands.

Notes

1. Laskey, H. A., Fox, R. J., & Crask, M. R. (1994, November/December). Investigating the impact of executional style on television commercial effectiveness. *Journal of Advertising Research,* 9–16.

2. Laskey, H. A. (1988). *Television commercial effectiveness as a function of main messages and commercial structure.* Unpublished doctoral dissertation, University of Georgia, Athens, GA. Cited in J. Ramaprasad & K. Hasegawa. (1992, January/February). Creative strategies in American and Japanese TV commercials: A comparison, *Journal of Advertising Research.* The classification was also used by Puto, C. P., & Wells, W. D. (1984). Informational and transformational advertising: The differential effects of time. *Advances in Consumer Research, 11,* 638–643.

3. Moriarty, S. E. (1991). *Creative advertising: Theory and practice* (2nd ed.). Englewood Cliffs, NJ: Prentice Hall, p. 82.

4. Kroeber-Riel, W. (1990). *Strategie und Technik der Werbung: Verhaltenswissenschäftliche Ansatze.* Kohlhammer, Edition Marketing, 2. Aflage. Stuttgart. Cited in U. Appelbaum & C. Halliburton. (1993). How to develop international advertising campaigns that work: The example of the European food and beverage sector. *International Journal of Advertising, 12,* 223–241.

5. Mueller, B. (1992, January/February). Standardization vs. specialization: An examination of Westernization in Japanese advertising. *Journal of Advertising Research,* 15–24.

6. Leiss, W., Kline, S., & Jhally, S. (1986). *Social communication in advertising.* London: Methuen.

7. Wells, W., Burnett, J., & Moriarty, S. (1992). *Advertising principles and practice,* pp. 398–400. Englewood Cliffs, NJ: Prentice Hall.

8. Appelbaum, U., & Halliburton, C. (1993). How to develop international advertising campaigns that work: The example of the European food and beverage sector. *International Journal of Advertising, 12,* 223–241; Katz, H., & Lee, W.-N. (1992). Oceans apart: An initial exploration of social communication differences in U.S. and U.K. prime-time television advertising. *International Journal of Advertising, 11,* 69–82; Cutler, B. D., & Javalgi, R. G.

(1992, January/February). A cross-cultural analysis of the visual components of print advertising: The United States and the European Community. *Journal of Advertising Research,* 71–80.

9.   Taylor, R. E., & Hoy, M. G. (1995). The presence of la séduction, le spectacle, l'amour and l'humour in French commercials. In S. Madden (Ed.), *Proceedings of the 1995 Conference of the American Academy of Advertising.* USA (http://advertising.utexas.edu/AAA/AAA95.html).

10.   Moriarty, 1991, 89–91.

11.   Franzen, G. (1994). *Advertising effectiveness.* Henley-on-Thames, Oxfordshire, UK: NTC Business Publications.

12.   In the first edition of this book, the original eight forms were presented with some additional subforms. In practice, when using the classification, the subform of Announcement/Pure presentation overlapped with Display, so I included the description of Display in Announcement, which changed the original eight forms into seven.

13.   Praet, C., Otaru University, Japan (personal communication, November 19, 2003).

14.   Wells, Burnett, & Moriarty, 1992, 398.

TEN

From Value Paradox to Strategy

Marieke de Mooij and Arne Maas

T he previous chapters have provided tools for understanding how culture influences consumer behavior, branding, and advertising. Marketing and advertising will only be successful if the values of consumers match the values of the product or brand, which means that strategies successful in one culture can be extended only to other cultures with similar relevant values. New strategies have to be developed for cultures with different values. Brand value means mindshare: the position the brand has in the mind of the consumer. To reach global mindshare, a brand must fit in the minds of consumers in different cultures. In global brand strategy, the choice is not between global and local but between ineffective global standardization and effective cultural segmentation strategy. We have learned that similar cultures can be clustered with respect to product-relevant values, needs, motives, and communication styles. This also applies to brand strategy.

A common perception is that a strategy can be global, but execution must be local. This is not correct. At the core of strategy is culture. Both mission statements and brand positioning statements appear to be culture-bound because they reflect the philosophy of a company's leaders. Any global corporate or brand strategy, to be effective, must incorporate not the values of its leaders but the values of all stakeholders—the shareholders of the company and consumers of the brand in all countries where the company operates. Already at the first levels of strategy development,

Authors' Note: Arne Maas, PhD, is president of Ameuse, his own consultancy and interim management firm, which cooperates with Cross Cultural Communications Company for strategic advice. Among his clients are Heineken, Royal Friesland Foods, KLM, and Philips. He has extensive international experience.

a company's mission and vision, culture is involved. This chapter sums up the various aspects of global strategy from a company's mission and vision to its communication strategy.

A Company's Mission and Vision

Worldwide, it is agreed that the *mission statement* is a crucial element in the strategic planning of a business organization. It is an explicit formulation of what the company stands for. In addition, the *vision* of a company states where the company wants to be sometime in the future. Some companies include *strategic intent* in the vision. Vision and mission should give focus to everyone who is involved with the company, be it directly (employees) or indirectly (e.g., shareholders).

The Western origin of the mission statement concept can be recognized in a definition by North American Christopher Bart:[1]

A good mission statement captures an organization's unique and enduring reason for being, and energizes stakeholders to pursue common goals. . . . It compels a firm to address questions like "What is our business? Why do we exist? What are we trying to accomplish?"

Next to the individualistic value of uniqueness, the statement reflects the practice of self-analysis of individualistic cultures.

Although the concept of the mission and vision are Western inventions, the practice has been embraced by companies worldwide. It has become global management practice to provide statements expressing a company's strategic intent, its philosophy, values and ethics, or operational effectiveness. This doesn't imply, however, that form and content are similar. The mission statement of American companies is an abstract statement of what the company stands for, its identity. In collectivistic, high-context cultures where companies function like families, what the company stands for is not necessarily made explicit, and if it is made explicit, it expresses the philosophy and vision of the company's leaders.

Any corporate mission or vision, in both form and content, reflects the worldview of its management, which usually represents the values of the culture of origin of the company.

The most famous examples of Japanese strategic intents were Canon's "Beat Xerox" and Komatsu's "Encircle Caterpillar."[2] Japan is a masculine and hence a competitive society; both companies pointed their arrows at one (bigger) competitor. An example of Asian *form* and *content* is formulating the company statement as a "Message from Top Management," as on Toyota's Web site. The subtitle of this message forms the content: "Harmony with people, Society and the Environment."[3]

The content of mission statements tends to include the typical values of the country of origin. American statements, for example, include hype, like American advertising does. Ford Motor Company[4] says, "We anticipate consumer need and deliver outstanding products." The U.S. company DDI[5] (Data Direction Inc.) states that it "will continue to staff the finest data processing professionals available, . . . use the highest standards . . . , use the best design and programming techniques . . . , attract and retain the best possible professionals." Microsoft's mission is "To enable people and business throughout the world to realize their full potential." This mission reflects the Anglo-Saxon value of self-actualization. The corporate philosophy of Canon is *kyosei,* or "All people, regardless of race, religion or culture, harmoniously living and working together into the future."[6] Korean Samsung's management philosophy is, "We will devote our human resources and technology to create superior products and services, thereby contributing to a better global society. . . . Our management philosophy represents our strong determination to contribute directly to the mutual prosperity of people all over the world. . . . We challenge the world to create the future with our customers."[7] Two elements of Toyota's *Vision 2010*—a real long-term perspective—is to realize a large increase in the number of Toyota fans and to be a truly global company that is trusted and respected by all peoples in the world.[8]

A global company that goes beyond universal statements and balances cultural values is Honda, who says,

> It is our mission to improve the lives of customers and communities where we all live, work and play. We will continue to develop and build products in local markets around the world to create value for all of our customers. Our established directions for the 21st century provide a balance of fun for the customer and responsibility for society and the environment. This is demonstrated through advanced technologies.[9]

Corporate Identity

From the vision and mission, a corporate identity can be distilled, which includes the core values of a company. This practice is also of Western origin. This is reflected in definitions of corporate identity that are based on the Western identity concept. The British communication consultant Nicholas Ind,[10] for example, defines *corporate identity* as "an organization's identity in its *sense of self,* much like our own individual sense of identity. Consequently, it is unique." Uniqueness and consistency of corporate identity in individualistic cultures is opposed to a collectivist's identity, which can change according to varying social positions and situations. When global companies define their corporate identities, they might consider including variations for the different cultural contexts in which they operate.

Usually the task of creating a corporate identity begins with the selection of an appropriate corporate name. Other factors that contribute to corporate identity include the logo of the organization and marketing communications. All this, including language, lettering, and associations, is logically a reflection of the home country of the organization. Many Western organizations prefer worldwide consistency of all these elements without realizing that this can be counterproductive, as not all elements are equally effective in all countries.

Some American companies in China have learned to adapt. Coca-Cola, for example, has changed its name to adapt to the visual orientation of the Chinese. The company renamed its brand into "Kokou Kole," which translates into "happiness in the mouth." The basis of the Western concept of corporate identity is that it should be perceived universally, but in reality it translates differently in different parts of the world. Perception of a corporate identity is also dependent on the use of the company name as a corporate brand. For example, Unilever (Netherlands) and Procter & Gamble (U.S.) are very big companies but hardly known to the general public because historically they have mainly marketed product brands. Other companies, such as Nestlé (Switzerland), Heineken (Netherlands), Yakult, Sony, Mitsubishi (Japan), Daewoo (Korea), and BenQ (Taiwan) are world players who use their corporate name on (almost) all of their products. Some Western companies such as Heineken (Amstel, Tiger) and Nestlé (Nescafé, Perrier, Nestea, KitKat), in addition to the corporate brand name, keep using other brand names of companies that they acquired. East Asian companies tend to stick to one corporate brand name.

Until recently, Unilever has chosen not to use its corporate name on its different brands and products. The reason for this was that a scandal (such as the nitrite in their Iglo frozen foods in 1980 in the Netherlands) could easily transfer consumer scare to other Unilever products. Driven by cultural specifics of collectivistic cultures like Russia, Japan, and China, however, Unilever has chosen to include its corporate name on all its brands. The very least that should be added to product brands in Asian advertising is the company's name. For some time, P&G in China has done so by adding a P&G signature, for example to Head & Shoulders in TV commercials; and Nippon Lever in Japan has done so for its Japanese products. For sweet biscuits (cookies), Danone uses the brand name Lu in Europe, but in Asia the corporate name Danone is also on this type of product.[11]

Brand values should fit the values in the overall company vision and mission. Brand vision should match corporate vision; they should enhance each other. This is of equal importance in individualistic and collectivistic cultures. If the brand and company vision are aligned and clear, trust in the company will transfer trust to the brand and vice versa. This strategy is more difficult for companies that have many brands such as Unilever or Procter & Gamble. For example, Unilever's mission (2004) is "to add vitality to life. We meet the everyday needs for nutrition, hygiene, and personal care with brands that help people feel good, look good, and get more out of life."[12] This vision must be translated to each individual brand. For example, the fundamental underlying consumer insight for the fabric softener Comfort/Snuggle is "Care for your second skin," which fits the corporate mission.

In order to develop a company and brand vision that is relevant to consumers on a global scale, the company must first listen to its consumers in all markets. Rather than doing market research in general, leading companies define consumer insights as the basis for their product development and brand-building activities. Consumer needs should decide which products or product extensions to develop for which markets. When developing a brand positioning statement, the first thing to know is your consumer's wants and needs.

Product/Market Development Across Cultures

Although some companies view themselves as pure marketing organizations that only focus on branding, the basis of existence of a global company is its product or service and the ability to develop or adapt product concepts for different markets. The most important decision of a company is which products or product variations to market to which markets. Therefore, marketers should work in close contact with research and development.

Many products sell better in some markets than in others. The cause of such variations can be wealth or culture. If the cause of low penetration of a specific product in a specific country is culturally defined, products should be adapted to better fit that culture.

New product-market combinations must be developed when products enter new markets of different cultural configurations. Life insurance, for example, is a product for individualistic cultures; entering a market with a collectivistic culture demands different products. An example could be offering parent-related pension insurance to the Singapore yuppies whose new mobile lifestyles make it more difficult to fulfill their obligations to look after their parents, a strong element of their collectivistic and Confucian values.

Well-defined cultural differences can help to develop more appropriate products or product adaptations for different cultures. If certain do-it-yourself products do not sell as well in strong as in weak uncertainty avoidance cultures, adapt the product to the need for competence. Add instructions, offer training, whatever helps the market to feel more competent. Similarly, electronic appliances such as remote control devices should be easy to use for weak uncertainty avoidance cultures, but may have complicated details for strong uncertainty avoidance cultures where people want to control the process.

Brand Positioning Across Cultures

A brand position is what the brand stands for in a world of brands. This position includes the associations it has in the mind of the consumer. It includes all aspects of a brand: the product attributes, benefits, and values. When developing brand strategies, companies tend to formulate the desired brand position in a brand positioning statement.

The *brand positioning statement* links the external aspects of the brand with the internal aspects. With the description of these two aspects, we cover the most used set of terms of Western branding theory. The *internal aspects* of a brand are the brand elements injected into the brand by the company. They include the brand identity and values attached to the brand by which people should be able to recognize its identity. The identity is what the sender (company, organization) wants to convey about the brand, which includes the brand's characteristics in terms of personality.

The *external aspects* of a brand include the take-out by the consumer, its image, or how the consumer perceives the brand, and usage, or how the brand's products

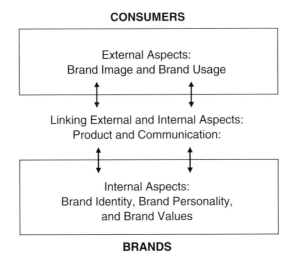

Figure 10.1　Elements of a Brand Positioning Statement

are used in daily life. The role of the brands and products in daily life contributes to the desired brand identity.

A brand is well positioned if there is a proper link between the external and internal aspects. This is visualized in Figure 10.1.

Several marketing mix elements contribute to transferring the identity to an image, of which the *product* itself and the *communication* are the most visible and culturally sensitive elements. The other marketing instruments, *price* and *distribution*, are also culturally relevant, in particular if price is used as a positioning strategy. A *value for money* positioning, for example, will be most appealing to longer-term-oriented cultures. As this book focuses on the effects of communication in branding strategies, we don't include price strategy in the brand positioning discussion, although price and distribution certainly emphasize the identity and image of a product or brand.

Before discussing the development of a multicultural brand positioning statement, we first recap a few cultural elements of the brand itself.

The Brand Concept and Culture

The brand concept, as such, is a Western, individualistic phenomenon because brands generally are positioned as unique personalities with abstract characteristics in terms of personal traits. Across individualistic cultures, personality traits vary, so one brand personality will not be equally attractive in all cultures. In Chapter 5, we showed that, for example, trustworthiness is an attractive brand characteristic in high uncertainty avoidance cultures, and a brand is preferably friendly in individualistic and masculine cultures. In collectivistic cultures, consumers are more attracted to concrete product features than to abstract brand concepts. They will select products from companies that they trust. As a result, *company brands* are more customary in Asia, whereas the *product brand* is a more Western, individualistic phenomenon (see also Chapter 6, the section on Personality and Identity in Marketing). Product brands are developed for positioning purposes, both against the competition and against other brands of the company's brand portfolio. In Asian collectivistic cultures, an important purpose of marketing is to build relationships and trust between companies and consumers. Developing strong company brands is a better strategy for this purpose than developing a portfolio of competitive product brands. Therefore, few East Asian companies carry more than one brand.

Because in Asia brands are most successful if they are linked to companies with a successful image, all sorts of products that in the West would not be considered fit for use under one brand name can be linked to a company brand name in Asia. Whereas in the West, a diaper by the Japanese cosmetics company Shiseido would be judged primarily in terms of whether cosmetics and diapers go together, in Asia the image of Shiseido would provide enough justification for giving the product a try.[13]

In collectivistic cultures, people associate best with concrete product features. Consider for example the Yakult products. In Western Europe, one is sold under the name Yakult (or Yakult Light), containing specific live bacteria (the lactobacillus *casei shirota*) that are supposed to be good for your intestinal flora. Yakult has many more products (e.g., Yakult Ace 80, Yakult Bansoreicha) on the market in Japan, all of them with bacteria or other ingredients that are supposed to be good for your body. Each of the Yakult products has some specific ingredient, and Japanese consumers know very much about all these different ingredients. Moreover, they trust the Yakult Honsha Company to deliver good and beneficial products. It is Yakult they trust, and they therefore consume its products.

Also, collectivistic cultures do not relate to brands as persons. They buy products with specific product features, not abstract brands. Illustration 10.1 shows outdoor advertising for the Super Sol retail chain in Barcelona, Spain, which mentions offering the leading products, not the leadership brands, as a north European retailer would.

Illustration 10.1 Super Sol, Barcelona, Spain

The lesson of all this is that a company that wants to work globally should consider the cultural specifics of the brand concept. When formulating the brand identity, be aware that Asian consumers are not so interested in an abstract brand identity or personality. They are more interested in what a company stands for, how reliable it is. A global company should align its corporate and brand identity in such a way that both north Europeans/Americans (brand identity) and Asians (corporate identity) can be addressed.

External Aspects: Product Usage and Brand Image

To enable the formulation of a brand identity, knowledge of the current brand image is needed, as well as how consumers deal with the brand and its product(s). These are the tools of the marketer. The image is what a consumer sees of the brand

and how she consequently perceives and mentally integrates all messages. It is the association network in the mind of the consumer. Ideally the image matches the identity, what the sender wants to convey about the brand.

Product Usage

Understanding how a global brand is perceived needs in-depth consumer research in many countries to really understand all the situations in which the brand is used. It not only includes talking with consumers but also walking with consumers: Go into their houses, see what they are doing and how the brand fits (or could fit) their needs. For years, Western companies have been selling their irons to Japanese and Korean consumers only to discover at a very late stage that they do not iron standing up but sitting down. This obviously asks for different ergonomic requirements. Another example: Indonesians like *teh botol* very much: to them it is the best thirst quencher thinkable. Although they like *teh botol* more than Coca-Cola, they do drink Coca-Cola because it is a status symbol, not because it is refreshing.

Large global companies like Procter & Gamble and Unilever have accumulated consumer insight by going inside the consumers' homes: P&G makes films of their consumers' toilet and showering behavior; Unilever puts on tape what consumers are doing in kitchens in countries as diverse as Nigeria, Vietnam, Paraguay, New Zealand, and Germany. They have learned that decision making based on assumptions about consumer behavior is one of the worst mistakes a company can make.

Knowledge of how a brand is perceived and how the brand's products are used is essential for defining the brand identity. There are many techniques such as "meet the consumer" sessions to develop knowledge and insight in brand/product perception and usage.

In general, product usage does not change overnight, although marketing and advertising people tend to think it does. They like to embrace the new. In this book, we have given several examples of the stability of people's behavior. Much of new behavior is only a new format of existing behavior as described in Chapter 2.

Because people's behavior is stable, past or current behavior can often explain future behavior. When developing and marketing new products, it is useful to analyze past behavior to predict the future. In Chapter 4, we showed how in countries where people are used to entertainment in bars and cafés they also access the Internet in the cyber café. If you want to sell advanced digital photo printers to people in different cultures, first analyze in which cultures people used the most analog films.

The above pertains not only to new technologies. For example, at the start of the twenty-first century, Unilever successfully marketed Bertolli olive oil and thus succeeded in convincing consumers in northern Europe to use olive oil instead of margarine for cooking and frying as they do in southern Europe. This change in cooking habits is consistent with northern European health awareness and does not imply a fundamental change in eating habits. In fact, in the past people had changed from frying with butter to margarine for the same reason.

An example of reinforcing existing habits is the introduction of the Senseo coffee machine in a joint venture between Philips and the coffee company Sara

Lee/Douwe Egberts. The Senseo is a new type of coffee machine that is a hybrid of the espresso machine and the drip-filter machine. Like the espresso machine, it makes one or two cups of coffee at a time, but it is cheaper. It is more convenient than a drip filter: one pad containing coffee is all you need. It appeals to individualistic cultures by individualizing the coffee experience. Every individual can select a coffee flavor according to his or her own taste because each cup is made separately. If your partner likes decaf while you like strong arabica, you are able to make each cup to your liking. This concept fits the trends of convenience and individualism: a hassle-free cup of coffee to your own liking in the shortest possible time. It reinforces individualistic values. Consumer behavior has slightly changed, but the coffee-drinking ritual in the home is maintained, as it is a typical machine for home consumption. In cultures where coffee consumption takes place more in the public domain, it is likely to be less popular. The reason for the success of Starbucks in Spain is not because it satisfies a need for the variety of coffee offered but because it confirms the existing need of young people to sit together at leisure and chat.

When predicting product usage in developing countries, one should not expect people to copy behavior of the developed world, in particular American behavior. They may copy some behavior because it delivers social status, but after some time people will return to behavior that fits their old values. Right after World War II, the Japanese adopted Western clothing. At the start of the twenty-first century, young Japanese rediscovered the kimono.

Modernization is not the same as Westernization. Also, social and political scientists tend to agree that the world is not Westernizing. Huntington[14] attacks the common assumption that modernization is Westernization and states, "Modernization is producing neither a universal civilization in any meaningful sense nor the westernization of non-western societies," and adds, "The spread of western consumption patterns and popular culture around the world is not creating a universal civilization." The opposite is the case: People may desire to think globally, but as a result of globalization, they actually become more aware of their specific local values.

People increasingly identify with their local or regional communities. We have yet to hear anyone from a European country say, "I am from Europe"; they always state their nationality.

In Chapter 2, we discussed that the wealthier countries become, the more manifest is the influence of culture on consumption and consumer behavior. Neither wealth nor technological development produces "new values." In post-scarcity societies, "old" values become manifest in consumption and consumer behavior. More discretionary income gives people more freedom to express themselves, and that expression will be based in part on their national value system. Wealth brings choice. It enables people to choose leisure time or buy status products or devote free time to self-education.

The more money people possess, the easier it is for them to stick to or refine their culturally determined behavior. People will select brands that comply with this cultural behavior. This means that the brand position should be multifaceted because a brand will mean something different to a Portuguese woman than a Vietnamese man.

The first visible aspect of a brand is the product itself. Therefore, analyzing and selecting the right product-market combinations is essential in defining your brand position.

Brand Image

Brand image is the representation of the brand in the mind of the consumer. In Western cultures, the image can be like a human being with unique characteristics. In collectivistic cultures, it can be quality and the representation of trust in a supplier—the product is part of a trusted family of products.

Ideally, the brand identity, the values the marketer puts into the brand, should be reflected in the image, which is the take-out of the consumer. Within cultures, discrepancies between identity and image occur, but across cultures the gap between identity and image is likely to be wider. Many marketing research agencies offer positioning models that help define brands in terms of human personality traits or values that are suggested to be universal, but the characteristics of their own culture often can be recognized in the descriptions (see Chapter 5). Consumers will attribute to the brand characteristics that fit their own mental maps and from there develop a brand image. This does not necessarily reflect the intended brand identity. So what is in the mind of the consumer, the brand image, is not necessarily the same as the brand characteristics the marketer uses to build the brand identity. Many global brands that desire a consistent brand identity and hope this will result in a consistent brand image end up with different brand images across cultures. Findings from the Crocus study (see Chapter 5) show that strong global brands have different, culturally relevant brand characteristics in different cultures. Coca-Cola is viewed as trustworthy in high uncertainty avoidance cultures, as prestigious in high power distance cultures, and as different in low uncertainty avoidance cultures. Mercedes is viewed as trustworthy in high uncertainty avoidance cultures, as prestigious in high power distance cultures, as friendly in low power distance cultures, and as different in individualistic cultures. L'Oréal is viewed as trustworthy in high uncertainty avoidance cultures, as friendly in low power distance cultures, and as prestigious and international in collectivistic cultures. Such different, culturally relevant images across cultures are a likely cause of success of these global brands, although the companies may not have intended this effect.

In-depth market research and cultural analysis are tools that help translate the brand image and product usage into a multicultural brand position.

Internal Aspects: Brand Identity and Personality and Brand Values

The internal aspects are the brand characteristics that the company inserts into the brand. Western global companies generally want to inject personality characteristics and values that are consistent across target groups and across countries, although in some cases some marketers also vary these characteristics by target group.

In national segmentation studies, brands often appear to have different meanings for different target groups or subcultures. For instance, Camel is a mainstream cigarette brand sold in all of Europe. During the mid 1990s, Camel organized "rave flights," where people could party (rave) on an airplane. Of course, the general public was not aware of these promotions, but Camel tried to become more popular in the younger age-groups where it was losing a battle against Marlboro. Camel is not alone in this approach. In trendy magazines that aim at youngsters, advertisements for mainstream brands send messages that deviate from their mainstream position and by which they try to reach the trendsetters. The idea behind this type of advertising is that a brand can have more than one face. Camel may be a trusted, adventurous, and humorous brand for adults and, at the same time, a cool, trendy brand for youngsters. Such dual strategies work as long as the different faces of the brand are not contradicting.

The same approach can be applied to international segmentation. Different brand values can be selected for different cultures. As long as the brand values selected for international exposure do not contradict with the brand values used in specific countries, several may well exist next to each other. In a similar way, it should be possible to develop an international brand identity with local variations that also make it culturally relevant locally. After all, how many consumers notice that a brand is communicating different values in different countries? The only consumers who do are probably your own employees.

Brand Identity and Personality

What has been said in this chapter regarding corporate identity also pertains to brand identity. The Western wish to develop a consistent brand identity leads toward labeling the brand personality with concepts that may mean different things in different languages or cultures. Instead, a better option is to find what is meaningful with respect to the brand and its role in people's lives in different culture clusters and to load the brand with different core values, although the product may be the same worldwide. International brands succeed when consumers in each market believe they are being spoken to by somebody who understands them, somebody who knows their needs and who talks and feels just as they do. In cultures in which trust in the company and long-term relationships between consumers and companies are important, focus on the company brand will be a more effective strategy than developing strong product brands. Corporate branding and endorsement strategies will be more effective in Asian markets than a product-brand approach of strongly positioned brand values. On the other hand, now that Asian products are increasingly entering Western markets, Asian companies may do better in Western markets by developing more differentiated product brands.

Because personal traits vary across cultures, personality descriptors for brand positioning across cultures will not lead to equal success in all countries. First, there are culture-specific personality dimensions such as ruggedness in the United States and peacefulness in Japan. Brand personalities fitting in such indigenous dimensions are not likely to be as successful in other countries as they are in the home country. In the Crocus study (see Chapter 5), we found that a brand characteristic like "friendly" is most attributed to strong brands in individualistic and low power distance cultures. "Trustworthy" was most attributed to strong brands in high uncertainty avoidance cultures. Second, similar trait labels can have different associations, so the meaning of seemingly similar trait descriptions can be very different. This poses a problem when brand personality traits are used for global brand positioning and particularly when they are used as a basis for marketing communications concepts.

Brand Values

As described in Chapters 2 and 5, there are three levels of communication: attributes, benefits, and values. Many international companies want to go beyond presenting product attributes or benefits and add values to the product to position the brand in the mind of the consumer. In particular, Anglo-American companies have propagated this approach to global advertising because of their belief in universal, global values. Thus, happiness is used to sell fast food, success to sell cars or wristwatch brands, unlimited human potential ("just do it") to sell trainers, and freedom to sell jeans.

Many global advertising campaigns of American origin reflect American values. Levi's, for example, focuses on freedom (of movement) in international advertising, as in Illustration 10.2, which shows images from an international TV commercial for Levi's in Spain. It shows two people running fast, as if in competition. The take-out of Spanish viewers was competition, not freedom. Most international brands of European origin have not adopted this approach.

Illustration 10.2   Levi's, Spain

One of the reasons for desired cross-cultural consistency in global branding strategies is the need for control. Companies want to be sure that their brand values are consistently similar across countries. Various studies are finding that the elements the company injects into the brand end up in different images in the minds of consumers in different countries. If consumers elsewhere perceive these global brands as having different values than the company intended, the process is out of control; to keep control, it may be better to define specific brand characteristics (product characteristics, brand values, traits, and company values) for the various cultures where the company operates.

Brand Positioning Matrix

Communication is supposed to convey the brand identity and its accompanying values to the consumer. This should result in a brand image in the mind of the consumer that will make him or her assess the possibility of buying the recommended product. It is the marketer's challenge to build a brand architecture that incorporates the internal and external aspects and to communicate this to consumers.

Benefits and values associated with the brands should be in line with the users' needs and motives. Brand consultant and professor Larry Percy[15] states that positioning a brand correctly requires careful attention to verifying the specific need, as consumers see it, and the benefits they associate with the brand. This means that across cultures brand positions need to adapt to the different needs and motives of consumers. In addition, the communication styles and formats must fit the culture of the consumer.

Next to attributes, benefits, and values, brands are differentiated from competitive brands by the type of presentation, consisting of advertising style and basic forms, as described in the previous chapters. The brand positioning variables are presented in the brand positioning matrix in Figure 10.2.

Analysis of 1,290 TV commercials from six European countries (Germany, Italy, the Netherlands, the U.K., France, and Spain) and the United States, demonstrates that the configuration of basic form and level of communication varies across cultures.

Basic Form / Level of Communication	Attributes	Benefits	Values	Emotion	Usage
Announcement					
Association Transfer					
Lesson					
Drama					
Entertainment					
Imagination					
Entertaining Presentation					

Figure 10.2   Brand Positioning Matrix

The standard three communication levels—attribute, benefit, and value—are not sufficient to distinguish communication strategies in these seven countries. Some commercials simply do not work at any of these levels. Examples are French, Spanish, and Italian commercials (as described in Chapter 7), which do not convey a message at the attribute, benefit, or value level but are simply playing with emotions. The advertiser apparently wants to induce a strong emotional bond between the consumer and the brand. This strategy is called "bonding." Other commercials are purely related to the moment of usage. In an abstract sense, this may be viewed as a product attribute or benefit, but it is not. The advertiser tries to find new ways of promoting his product without introducing new attributes or attribute-related benefits.

Analysis of the configuration used by international European brands shows that few communicate at the value level. In the culturally diverse Europe, international companies have learned that international advertising based on values is not equally effective everywhere. Most successful international brands of European origin focus on continuously innovative product attributes or benefits and employ culturally relevant advertising forms and styles. Examples are L'Oréal, Nivea, Bounty kitchen disposables, Actimel (by Danone), and Volkswagen. Illustrations 10.3 and 10.4 show TV images from Volkswagen commercials in Germany and France. The product attribute is 4-Motion. The German commercial (Illustration 10.3) reflects the typical German need for testing and demonstration. The driver by accident gets on a toboggan run and drives down the mountain that way to a coffee bar. When he orders a cup of coffee, he discovers he has lost his wallet and he returns driving upward. This is the extreme test. The French commercial (Illustration 10.4) uses the metaphorical approach and associates the 4-Motion technique with all sort of tricks, like cutting a woman in two, boxing tricks, and film tricks.

Illustration 10.3 Volkswagen, Germany

Illustration 10.4 Volkswagen, France

Formulating a brand positioning statement based on cultural analysis early in the process will lay the foundation for building strong international or global brands. Any marketer who has traveled abroad and has analyzed markets thoroughly will agree that there are big differences. Only a few companies have successfully formulated and executed a global brand positioning statement with a very limited set of brand values and benefits. An example is the recent worldwide campaign by Shell. They have adopted the sea as their brand world and fishes as the characters. Because nature is viewed as important in every culture (although in different ways), this analogy is very strong and scores well worldwide. Coca-Cola is an example of a brand that has defined its essence in terms of a thirst quencher that is available everywhere. The take-out by consumers in some places in the world has been fun and happiness, in others social status. Coca-Cola and Shell have defined a worldwide uniform identity, but they allow the message consumers take out, the image they have of the brands, to differ across countries. Because they continuously monitor the take-out by consumers, they are in control. There is no problem with different take-outs as long as companies are aware of these differences and the take-out by consumers fits their mental maps. If this is not the case, a company should work on obtaining a better fit cross-culturally.

Once the brand positioning statements have been formulated for different culture clusters, they should be applied to all marketing mix elements, in particular marketing communications.

Marketing Communication Strategy

In Chapter 2, six strategies that companies use for internationalization were described. For each of these strategies, a multicultural brand positioning statement is important, as it must provide competitive advantage in various cultures. Depending on the brand strategy, a configuration of form and style must be decided to communicate the desired brand position. The selected form, as we learned in Chapter 9, can be related to culture or, historically, to the product category. Time and again, marketers need to ask themselves whether they want to stick to one format (as for example P&G does for some brands) or to give freedom (as Volkswagen does with completely different styles in different countries). Several brand-communication configurations are possible, which also vary by stage of market development. Each strategy uses a different combination of basic forms and execution. Global advertising eventually boils down to six different strategies.

1. Fully Standardized: One Product or Brand, Display

There is one product or brand that is sold across borders. The product is the message. Advertising focuses only on the product attributes. This is export advertising. It will be in one language. This strategy is used in umbrella campaigns, additional to local advertising, as for example for perfumes and alcoholic beverages. Examples are Clinique and Bacardi. It is also recognized in corporate advertising.

Be careful not to include any values, or it will run into cultural problems. Focusing on product attributes alone can be a successful strategy when introducing a new product. In a world of growing parity in products and brands, such a strategy is rarely effective at long term.

2. Semistandardized: One Brand, One Advertising Form, and Standard Execution (Voice-Over and/or Lip Sync)

Innovative product attributes and benefits are central to the advertisement. In some countries, the original language is used (often English); in others voice-over or subtitles are added. As not all countries are used to lip sync, showing a person's lips while talking is not advisable, as it shows too clearly that the advertising is "imported." In countries where people are not used to voice-overs in television programs, this irritates consumers. This strategy is most used for international personal care brands (e.g., Gillette and L'Oréal). Using only a voice-over and not showing interaction with dialogue between people allows for cross-border usage. It is the strategy for brands that thrive on distinct product attributes or benefits and continuous innovation.

3. One Brand, One Form, Varying Standard Executional Elements

This strategy, also called pattern standardization, uses one advertising form, including a number of executional elements that can be used in different configurations. The executional elements reflect different values (e.g., expressed by different user benefits). The risk of this strategy is in the combination of opposing values in one advertisement because the concept tends to reflect the values of the country of origin and contrasting values can be added in the execution. An example would be focusing on value for money in the Netherlands and adding a line about testing, which is not culture-fit for the Netherlands. In such cases, the cultural specifics are compromised. The combination of appeals may not be as effective as each separate appeal would have been in the countries where it fits. Such combinations of appeals are found in pan-European campaigns, for example for shampoo, toothpaste, and household products.

4. One or Different Brand Names, One Advertising Form, Different Executions

This is a strategy used by many Anglo multinationals like P&G, advertising similar products with different brand names using one consistent basic advertising form such as comparison, testimonial, or drama but adapting to people, languages, and culture. It is used for sanitary napkins and detergents or cleaning liquids (Dreft,

Fairy, Ace). P&G has been very successful with this strategy. Based on one form, different commercials are made for each country, and the execution reflects appropriate cultural values. An example is how in large power distance cultures the elder advises the younger and in small power distance cultures the opposite occurs.

5. One or Different Brand Names, One Concept, Different Executions, Based on Culture-Fit Advertising Styles

One abstract platform or idea is the basis for different local executions. Examples are campaigns for Actimel by Danone and for Axe, a male deodorant, by Unilever. The Actimel concept is that it regenerates people in bad times, such as in winter or in hectic life. The Axe concept is that it attracts women vigorously. Many different executions are used to express the concepts. There will be recognizable elements such as the brand name and package, the payoff, music, a symbol. Different executions based on the concept can be developed in different countries and adopted by others of similar cultural configurations. The advantage of this strategy is the combination of local values and a centrally recognizable idea. Actual ads may be used globally, regionally, or locally depending on the need for cultural adaptation.

6. Cultural Segmentation: Act Global, Think Local

This is the opposite of the "think global—act local" paradigm. It means reaping all the benefits of globalization in production, sourcing, distribution, marketing, and the connected benefits of economies of scale in production and organization but with the exception that mental images cannot be standardized. Advertising is mostly local but endorsed by the company. This is the global strategy of companies that have learned to exploit local cultural values. These companies build relationships with local consumers. The company's name is used as endorsement. This is Nestlé's strategy; it can be recognized in Volkswagen's strategy and in strategies of many Japanese companies. The product is central, so focus is on product attributes, but the advertising style varies by culture cluster (Volkswagen 4-Motion).

Levels of Communication by Stage of Market Development

In global marketing for new products in all sorts of durable goods and technology categories, but also for advanced food products, worldwide income will be the main driver of penetration across national markets. In economically homogeneous areas, acceptance of new products will vary with the degree of uncertainty avoidance. After introduction, further penetration will depend on needs and motives of different cultural configurations. Knowledge of these differences can help structure marketing communications programs in the developed world.

Increased economic homogeneity has consequences for product development and marketing communication strategy across markets that should vary by stage of market development. At the time of introduction of a new product, when it still is more or less generic, for many products advertising can focus on product attributes, and both product and advertising can be standardized. With increased competition, product differentiation takes place, and advertising must differentiate by focusing on benefits or values. Customer demand becomes more heterogeneous, and because of varying consumer needs across cultures, the benefits and values used in communications can be better adapted to varying needs. We suggest three stages of international market development with different consequences for international marketing communications in each stage.

Stage 1: Global Products, Global Marketing Communications

Market penetration of the generic product will depend on national wealth in economically heterogeneous areas and on cultural factors in economically homogeneous areas. An example was the penetration of the television set when it was introduced. A more recent example is penetration of mobile phones. In this first stage, marketing communications can be based on product attributes and can be relatively standard. The success of Coca-Cola in foreign markets was in this first stage, when there was relatively little competition in the category and their global advertising was effective. Nokia introduced mobile phones with standardized international advertising. Nokia claimed the generic attribute for mobile communications by saying "Connecting people," a statement that also reflects the basic value of human communications. The mobile phone producers piggybacked on the mobile phone service providers, who were the national telecom companies and who penetrated their own markets by offering locally meaningful services with culturally meaningful local advertising. The messages of the mobile phone producers in this stage remained generic, introducing new product attributes, for example small or well-designed phones.

Stage 2: Global Products, Adapted Marketing Communications

When markets become saturated, differentiation takes place within and across markets, which is likely to follow different patterns across markets. Although the same differentiated products are sold everywhere, some are sold better in some cultures than in others. Following the example of the television set, all producers developed wide-screen TV and teletext reception features; but in the high uncertainty avoidance cultures, more wide-screen televisions were sold, and in the individualistic cultures teletext was more used. In this stage, the mobile phone service providers differentiated their services. SMS messaging was first adopted in the individualistic cultures. In a collectivistic culture like Spain, special services were offered to mothers to communicate with their children. In high power distance

Belgium, schoolchildren were offered special after-school rates in order not to conflict with the authority of school teachers who wouldn't want children to use the phone during school hours. In the feminine cultures, electronic banking services by phone were introduced. New services followed existing habits and preferences. In this stage, because markets are not saturated for the generic product, products can still be standardized; but marketing communications must be adapted, and this can be done by defining culture clusters. The mobile phone producers adapted their products and advertising only with respect to language. Advertising went to a level higher, at the benefit level, with messages like Nokia's, "You have information under control." When Coca-Cola entered this stage, they continued their strategy of Stage 1, which became less effective. They thereby created room for local brands such as Mecca-Cola (France), Raak (Netherlands), and Virgin (U.K.).

Stage 3: Local Products, Local Marketing Communications

This is a stage when markets become saturated for the generic product, and strong competition forces companies to differentiate both products and marketing communications. It will be profitable to develop product extensions for specific applications to comply with cultural differences in usage and motives across national markets. These can be single markets or clusters of markets following the product-relevant cultural values. In the television category, the example is interactive television or broadcasting by computer and Internet. The VCD (video CD) player—a system that can play compressed video on a TV, offering the possibility of random access playback—penetrated much faster in Asia than in the United States because it was used for karaoke. In 2002, the mobile phone had entered Stage 3, but in Europe mobile phone producers kept standardizing their products and advertising as if they were still in Stage 1. Only in large developing markets like China did Nokia market its cellular phones with features that appealed to local tastes such as greeting cards with popular Chinese astrological symbols.[16] Nokia did not, however, develop specific handset designs to specific markets. Via a subsidiary, Nokia did offer an expensive luxury subbrand (Vertu) in gold or platinum that should appeal to the rich and famous of this world, and Siemens offered "fashion accessory phones" under the name Xelibri.[17] In China, a taste for faux diamond-studded handsets developed that was considered kitschy and thus bad taste in the West. As a result, in China handset brands such as TCL, Ningbo Bird, and Amoisonic quickly gained market share, and Nokia and Motorola were losing. Too late Motorola started copying the diamond-studded phone designs so popular in China.[18] Coca-Cola, which had entered Stage 3 long ago, changed its strategy only at the end of the twentieth century into one of local product development.

In Stage 3, marketing communications should be multilocal or differentiate by culture cluster. In this stage, both Nokia and Ericsson used pan-European advertising based on the "You can work where you want" appeal, which fits the cultural configuration of the Scandinavian countries of origin of the brands, not the south of Europe.

Of the three development stages, Stage 2 is the most important for international marketing because in that stage markets start to differentiate, while the company still reaps the benefits of their successful Stage 1. If a company understands local consumer behavior in this stage, it is an investment that will pay off in Stage 3.

Global Integrated Marketing Communications

The need for integrating the various marketing communications instruments originated in the 1990s in the United States as a response to the sender-oriented approach of marketing. As a countermovement, global integrated marketing communications (IMC) should build positive relationships by placing consumers or stakeholders first. There also was an organizational problem. Each discipline—advertising, promotions, and public relations—had its own compensation structure that resulted in different objectives and practices, and there was little contact between the different disciplines. An orchestrated approach should be more effective than several competing disciplines. In other countries, the problem never was as pronounced as in the United States because budgets tend to be lower and competition between disciplines less strong.

In the United States, opinions vary concerning whether the concept is really a new paradigm, as definitions of IMC have been weak. Two elements can be distinguished, of which one is basically the same as the original marketing paradigm: "Beginning with the needs and wants of a defined market segment before developing products and marketing approaches." The other element is the organizational one: "Coordinating all marketing communication and promotion through traditional and developing media so that the organization's messages *speak with one voice*." Other elements are practical, like researching the consumer, developing databases, and coordinating the contacts with the consumer.[19]

The two elements are conflicting when IMC is applied to global marketing. Placing consumers and stakeholders ahead of the marketer's need confirms the need for cross-cultural sensitivity. But IMC also preaches consistency in communicating a central message, which goes against cultural sensitivity. The best approach is to speak with one voice within one country and listen to your consumer in each country separately.

The more companies want to integrate their marketing communications, the more elements need to be culturally relevant for culturally very different consumers. Indeed, when both the promotion of an item and the international advertising should be integrated, this either does not leave much room for the promotion (which will eventually fail in many countries), or it would lead to a gray middle-of-the-road advertising campaign that leaves room for local promotions. The principles mentioned in this chapter and throughout this book only become more relevant in IMC.

Conclusion

For global advertisers, the choice used to be between global and local. In this book, we have argued that the real choice is between failure and success. One standard strategy has been assumed to reduce costs because of economies of scale. What is gained by cost reduction, however, is lost by loss of effectiveness. Consistency in presentation is another frequently heard argument for standardization. This reflects a Western frame of mind that is not shared globally. If you want to reach consumers in different parts of the world, speak to them in a way they understand.

The new paradigm is cultural segmentation—defining markets based on their cultural specifics and developing culture-fit strategies. A strong corporate identity can go with cultural sensitivity. Instead of being consistent, brands should be pragmatic and adapt to the cultural mind-sets of consumers. This will be the future of global branding and advertising.

Notes

1. Bart, C. (1998). Mission matters. *CPA Journal 8,* 56–57.

2. Murphy, J. J. (2004, August 8). The concepts of vision and mission revisited. Negotiation Academy. Retrieved November 21, 2004, from http://www.negotiationeurope.co.uk/articles/

3. Retrieved August 3, 2004, from www.toyota.co.jp/en/about_toyota/message/index.htm

4. Retrieved August 3, 2004, from www.ford.com

5. Retrieved August 3, 2004, from www.data-directions.com

6. Retrieved August 8, 2004, from www.canon.com

7. Retrieved August 8, 2004, from www.samsung.com

8. Retrieved August 3, 2004, from www.toyota.co.jp

9. Retrieved August 3, 2004, from www.hondacorporate.com

10. Ind, N. (1992). *The corporate image: Strategies for effective identity programmes.* London: Kogan Page, p. 19.

11. A C Nielsen. (n.d.). *Global mega brand franchise: Extending brands within a global marketplace.* Retrieved June 25, 2004, from www.acnielsen.com/download/html/Global_Mega_Brand_Franchises.htm

12. Unilever mission as formulated on their Web site. Retrieved August 1, 2004, from www.unilever.com

13. Schmitt, B. H., & Pan, Y. (1994). Managing corporate and brand identities in the Asia-Pacific region. *California Management Review, 36,* 32–48.

14. Huntington, S. P. (1996). *The clash of civilizations and the remaking of world order.* New York: Simon & Schuster, pp. 20, 58.

15. Percy, L. (n.d.). *Tools for building strong brands.* Retrieved December 2003 from http://www.larrypercy.com/tools.html

16. Cai, Y. (2001, Fall). Design strategies for global products. *Design Management Journal,* 59–64.

17. The origins of Vertu. (2003, February 22). *Economist,* 66–67.

18. The local touch. (2003, March 8). *Economist,* 62.

19. Swain, W. N. (2003). An exploratory assessment of the IMC paradigm: Where are we, and where do we go from here? *Integrated Marketing Communication Research Journal, 9,* 3–11 (see p. 6).

Appendix A

GNI/Capita 2001 (US$) and Hofstede Country Scores for 64 Countries

Country	Abbreviation	GNI/cap	PDI	IDV	MAS	UAI	LTO
Argentina	ARG	6,960	49	46	56	86	
Australia	AUL	19,770	36	90	61	51	31
Austria	AUT	23,940	11	55	79	70	31
Bangladesh	BAN	0,370	80	20	55	60	40
Belgium	BEL	23,340	65	75	54	94	38
Brazil	BRA	3,060	69	38	49	76	65
Bulgaria	BUL	1,560	70	30	40	85	
Canada	CAN	21,340	39	80	52	48	23
Chile	CHL	4,350	63	23	28	86	
China	CHN	0,890	80	20	66	30	118
Croatia	CRO	4,650	73	33	40	80	
Czech Republic	CZE	5,270	57	58	57	74	13
Colombia	COL	1,910	67	13	64	80	
Costa Rica	COS	3,950	35	15	21	86	
Denmark	DEN	31,090	18	74	16	23	46
Ecuador	ECA	1,240	78	8	63	67	
Estonia	EST	3,880	40	60	30	60	
Finland	FIN	23,940	33	63	26	59	41
France	FRA	22,690	68	71	43	86	39
Germany	GER	23,700	35	67	66	65	31
Great Britain	GBR	24,230	35	89	66	35	25
Greece	GRE	11,780	60	35	57	112	
Guatemala	GUA	1,670	95	6	37	101	
Hong Kong, China	HOK	25,920	68	25	57	29	96
Hungary	HUN	4,800	46	80	88	82	50

(Continued)

Country	Abbreviation	GNI/cap	PDI	IDV	MAS	UAI	LTO
India	IND	0,460	77	48	56	40	61
Indonesia	IDO	0,680	78	14	46	48	
Iran	IRA	1,750	58	41	43	59	
Ireland	IRE	23,060	28	70	68	35	43
Israel	ISR	16,710	13	54	47	81	
Italy	ITA	19,470	50	76	70	75	34
Jamaica	JAM	2,720	45	39	68	13	
Japan	JPN	35,990	54	46	95	92	80
Korea, Rep.	KOR	9,400	60	18	39	85	75
Malaysia	MAL	3,640	104	26	50	36	
Malta	MLT	9,120	56	59	47	96	
Mexico	MEX	5,540	81	30	69	82	
Morocco	MOR	1,180	70	46	53	68	
Netherlands	NET	24,040	38	80	14	53	44
New Zealand	NZL	12,380	22	79	58	49	30
Norway	NOR	35,530	31	69	8	50	44
Pakistan	PAK	0,420	55	14	50	70	0
Panama	PAN	3,290	95	11	44	86	
Peru	PER	2,000	64	16	42	87	
Philippines	PHI	1,050	94	32	64	44	19
Portugal	POR	10,670	63	27	31	104	30
Poland	POL	4,240	68	60	64	93	32
Romania	ROM	1,710	90	30	42	90	
Russia	RUS	1,750	93	39	36	95	
Salvador	SAL	2,050	66	19	40	94	
Singapore	SIN	24,740	74	20	48	8	48
Slovak Republic	SLK	3,700	104	52	110	51	
Slovenia	SLV	9,780	71	27	19	88	
South Africa	SAF	2,900	49	65	63	49	
Spain	SPA	14,860	57	51	42	86	19
Sweden	SWE	25,400	31	71	5	29	33
Switzerland	SWI	36,970	34	68	70	58	40
Taiwan	TAI	n.a.	58	17	45	69	87
Thailand	THA	1,970	64	20	34	64	56
Turkey	TUR	2,540	66	37	45	85	
United States	USA	34,870	40	91	62	46	29
Uruguay	URU	5,670	61	36	38	100	
Venezuela	VEN	4,760	81	12	73	76	
Vietnam	VTN	0,410	70	20	40	30	80

SOURCE: Hofstede (2001)

Appendix B

Data Sources

Many secondary data sources were used for the cultural analysis in this book. Databases are of several types.

1. Consumer surveys sponsored by the media that ask questions about consumption of products and media usage. The surveys used are the Reader's Digest Surveys *A Survey of Europe Today 1970* and *Eurodata 1991*, and the *European Media and Marketing Surveys (EMS)* of 1995, 1997, and 1999.

2. Statistical data on sales of various products measured in value and liters or kilograms per capita from commercial sources like Euromonitor.

3. Economic statistics published by governmental or nongovernmental organizations: World Bank, United Nations, OECD, and Eurostat.

4. Surveys of opinions and habits of citizens of countries published by governmental organizations. The major studies used are the Eurobarometer reports published by the European Commission Directorate.

5. Academically driven value studies. Examples are the *World Values Survey* and the *European Value Study*.

6. Industry-driven studies, for example, by the tourism trade, car industry, or telecommunications industry. Examples are ITU (International Telecommunications Union) that offers data on telephones, Hotrec on tourism, and the Beverage Marketing Corporation of New York.

7. Studies on specific areas of consumer behavior conducted and published by market research agencies, media, or companies. Examples are studies by Roper Starch or TGI, and the "Trusted Brands" study by Reader's Digest.

This appendix describes the studies in categories 1 through 6. In addition to these, the notes at the end of each chapter mention various other studies from which data were drawn.

1. Media-Sponsored Consumer Surveys

The Reader's Digest Surveys. Studies of the lifestyles, consumer spending habits, and attitudes of people in 17 European countries, published in 1970 and 1991. The data of the 1970 survey were the results of a probability sample representative of the national population aged 18 and over. Comparable sample surveys were conducted in 16 western European countries in early 1969. Approximately 24,000 personal interviews were involved. *Eurodata 1991* was based on comparable sample surveys conducted in the early summer (May/June) of 1990. Approximately 22,500 personal interviews were involved. The study was commissioned by the Reader's Digest Association, Inc., in cooperation with its editions and offices in Europe. With the exception of Sweden, it was conducted by the Gallup-affiliated companies and institutes in Europe and was coordinated by Gallup, London. Probability samples were employed in each of the 17 countries, representative of the population aged 18 and over, living in private households. (Reader's Digest Association Limited, London).

Countries surveyed were Austria, Belgium, Denmark, Finland, France, Germany, Greece, Ireland, Italy, Luxembourg, the Netherlands, Norway, Portugal, Spain, Sweden, Switzerland, and the United Kingdom.

The European Media and Marketing Survey (EMS) (conducted by Inter/View-NSS [www.interview-nss.com], Amsterdam, the Netherlands, in 1995, 1997, and 1999). A European "industry" survey, which collects three broad types of data in 17 European countries simultaneously: (a) advertising effect data based on corporate and brand management, (b) media data, and (c) classification data covering the respondent in both his business and personal environment. The data are drawn from random digit dialing samples. The universe is main income earners in the top 20% of households by household income within each of the 16 countries surveyed—an estimated population of almost 40 million people (18 years or older) in the EU (excluding Greece), Switzerland, and Norway. *EMS 1996* achieved 16,823 interviews and 8,221 self-completion questionnaires. *EMS 1997* achieved 17,844 telephone interviews and 7,711 postal questionnaires. In total in 1996/1997 (report 1997), 34,667 telephone interviews and 15,940 postal questionnaires were completed. Reports are available to subscribers only.

Countries surveyed were Austria, Belgium, Denmark, Finland, France, Germany, Greece, Ireland, Italy, Luxembourg, the Netherlands, Norway, Portugal, Spain, Sweden, Switzerland, and the United Kingdom. In 1997 and 1999, Greece was not included.

2. Commercial Statistical Databases

Euromonitor. Consumer Europe 1997 is a compendium of pan-European market information on sales, in value and volume, of a large number of products; and *Consumer International 1997,* by Euromonitor PLC, London. Euromonitor publishes databases on consumption and ownership of products worldwide (*Consumer World*) and category-specific data reports (www.euromonitor.com).

Countries included in *Consumer Europe 1997* were Austria, Belgium, Denmark, Finland, France, Germany, Greece, Ireland, Italy, Luxembourg, the Netherlands, Norway, Portugal, Spain, Sweden, Switzerland, and the United Kingdom.

3. Economic Statistics

World Bank. Annual World Development Reports include economic data and data on infrastructure; separate reports on world development indicators; data on most countries in the world (World Bank, New York: http://econ.worldbank.org/wdr/).

United Nations. UN Statistical Yearbooks include economic data and data on product ownership and media, data on most countries in the world. United Nations, New York: http://unstats.un.org/unsd/methods/inter-natlinks/refs3.htm)

Eurostat. (a) Annual Reports include demographic data and data on consumption. Data cover the member states of the European Union. (b) Social Indicators Reports. (c) Family Budgets Surveys. The report *Consumers in Europe: Facts and Figures* (2001) covers data from 1996 to 2000, published by the Office for Official Publications of the European Communities, Luxembourg (http://eur-op.eu.int/general/en/index_en.htm).

Data on European Union member countries Austria, Belgium, Denmark, Finland, France, Germany, Greece, Ireland, Italy, Luxembourg, the Netherlands, Portugal, Spain, Sweden, the United Kingdom, and some data for candidate member countries Bulgaria, Cyprus, Czech Republic, Estonia, Hungary, Lithuania, Latvia, Malta, Poland, Romania, Slovenia, Slovakia, and Turkey.

4. Governmental Opinion Surveys

Eurobarometer. The standard Eurobarometer reports cover the resident populations (aged 15 years and over) of the European Union member states. The basic sample design applied in all member states is a multistage, random (probability) one. The number of interviews for the Report 53 (October 2000) was 16,078. The results of Eurobarometer studies are reported in the form of tables, data files, and analyses and published by the European Commission Directorate, Brussels. The results are published on the Internet server of the European Commission: http://europa.eu.int/comm/dg10/epo. Several special reports are published. Examples are *Measuring the Information Society 1997 and 2000, The Young Europeans 1997 and 2001, Trend Variables 1974–1994* (November 1994), *How Europeans See Themselves* (September 2000), and *Consumer Survey,* Flash Eurobarometer 117 (January 2002).

5. Academically Driven Value Studies

World Values Survey. A study of values via public opinion surveys was started in the early 1980s as the *European Values Survey.* In 1990, a second round was started, renamed the *World Values Survey (WVS)*. It eventually covered some 60,000 respondents across 43 societies, representing about 70% of the world's population, with a questionnaire including more than 360 forced-choice questions. Examples of areas covered are ecology, economy, education, emotion, family, health, happiness, religion, leisure, and friends.

The 1990 data are published in the following:

Inglehart, R., Basañez, M., & Moreno, A. (1998). *Human values and beliefs: A cross-cultural sourcebook*. Ann Arbor: University of Michigan Press.

Data for Europe of 1999/2000 are published in the following:

European Values Study: A Third Wave. Source Book of the 1999/2000 European Values Study Surveys. Loek Halman, Tilburg University, PO Box 90153, 5000 LE Tilburg, The Netherlands (evs@uvt.nl).

Countries covered by the European Values Study are Austria, Belarus, Belgium, Bulgaria, Croatia, Czech Republic, Denmark, Estonia, Finland, France, Germany, Greece, Hungary, Iceland, Ireland, Italy, Latvia, Lithuania, Luxembourg, Malta, the Netherlands, Northern Ireland, Poland, Portugal, Romania, Russia, Slovakia, Slovenia, Spain, Sweden, Ukraine, and the United Kingdom.

The European Social Survey 2002/2003 (R. Jowell and the Central Co-ordinating Team, Centre for Comparative Social Surveys, City University, London) is conducted in cooperation among universities in Norway, the Netherlands, Belgium, and Germany and covers 23 mostly European countries: Austria, Belgium, Czechia, Denmark, Finland, France, Germany, Greece, Hungary, Ireland, Israel, Italy, Luxembourg, the Netherlands, Norway, Poland, Portugal, Slovenia, Spain, Sweden, Switzerland, Turkey, and the United Kingdom. It provides answers to value questions that can be isolated for the various provinces of the participating countries. At the time of writing this book, the full data file (in SPSS) could be downloaded from http://ess.nsd.uib.no

6. Industry-Driven Organizations

ITU (International Telecommunications Union) offers data on telephony worldwide (www.itu.org).

The Beverage Marketing Corporation of New York sells worldwide data on soft drinks (www.beveragemarketing.com).

Hotrec publishes data for the tourism trade: hotels, restaurants, and cafes in Europe (www.hotrec.org).

Index

Italicized numbers indicate illustrations.

About the Author

Marieke de Mooij, PhD, is President of Cross Cultural Communications Company, her own consultancy based in the Netherlands. She is a consultant to companies for their international communications strategy and conducts seminars and workshops for global companies and advertising agencies. She is a doctor in communications and visiting professor to various universities in Europe: the University of Navarra, Spain; Vaasa University, Finland; and the European University Viadrina, Germany.

Since 1980, she has been involved in international advertising education as Director of Education, International Advertising Association (IAA), and as Managing Director of BBDO College. She is the author of several publications on the influence of culture on marketing, advertising, and consumer behavior. Her previous book was *Consumer Behavior and Culture: Consequences for Global Marketing and Advertising* (2004), Sage Publications.